# Exploring
# Speaking-Writing
# Relationships

# Exploring Speaking-Writing Relationships

## Connections and Contrasts

Edited by

**Barry M. Kroll**
Iowa State University

**Roberta J. Vann**
Iowa State University

National Council of Teachers of English
1111 Kenyon Road, Urbana, Illinois 61801

NCTE Stock Number 16493

© 1981 by the National Council of Teachers of English. All rights reserved. Printed in the United States of America.

Library of Congress Cataloging in Publication Data

Main entry under title:

Exploring speaking-writing relationships.

   Bibliography: p.
   1. Speech—Addresses, essays, lectures.
2. Writing—Addresses, essays, lectures. I. Kroll, Barry M., 1946-     . I. Vann, Roberta J., 1947-     . III. National Council of Teachers of English. Commission on English Language
P95.E9     001.54     81-11265
ISBN 0-8141-1649-3    AACR2

# Contents

        J. G. Kyle

12. Integrating Oral and Written Business Communication              184
        Don Payne

13. Speaking, Writing, and Teaching for Meaning                      198
        James L. Collins

    *References*                                                     215

    *Contributors*                                                   234

# Introduction

A deaf child learns to read, a young boy teaches his illiterate father to write his name, a freshman struggles to find the right "voice" for her first theme, a native speaker of Arabic makes a journal entry in English. In its own way, each of these different events directs our attention to the relationships between oral and written language. These relationships—the connections and contrasts between speaking and writing—are the focus for the essays in this book.

In spite of the long history of interest in oral and written language among philosophers and linguists, until recently little research dealt directly with the relationship between the two modes, and very few studies approached the topic from a pedagogical perspective. Nevertheless, certain implicit assumptions about oral and written relationships have influenced the teaching of English. Often these assumptions have led to the kind of dogmatic tone used by the Harvard committee on composition and rhetoric (1902), which asserted that it was "little less than absurd to suggest that any human who can be taught to talk cannot likewise be taught to compose. Writing is merely the habit of talking with the pen instead of the tongue." This notion is still current, appearing in composition texts as advice to "write like you speak." The underlying assumptions are that writing is highly dependent upon speaking and that speaking is primary, not only in the obvious sense that it is acquired earlier than writing, but also that it is somehow closer to "true" language. The need to examine this and other assumptions about oral and written language relationships was recognized as early as 1963, when the authors of the NCTE report *Research in Written Composition* called for investigations into rhetorical and syntactic relationships between oral and written language. Since that time, a growing number of scholars from a variety of disciplines have dealt with the question of how speaking and writing are related.

Each of the essays in this volume explores what we know and what we still need to learn about the complex relationships between speaking and writing. Such efforts at clarifying basic concepts, explicating key theories, reviewing research, suggesting pedagogical implications, and posing new questions seem to us a necessary step in advancing our understanding of oral and written relationships, and a step which is logically prior to new empirical work. In our view—a view reiterated in nearly every essay—much of the research on these relationships has been insubstantial and unhelpful, largely because the perspectives of the researchers have been too restricted. In contrast, the essays in this book range widely in the perspective each takes on oral and written language. Such diversity is necessary because the basic question of how speaking and writing are related is multidisciplinary in nature, encompassing such fields as linguistics, developmental psychology, cultural anthropology, philosophy, brain physiology, sociology, and, of course, education.

The first chapter in the book provides a detailed overview of linguistic studies of oral and written language relationships. This essay comes first because it provides an important context for understanding many of the following chapters. Schafer begins with a historical explanation of why there have been so few linguistic comparisons of speaking and writing. He suggests that three assumptions underlie this neglect: that one of the language modes is primary, that linguists should work with idealized language data, and that linguists should describe language systems rather than language events. He then considers those linguistic studies which do compare speaking and writing, extending from the phoneme-grapheme to the rhetorical level. Schafer concludes by exploring what a knowledge of similarities and differences between speaking and writing can contribute to our understanding of students' writing problems.

The next three chapters focus on the relationships between children's oral and written language skills, and what these relationships imply about the teaching of writing and reading. In chapter 2, Kroll proposes a general developmental model based on the concepts of "integration" and "differentiation." During the first phase of writing development, children learn the skills which will prepare them to use written language. During the second phase, which involves consolidation of oral and written language skills, children's written utterances rely heavily on their spoken language repertoire. During the third phase, children learn to differentiate important aspects of their oral and written language resources. And finally, during the fourth phase, speaking and writing become both appropriately differentiated and systematically integrated. In chapter 3, Kantor and Rubin provide a detailed discussion of the differentiation phase of development, a phase which they believe characterizes the majority of writers, who are "suspended awkwardly between speech and writing." The authors discuss a rich array of compositions from students in grades four to twelve, illustrating the various patterns of differentiation between speech and writing. In chapter 4, the focus shifts from how children learn to write to how they learn to read. Cambourne outlines two divergent views of reading based on two different conceptions of the relationship between speaking and writing. Using evidence from psycholinguistic research, he argues for the view that comprehension of written language is similar to comprehension of spoken language and hence that children can learn to read in very much the same way they learn to talk, thus suggesting that the task could be less complex than it sometimes is.

The next two chapters consider oral and written language in a societal context. Olson, in chapter 5, discusses ways in which our conceptions of speech and writing underlie aspects of our sociopolitical existence, particularly our system of schooling. The author views writing not only as a means of communication, but also as an archival resource for a literate society, playing much the same role as ritualized speech does in oral societies. Focusing on the textbook as archival resource, Olson hypothesizes that it represents a distinctive register of language which may contribute to the distinctive mode of thought associated with literacy and schooling. Gere, in chapter 6, points out the definitional problems of the term "literacy" and stresses that our assumptions about its relationship to cognition need reexamining. Arguing that the most appropriate definition of literacy is a broad one, she suggests that the English teacher's task must be to go beyond manipulation of language to include facilitating the transition from a simple to a complex world.

Chapters 7, 8, and 9 are concerned with methodological issues in the study of speaking-writing relationships, and each suggests a way to broaden our understanding of these relationships. Barritt, in chapter 7, challenges traditional methods of researching speaking and writing by arguing for the relevance of a "descriptive phenomenological" approach. In this approach the researcher attempts to "bracket" prior assumptions so that he or she can explore, from a fresh perspective, a phenomenon as it is experienced. Barritt describes five aspects of the writing experience and shows that there are important differences between the experiences of speaking and writing. O'Keefe, in chapter 8, also critiques previous research on oral and written language relationships. She bases her criticism on researchers' insensitivity to speaking and writing as language-in-use: discourse shaped by the practical activities, contexts of action, and communicative purposes of which it is a part. O'Keefe's point is that the conditions under which any discourse act takes place are powerful shapers of the form and function of that discourse. The fact that a discourse is produced by talking or writing *may* also shape discourse, but there is no substantial evidence for this, given the inadequate control of the major discourse factors in extant research. In chapter 9, Glassner reviews work in the neurosciences, showing how the "black box is being opened." Glassner's review suggests that basic research in brain physiology may well illuminate the role that writing plays as an integrator of hemispheric activity and hence as a facilitator of learning.

The next two chapters broaden our understanding of oral-written relationships by considering two special groups of individuals who often struggle to learn English: speakers of other languages and the profoundly deaf. In chapter 10, Vann focuses on students who are non-native speakers of English. She proposes a model for the development of their writing skills (a model which parallels, in certain respects, models describing the relationships between children's oral and written language development), and she offers an alternative to the static notion of oral interference as an explanation for the writing problems of ESL students. Vann concludes by discussing instructional strategies for bridging the gap between the spoken and written communication skills of EFL students. In the next chapter, Kyle suggests that we may be able to derive fundamental insights into the relationship between oral and written language if we look at a group of people without spoken language: the profoundly deaf. Kyle points to an important relationship between the ability to use oral language coding (or "inner speech") and the ability to read and write. However, he shows that this relationship is complex: some profoundly deaf people, without oral language, learn to use sign language coding for reading English. Kyle's point is that it is the principle of internal coding, rather than a particular code, which is important for achieving literacy. Nevertheless, the deaf have a great deal of difficulty learning to use written English, and many of their problems seem to stem from the lack of correspondence between English and sign languages.

The final two chapters focus on pedagogy. Payne, in chapter 12, considers a number of ways in which speaking and writing might be integrated in a particular kind of writing course—a course in business communications. Payne raises intriguing questions about the ability of such technological advances as computerized text-editing systems to make connections between students' oral and written composing abilities. In the last chapter, Collins attempts to draw together some of the practical implications of issues considered in preceding essays. He focuses particularly on pedagogical implications for teaching unskilled writers at the high school and college levels. In part, such writers are "weak" because they produce writing through the mediation of spoken language. What is adequate elaboration of meaning for spoken interaction is often insufficient for written discourse. Collins' central premise—a premise implicit in a number of the preceding essays—is that teachers must place a priority on the elaboration of *meaning* if they want to help students develop as writers.

The essays in this book provide a broad foundation for further examinations of oral and written language relationships. This is a rich and diverse set of explorations, not a tightly focused group of empirical studies. These essays raise questions about our assumptions rather than merely elaborate a particular approach or a single "received" view. In sum, the essays provide the kinds of detailed theoretical explication and rigorous conceptual analysis which are essential for clear thinking, sound research, and good teaching. These essays aim to be provocative. Our hope is that they will indeed provoke a good deal more discussion of the many issues raised by exploring the relationships between speaking and writing.

## Acknowledgments

We are grateful to our colleagues in the Iowa State University Department of English for their support, to our typist Marilyn Dale for her patience and help in meeting deadlines, to the NCTE Editorial Board for their perceptive comments, and, finally, to Paul O'Dea for his help in seeing this project through to completion.

# 1 The Linguistic Analysis of Spoken and Written Texts

John C. Schafer
Tulane University

My purpose here is to describe the work of linguists who have tried to account for similarities and differences between spoken and written texts. Since only a few linguists have addressed this topic, my first task is to explain this neglect. I offer three reasons, which relate to certain assumptions that have guided linguistic research in recent years: that spoken language was primary, that linguists should describe language systems not language events, and that researchers should work with idealized language data. Some linguists have challenged these assumptions, however, and have developed approaches that help us understand speech and writing. I survey these approaches, beginning with those that concentrate on differences between speaking and writing at the phoneme-grapheme level and ending with those that make their comparisons at the more global levels of context of situation and code.[1] I also discuss the work of researchers who treat speaking and writing not as modes of communication but as noetic processes, stages in what Ong (1977) calls the "evolution of consciousness." Although not linguists these researchers increase our awareness of underlying assumptions which have influenced linguists in their research. Throughout, my emphasis is on what a knowledge of differences between speaking and writing can contribute to our understanding of why students find writing so difficult. My paper concludes with a discussion of work on dialogue and monologue because I believe these studies contain the most useful insights for teachers of writing.

## Why Linguistic Comparisons of Speaking and Writing Are Few

There has been little comparing of the two modes, first of all, because the assumption has been that one or the other was primary;

1

the nonprimary member of the pair was not considered worthy of serious attention. In this century linguists have regarded spoken language as primary. Traditional grammarians, however, believed in the primacy of writing; the term "grammar," in fact, comes from a word meaning someone who could read and write (Robins, 1967, p. 13). By the third century B.C. texts of the poems of Homer and other famous writers had become corrupt and Alexandrian scholars, using the resources of the library in Alexandria, applied linguistic scholarship in an attempt to produce correct versions. These scholars assumed that the language of written classical texts was purer than colloquial Greek and that oral speech was derived from the written language (Lyons, 1968). Dionysius Thrax (ca. 100 B.C.), a Greek from Alexandria, wrote the first description of the Greek language. His *Techne grammatike* remained a prominent work for thirteen centuries and influenced later Latin and European grammars. Thrax took his illustrations from the texts of classical authors and considered "the appreciation of literary compositions" to be "the noblest part of grammar" (quoted by Robins, p. 31).

Since the Greeks believed in the primacy of the written language, it is not surprising that their system of phonetics was letter-based. A confusion of letters with sounds persisted for centuries, exasperating many linguists. For example, Sir William Jones in the nineteenth century protested references to the "five vowels" in English (Robins, p. 202).

## Langue *and* Parole: *de Saussure and Bloomfield*

No one was more exasperated by this confusion of spoken and written forms than de Saussure, the generally acknowledged founder of modern linguistics. De Saussure (1916/1959) argued that

> language and writing are two distinct systems of signs; the second exists for the sole purpose of representing the first. The linguistic object is not both the written and the spoken forms of words; the spoken forms alone constitute the object. (pp. 23-24)

De Saussure complained of the tendency of the written image "to usurp the main role" which belongs to speech. Considering written signs primary is comparable, he argued, to "thinking that more can be learned about someone by looking at his photograph than by viewing him directly" (p. 24). Bloomfield (1933), the founder of American descriptive linguistics, echoed de Saussure's point regarding the primacy of the spoken language: "Writing is not language," he stated, "but merely a way of recording language by means of visible marks" (p. 21).

In what sense, according to de Saussure and Bloomfield and their followers, was the spoken language primary? First, in the sense that it was older and more widespread. Bloomfield explains that writing is a "relatively recent invention," existing in only a few speech-communities for a long period of time and in these communities only a small percentage of the population has known how to write (p. 21). Linguists also considered the spoken language primary because they observed that all three of the common systems of writing were based on different units of the spoken language. The alphabetic system used for English, for example, is based on sounds, the syllabic systems are based on syllables (Amharic, the official language of Ethiopia, for example), and ideographic systems are based on words (Chinese, for example). Since these units are present first in spoken language, linguists concluded that it was primary and written language derivative (Lyons, 1968, p. 39).

A challenge to the view that the spoken language is primary has been mounted by Vachek (1973) who argues that neither speaking nor writing is primary. They are "functionally complementary" systems: in some situations speech serves a society's communicative needs best, in other situations writing does. Since, however, the situations in which writing is preferred "have always something specialized about them," writing should be considered the marked member of the opposition (p. 16). By "specialized" Vachek means situations in which cultural and administrative tasks are conducted. The fact that people use writing for these civilizing purposes proves, Vachek maintains, that it is not the inferior mode of communication. He also dismisses the argument that writing is secondary because it is a recent invention, used today by only a minority of language communities: even in communities that have no system of writing, he points out, writing exists as a latent possibility. In all communities language develops in the direction of a maximum realization of communicative possibilities. "Universals," he argues, should not be ranked higher than "optimals" in discussions regarding the status of spoken and written language (p. 17). In the next section I will discuss other conclusions Vachek derives from his perception that writing serves some special needs of societies, particularly their need for a mode that allows "quick and easy surveyability" without regard for sound.

Few linguists, however, have compared speech and writing as
carefully as Vachek. Most have neglected such studies not only
because they have assumed that the spoken language was primary
but also because they have felt that they should describe language
systems not language events.

De Saussure, who believed that the spoken language was primary and was therefore the proper object of linguistic study, did
not recommend that linguists study speech events, or *parole*. What
linguists should describe, de Saussure said, was the system of a
language, *langue,* that made communication in a speech act possible. In describing this system linguists must isolate what is crucial
from what is "accessory and more or less accidental" (p. 14). "In
French," de Saussure points out, "general use of a dorsal *r* does
not prevent many speakers from using a tongue-tip trill; language
is not the least disturbed by it" (p. 119). These variations are accidental. All that is important is that the sound /r/ be distinguishable
from other sounds in the system of the French language. The same
principle applies in writing which, according to de Saussure, is
simply another system of signs, an alternative manifestation of the
same formal units. One can write *r* in different ways; all that is
necessary is that it not be confused with other letters in the al-
phabet. What is primary is the unit of form, not the substance of
the physical sound or the written letter. This distinction between
form and substance and the identification of *langue* not *parole* as
the object of linguistic investigations were de Saussure's great
contributions to modern linguistics. Linguists who followed in his
footsteps constructed inventories of the formal units of a
language—phonemes, morphemes, words—and sought out the
rules for their combination. They did not attempt to describe how
these units were realized in speech and text acts.

When Bloomfield in *Language* (1933) announces that not writing, literature, philology, or usage but "speech-events" are the
proper object of linguistic study, he appears to be departing from
de Saussurean principles, opting for *parole* rather than *langue*.
Elsewhere (1927), Bloomfield had made it clear that he agreed
with de Saussure:

> ... all this [language as a means of expressing and com-
> municating thoughts and feelings], de Saussure's *la parole,*
> lies beyond the power of our science. We cannot predict
> whether a certain person will speak at a given moment, or
> what he will say, or in what words and other linguistic forms
> he will say it. Our science can deal only with those features of
> language, de Saussure's *la langue,* which are common to all
> the speakers of a community—the phonemes, grammatical
> categories, lexicon, and so on. (pp. 444-6)

Bloomfield and post-Bloomfieldians did study speech in the sense that they started with a corpus made up of spoken utterances. But instead of accounting for how these utterances functioned in a context of situation, they abstracted from their corpus a grammar which consisted of a taxonomy of formal units and rules for their combination (Levin, 1965).

Many post-Bloomfieldians studied American Indian languages which had no system of writing and hence no written literature. Working with these languages reinforced their notion that the spoken language was primary and the proper object of investigation. It also had another consequence. In studying these languages linguists generally dealt with linguistically naive informants who could, of course, volunteer utterances for a corpus but who could seldom offer much information regarding them. Even if the informant were capable of communicating additional information, the rigid rules for eliciting data that post-Bloomfieldians were supposed to follow would prevent linguists from recording it (Levin, 1965). The result was an impoverished conception of what a native speaker knows regarding his language. Post-Bloomfieldian grammars were, in effect, descriptions of the discovery procedures linguists used in the field. The aim of the whole enterprise was to produce a taxonomy of the formal units of a language. These grammars did not account for the creativity of language users.

## Competence and Performance: The Chomskyeans

Chomsky's distinction between competence and performance parallels de Saussure's *langue-parole* distinction; but by locating competence in the individual rather than in the collective consciousness of a speech community, Chomsky pushed linguistics toward the kinds of investigation that illuminate differences between speaking and writing. In separating *langue* from *parole* de Saussure said he was separating "what is social from what is individual" (p. 14). According to de Saussure, languages work because the same storehouse of conventions exists in the brain of everyone in a speech community. Grammars of *langue* are inventories of these conventions. Chomsky argued, however, that people who are said to know a language possess much more than an inventory of signs: they also have the ability to produce sentences they have never heard before, to distinguish well-formed sentences from deviant ones, to recognize sentences that are grammatically related, and to identify sentences that are ambiguous. More than *langue* and *parole*, competence and performance suggest individuals and concrete actions. Although he wasn't recommending that linguists

explore how language is used in situational contexts, he did, in
reaction to de Saussure, individualize linguistics and pave the way
for such explorations.

By competence Chomsky meant grammatical competence: the
ability to produce and comprehend, and make judgments about,
well-formed sentences. There is no place in his theory of competence for the concept of appropriateness: the ability of speakers to
recognize whether an utterance is appropriate to the communicative situation in which they find themselves. Thus his theory was
a-rhetorical; it excluded knowledge essential to effective speaking
and writing. As Hymes (1972b) points out, Chomsky presented us
with an inspiring image, an image of a child who by the age of five
has mastered a complex linguistic system. This image, Hymes explains, was a necessary corrective to the view that some children,
because of their race or social background, are so linguistically
deprived that little can be done for them. But, Hymes continues,
this image becomes if not "irrelevant" at least "poignant" when
compared to children in our schools—"poignant, because of the
difference between what one imagines and what one sees; poignant too, because the theory, so powerful in its own realm, cannot
on its terms cope with the difference" (p. 271).

To help us cope with these differences, Hymes argues, we need
to replace grammatical competence with communicative competence. Central to the latter would be the ability to judge whether
an utterance was appropriate to the context in which it was used.
In elaborating this concept of communicative competence Hymes
and other sociolinguists provided a theoretical justification for the
study of oral and written language in contexts of situation.

Another aspect of Chomskyean linguistics that prevented investigations of speaking and writing was its concentration on
idealized language data—on perfectly formed sentences that the
Chomskyeans made up and used to prove the validity of their
theory. Transformational grammarians idealized language in all
three of the ways distinguished by Lyons (1977): first, they regularized it—purged it of hesitations, slips of the tongue, and
stammering; second, they standardized it—ignored all dialectal
variation, taking as their task the description of the language system underlying the variation; third, they decontextualized it—
eliminated all context-dependent features. The natural unit of language is not the sentence but the discourse or text, which in turn
may be made up of sentences—or it may consist of a single sentence, clause, fragment, or word. In short, by electing to study
only isolated sentences, transformational grammarians ruled out of

consideration two sets of relations crucial to the successful production of spoken and written texts: inter-sentence relations and the relations of a text to context.

By rejecting context-dependent sentences transformational grammarians removed from consideration many of the types of utterances found in conversation because talk, as Emig (1977) puts it, "leans on the environment" (p. 124). An elliptical utterance such as *As soon as I can,* for example, an utterance that can be accurately interpreted only if one knows the utterance preceding it, would be too context-dependent to be studied by most transformational grammarians. The linguistic context this utterance is dependent on is sometimes referred to as the co-text. Another kind of utterance, for example, *I haven't seen him before,* could be dependent not on the preceding co-text but on the context of situation: the person referred to could be visible to the speakers and indicated by a gesture (Lyons, 1977).

A sole focus on decontextualized sentences fails to provide a satisfactory account of a variety of linguistic elements. The sentence *I haven't seen him before* exemplifies a difficulty with pronouns. Linde (1974) in her study of apartment layout descriptions reveals a difficulty with definite and indefinite articles. According to the traditional view, the definite article is used with nouns the second time they are mentioned in a discourse, as in the following example:

> Once upon a time there was an old tailor in a village. The old
> tailor was known all over the village as Old Harry.

Linde found, however, that in describing their apartments speakers often use the definite article with rooms the first time they are mentioned. She also found that major rooms (living rooms, bedrooms, kitchens) are introduced with the definite article more often than minor rooms (dens, libraries, studies, laundry rooms). In other words, speakers are more likely to say

> The kitchen is next to the living room.
> Next to the living room is a den.

than

> A kitchen is next to the living room.
> Next to the living room is the den.

Linde concludes that in introducing rooms speakers tend to use the definite article with rooms that can be treated as given—not given in the sense of mentioned in the preceding discourse, but given in the sense of not being new information to hearers who are familiar with American apartments. Thus her study demonstrates that one must consider not only the preceding co-text and context of situation, but also the cultural knowledge shared by the participants, what some linguists call the context of culture.

Using decontextualized data leads to another problem: the misleading assumption that if one knows the form of an utterance one also knows its function. Schegloff and Sacks (1973) offer the following example from a conversation:

> B has called to invite C, but has been told C is going out to dinner:
>
> B: Yea. Well get on your clothes and get out and collect some of that free food and we'll make it some other time Judy then.
> C: Okay then Jack
> B: Bye bye
> C: Bye bye

B's first utterance is by form an imperative, but, Schegloff and Sacks observe, it functions in this dialogue not as an imperative but as a closing invitation and "C's utterance agrees not to a command to get dressed . . . but to an invitation to close the conversation" (p. 313).

Chomsky and his followers knew, of course, that to understand utterances speakers need to know more than phonological and grammatical rules and the dictionary meaning of words. They never doubted that knowledge of linguistic and extralinguistic context was involved, but they wondered how much of this knowledge linguists should try to include in their descriptions. Katz and Fodor (1964) concluded that they could hope to account for only a small fraction of it—that fraction which would enable speakers to identify semantically ambiguous sentences, anomalous sentences, and sentences that were paraphrases of each other. To represent in their theories all the knowledge a speaker uses in understanding an utterance, linguists would have to represent *"all the knowledge speakers have about the world,"* clearly, they said, an impossible task (p. 489).

## Context Dependence: Malinowski and Firth

Some linguists, of course, have opposed Katz and Fodor's approach to semantics. The most influential opposing view originates in the work of the anthropologist Malinowski. It was further developed by Firth and is espoused today by Halliday and Hasan and other members of the Neo-Firthian or London School of Linguistics. After spending many years studying the culture of the Trobriand Islanders in Melanesia, Malinowski (1923) concluded that in regard to the language of primitive peoples

> the conception of meaning as *contained* in an utterance is false and futile. A statement, spoken in real life, is never detached from the situation in which it has been uttered. . . . [U]tterances and situation are bound up inextricably with each other and the context of situation is indispensible for the understanding of words. (p. 467)

In regard to "a modern civilized language, of which we think mostly in terms of written records," however, Malinowski believed—in 1923—that context of situation was not crucial to meaning. The meaning of written texts, he said, is more "self-contained and self-explanatory" (p. 466). Later (1935), however, he said this distinction between primitive speech and modern, scientific writing was a serious error: context was important to the meaning of both types of texts.

Firth developed Malinowski's approach to meaning in an article entitled "The Technique of Semantics" (1935/1957) in which he explained what he meant by the "semantic function" of language. For Firth there were three categories of functions in language: the minor functions of sounds for which one needed only a phonetic context to study; the major functions—lexical, morphological, and syntactical—for which one needed a linguistic context but not a context of situation; and the semantic function for which one needed a context of situation. One could, he pointed out, determine which syntactic category the two utterances *Not on the board!* and *Not on the board?* belonged to without knowing the context of situation in which they were spoken—by simply attending to their intonation. But take the utterance bɔːd? (Bored? or Board?). A linguist cannot, Firth maintained, determine the semantic function of this utterance unless he knows the context of situation. In addition, argued Firth, "since every man carries his culture and much of his social reality about with him wherever he goes," we must also know the context of culture[2] (p. 27).

The linguists and sociolinguists surveyed below who provide the most useful framework for the consideration of speech and writing have rejected decontextualized data and adopted Firth's theory of semantics. In distinguishing spoken from written texts, researchers discuss degree of dependence on contexts more than any other feature. In introducing and elaborating the concept of context of situation, Firth and his followers have therefore contributed greatly to the study of spoken and written texts.

## Some Studies of Spoken and Written Language

For the reasons just described, there are not many linguistic
analyses of the differences between spoken and written language,
but there are some studies; and there are other studies which, although they do not address the subject of spoken and written language directly, do allow for consideration of the two modes within
their conceptual apparatus. In surveying these studies I will start
with the work of researchers who describe the lower levels of the
linguistic hierarchy—the levels of phoneme-grapheme relations,
for example—and proceed upward through studies that focus on
syntax, text, context, and code. Often researchers identify
relations—often causal relations—they see existing between different levels of the hierarchy. Hasan (1973, 1978), for example,
argues that the structure of certain texts is causally related to the
context of situation; Bernstein (1971) argues that features of a person's speech are causally related to code. In surveying these
studies I will explain the relation, if any, the researcher posits as
existing between the different levels.

### *Phoneme-Grapheme Level*

Because he is interested in the reform of orthographic systems,
Vachek (1973) concentrates his study at the phoneme-grapheme
and word levels. Vachek, however, was able to arrive at certain
insights concerning relations between the two modes at these
levels only after he had broadened his frame of reference to consider how speaking and writing function in a context of culture.
He observes that the function of the written mode "is to react to a
given stimulus (which as a rule, is not an urgent one) in a static,
i.e., preservable and easily surveyable manner" (p. 16). Vachek
then explains certain "structural" relations between the spoken
and written mode as resulting from this ability of the written mode
to function as an easily surveyable medium. He argues that while
the common characterization of written language as symbols of
symbols is correct in reference to languages that have only recently had a written form, it is not an apt description of the written
languages of culturally advanced societies. In these societies,
Vachek argues, people customarily read silently; they take meaning directly from writing. Since in silent reading there is no "de-
tour via the corresponding spoken utterances," written symbols
become "signs of the first order" (p. 37). The most economic system of correspondence between the two modes—economic be-

cause it would require a minimum of symbols and the simplest rules for their combination—would be to have one grapheme for every phoneme. If we understand how the written language functions, then we can understand why this principle is not implemented consistently in any written language. Deviations from it are necessary, says Vachek, to enable writing to accomplish its function of "quick and easy surveyability."

By deviating from the principle of one grapheme for every phoneme and applying instead what Vachek calls the "logographic principle," the written mode of English is able to differentiate homophones such as *right, rite, wright,* and *write* (p. 23). Here the correspondence between the two modes is at the level of the word. Sometimes surveyability is provided by a correspondence at the level of the morpheme, as in the case of the English graphic morpheme for the plural of nouns—(e)s—which, if the one phoneme-one grapheme principle were followed, would require a separate symbol for each of its allomorphs—/-s/, /-z/, and /-ɪz/. If it possessed these separate symbols, however, the plural marker in English would be less easily surveyable. According to Vachek, attempts to reform orthography based on the principle of strict phoneme-grapheme correspondence would make English easier to write but harder to read. Writers, for example, could use the same spelling for homophones like *rite* and *right,* but if they did, the spelling wouldn't convey the meaning quickly to readers, who would have to rely instead on syntactic or contextual clues.

## Syntactic Level

Another category of studies concerning spoken and written English deals with syntactic analyses of spoken and written texts. Typically in these studies the researchers don't try to prove that causal relations exist between linguistic features and some larger context; they are content to describe differences between texts in the two modes. One such study is O'Donnell's (1974) analysis of the syntactic differences between the oral and written language of a man who was both an author and television talk-show host. The sample of oral language was taken from a TV program in which the subject was responding to questions on different topics put to him by three journalists. The written sample was taken from four newspaper columns the author had published. After analyzing his two samples, O'Donnell concludes that in comparison to speech, writing has longer T-Units (an independent clause plus any dependent clauses attached to it), more T-Units containing dependent clauses, and more non-finite verbals, passive constructions, auxiliaries, and attributive adjectives.

Many similar studies have been conducted, often with conflicting results. Researchers have isolated various features—sentence units, thought units, and personal references, for example—and then, after analyzing their data, have concluded that one mode has fewer of these units, or shorter units, than the other mode. Other researchers, however, studying the same features, come up with contradictory results (see Einhorn, 1978). A frustrating aspect of these studies is that while they are based on texts produced in particular circumstances by only a few subjects (in O'Donnell's study by only one subject) speaking and writing in only one situation, this doesn't prevent researchers from offering their results as accurate generalizations of universal differences between speaking and writing. More careful than most researchers, O'Donnell admits in his conclusion that there are dangers in generalizing from the results he obtained from his single speaker-writer. But the text of his article includes statements like "Table 1 shows that T-Units in writing have greater average length than those in speech" (p. 105).

It is also difficult to draw conclusions about universal differences between speaking and writing from this group of studies because different researchers have used different types of oral language texts. O'Donnell takes his sample of oral speech from an interview situation in which the author responds to questions from three people. Other researchers have used a variety of oral texts including: the formal speeches of nationally known lecturers delivered at a university campus (Blankenship, 1962); tapes of dyadic conversations on women's liberation and the future of the family between community college students and a partner of the same sex and race (Cayer & Sacks, 1979); the prepared five-minute speeches of beginning speech students who were instructed to prepare their talks using a "key-word" outline (Gibson et al., 1966); personal narratives in response to the question "Were you ever in a situation where you thought you were in serious danger of getting killed?" (Kroll, 1977). All we learn from these studies is that one particular type of speech (dyadic conversation, prepared speech, or whatever) of a particular sample of the population differs in certain ways from the written sample to which it is compared. Usually the researchers try to control for the influence of topic by having the subjects write on the same topics they speak on, but some do not. These latter studies therefore not only tell us nothing useful about universal differences between speaking and writing, they also don't tell us whether the discovered differences between the particular types of spoken and written texts compared in the experiment are attributable to differences in mode or to some other factor in the context of situation.

In short, these researchers seem limited by the narrow sentence-based perspective of the linguistic models they draw on for definitions of the features they look for. A more fruitful approach would be to elicit from the same subjects different spoken texts on the same topic—dyadic unstructured conversations, more structured dyadic conversations (interviews, for example), extemporaneous speeches, prepared speeches—and attempt to specify the different strategies the speakers use to structure their texts in these different situations. Moffett argues that in moving from dialogue to monologue a speaker, no longer able to rely on social interaction to structure his discourse, must begin to "enchain his utterances according to some logic" (1968, p. 85). It would be interesting to learn what linguistic devices are used to achieve the enchaining. For the definition of such devices researchers will need to draw on text-based, not sentence-based, grammars; they will also have to abandon the opposition between speech and writing and let other oppositions—dialogue vs. monologue, planned vs. unplanned discourse—guide their research efforts.

## Text Level

What studies concentrating at the level of text illuminate best the differences between speech and writing? Few text analysts have set out to compare spoken and written texts; usually the analyst prefers to work with texts of one mode. Thus there are analysts of conversation such as Sacks and Schegloff (1973, 1978), who focus on dialogue; and structuralists such as Barthes (1970/1974), who concentrate on written texts, usually literary ones. Some text analysts have devised approaches that are applicable to texts in both modes, however, and the terminology and methods of these approaches can be used to compare spoken and written texts.

### Cohesion

One useful approach is Halliday and Hasan's treatment of cohesion. In *Cohesion in English* (1976) they explain that "text" is "used in linguistics to refer to any passage, spoken to written, of whatever length, that does form a unified whole" (p. 1). They set out to describe what makes a passage a unified whole—a text—and conclude that one aspect of texture is cohesion, "a set of semantic resources for linking sentences with what has gone before" (p. 10). They identify five cohesive devices:

Reference:      1. Wash and fix *six cooking apples*. Put *them* in
                   a fireproof dish.

Substitution:   2. *My axe* is too blunt. I must get a sharper *one*.

Ellipsis:       3. This is *a fine hall* you have here. I've never
                   lectured in a finer *[φ]*.

Conjunction:    4. For the whole day he climbed up the steep
                   side, almost without stopping. *Yet* he was
                   barely aware of being tired.

Lexical:        5. I turned to *the ascent* of the peak. *The climb*
                   is perfectly easy.

Students of spoken and written language have been most interested in Halliday and Hasan's distinction between exophoric and endophoric reference. Exophoric reference is reference to something in the context of situation (or context of culture); endophoric reference is reference to something in the text. Thus if someone is conversing with a friend and says, "That must have cost a lot of money," meaning by "that" an antique silver collection on the table in front of the friend, the reference is exophoric; if this person says the same sentence after her friend has commented, "I've just been on a holiday in Tahiti," the reference is endophoric (p. 33).

Bernstein, who read early chapters of *Cohesion in English* first published by Hasan in 1968, adopted this distinction, arguing that working-class youths were oriented toward the use of a restricted speech variant which had more exophoric reference than the elaborated speech of middle-class youths (1971). Bernstein was interested in the sociological causes of particular speech variants, not in variation across modes, and studied only spoken texts—tapes of discussions. In *The Philosophy of Composition*, however, Hirsch (1977) argues that Bernstein's distinction can be used also to distinguish oral and written texts: the former, he says, typically contain more exophoric reference than the latter. Context-free speech correlates with economic class, Hirsch argues, because middle class children "will normally be more intensively educated in reading and writing" than working class children (p. 26). They will have been forced to operate more often in situations in which exophoric reference is less often a possibility because school talk and writing typically concern things not present in the context of situation.

Patterns of Thematization

For Halliday and Hasan a passage that native speakers identify as
a text exhibits other relations besides cohesive ones. There are, for
example, patterns of thematization, a cover term for a range of options concerning where in the clause the given and new information and the theme and rheme are placed (Halliday, 1967). These
options have their point of origin in the clause but speakers and
writers must consider the preceding discourse in choosing their
options. Consider the second sentence in the following two pairs
of illustrative sentences from an article by Walpole (1979) on the
uses of the passive:

1. (a) Napoleon was not a bogeyman until Austerlitz. (b) Napoleon won the battle and quickly became a name of fear to
   all European monarchs.
2. (a) The battle of Austerlitz changed the course of European
   history. (b) The battle was won by Napoleon and became
   the first in a long series of striking victories for the Little
   Corporal. (p. 252)

In 1-b Napoleon is the given information: he is mentioned in the
preceding sentence. Napoleon is also the theme—what the writer
is writing about. (Generally theme is identical with the given information; see Halliday, 1967.) The theme almost always precedes
the rheme. It is also the subject of the sentence—except in marked
cases: That man I don't like. In London you'll find some nice res-
taurants.

If (1) and (2) were sentences in a history book, the author
should not use the passive and begin 1-b "The battle was won by
Napoleon ..." because the author's theme is Napoleon not the
battle, as the rest of the sentence makes clear. Putting battle in the
theme slot would impair comprehension. It would be appropriate,
however, for the author to begin 2-b in this way because in this
second pair of sentences battle *is* the theme and the given information. The oft denigrated passive voice is then, as Walpole
points out, a useful device because it allows a writer to say what
he wants to say while satisfying expectations regarding theme:
that it heads, and is the subject of, the sentence.

Many student paragraphs are comprehensible but difficult to
read because themic material is poorly arranged (for examples, see
Williams, 1979). The problem is not unique to writing. Scinto
(1977) studied oral answers to an interviewer's question (Are
things on television real or pretend?) and concluded that the an-

swers of younger interviewees were difficult to understand in part because of faulty pronoun reference but primarily because of poor theme-rheme structuring. In particular Scinto found that the younger interviewees rarely structured their texts by making the rheme of one sentence the theme of the following sentence. Thus their answers seldom took the form:

> John bought a car yesterday.
> It was a green Volvo.
> Volvo was a wise choice . . . etc.

Since the adult interviewee used this pattern almost exclusively, and his answer was the clearest, Scinto wonders whether this is a "highly valued" structure in producing cohesive texts (pp. 30-31).

Students may have trouble with theme-rheme patterning because they are used to dialogue, which doesn't require a speaker to develop a topic unilaterally through a series of statements. Dialogue also doesn't provide practice in making the kinds of topic shifts and changes one has to make in writing. In dialogue, as Schegloff and Sacks have shown (see below), topic shifts and changes are carefully negotiated in a process that is as social as it is linguistic. In monologue, however, transitions must be achieved unilaterally and linguistically by the creator of the text. Theme-rheme patterning is important to the process. Becker (1965) argues that when the theme of a set of sentences appears in a new grammatical role in a sentence following this set, this often signals the start of a new division of a paragraph, or a completely new paragraph. In other words, a change in theme-rheme patterning appears to signal a shift or change in topic. Walpole's example sentences can be used again here to illustrate Becker's point. Becker is saying that it might be effective to begin 2-b "Napoleon won the battle . . ." if 2-b were the first sentence in a new paragraph about Napoleon, instead of the second sentence in a paragraph about the Battle of Austerlitz.

Since theme-rheme patterning is realized syntactically, it is achieved the same way in both oral and written monologues. Another aspect of thematization, information focus, however, because it is realized by intonation, is not achieved the same way in both modes. Speakers use intonation to chunk their texts into information units and to focus hearers' attention on the new information in the unit. Writers can use punctuation to guide readers toward the desired rhythm and intonation but there is rarely enough punctuation for it to be authoritative (Bolinger, 1968). Sometimes, too, the rules force writers to punctuate grammatically not phonologically. Scott (1966) gives the following example: *It is common knowledge that, if we are to learn to speak another language well, we must spend a great deal of time practicing it.* The rules don't allow a writer to place a comma after *knowledge,* where most readers would pause, but force him to place one after *that,* where most readers would not. Information focus, like the division of a text into information units, is achieved differently in writing. A speaker could make clear that the italicized items in the following sentences were new information by stressing them in an oral reading: John painted the shed *yesterday. John* painted the shed yesterday. A writer, however, must use other devices—italic type or syntactic rewordings—to raise these items to prominence.

## Contexts of Situation Level

In *Cohesion in English* Halliday and Hasan discuss cohesive ties between sentences in a text, not the relation of features of a text to the context of situation. (In their discussion of reference, for example, they distinguish exophoric from endophoric reference, but discuss only the latter in detail.) They make clear, however, that to distinguish text from non-text one must know the context of situation. A set of citation forms exhibiting a particular grammatical feature would in most situations be non-text, but if placed in a grammar book we would be able to accept it as text. Halliday and Hasan argue therefore that in addition to cohesion we need a notion of register, their term for "the linguistic resources which are typically associated with a configuration of situational features" (p. 22). The categories they suggest for distinguishing registers—field, mode, and tenor—represent their attempt to give form to the elusive concept "context of situation." If we know the information subsumed under these three headings, they argue, we can predict the structure of texts. *Field* includes the event in which the text is functioning and the subject of the discourse; *mode* refers to the channel (spoken or written, extempore or prepared) and the genre, or rhetorical mode—narrative, persuasive, didactic; *tenor* refers to the social relations among the participants (p. 22).

To support the assertion that knowing these factors enables one to predict a text's structure, Hasan (1978) asks us to imagine a person contacting a doctor's office for an appointment. If this person makes the request by telephone and is not known by the secretary, the text must have an identification element (italicized):

> Good morning. *Dr. Scott's Clinic.* May I help you?
> Oh, hello. Good morning. *This is Mrs. Lee speaking.*

If instead of telephoning this same patient makes a written request, the identification element is still obligatory, but it may occur in a different place in the message—in the closing, for example. If another patient who is a good friend of the secretary makes the request in person, the text, to be appropriate, must *not* have an identification element. One wouldn't come up to a secretary who was a close friend and say, "This is Mr(s). _____ speaking."

## Contexts of Culture Level

Bernstein's restricted and elaborated codes are like Hasan's registers: essential to both is the idea that extralinguistic factors correlate causally with the structure of texts. But code is a much more abstract and global construct than register (Hasan, 1973). It's not a term for a variety of language or a context of situation; it refers instead to a way of socializing children. More specifically, it refers to a "regulative principle" which controls the way parents and other adults talk to children when they discipline them, teach them, and discuss their feelings with them (Bernstein, 1971, p. 15). Speech regularized by a restricted code is a restricted speech variant; speech regularized by an elaborated code is an elaborated speech variant.

How do the two variants differ? Early in his career Bernstein conducted an experiment to determine whether the speech of working class youths, which he presumed to be influenced by a restricted code, differed grammatically and lexically from that of middle class youths. He found that working class youths used less subordination, fewer complex verbal stems, less passive voice, fewer uncommon adjectives, adverbs, and conjunctions, and more "sociocentric" expressions *(you know, ain't it, isn't it)* than middle class youths (1971, pp. 115-17). But Bernstein's main interest has been in the semantic not the formal differences between restricted and elaborated variants. He did his grammatical and lexical analysis in search of more evidence to prove his primary hypothesis: that the two classes are oriented to different orders of meaning. Sociocentric expressions, used frequently by the working class youths in his experiment, interest him because he sees them as "a response of the speaker to the condensation of his own meanings" (p. 111). Since the working class speaker is relying heavily on shared understanding, he needs to use these expressions, Bernstein argues, to check if his hearers are with him.

Bernstein summarizes the semantic properties of the two variants as follows:

> Restricted speech variants are context-dependent, give rise to particularistic orders of meaning, where principles are verbally implicit or simply announced; whereas elaborated speech variants are context-independent, give rise to universalistic orders of meaning, where principles are made verbally explicit and elaborated. (p. 14)

Bernstein's three qualities of meaning are closely related. If a variant is context-dependent, so full of exophoric reference, for example, that it is understandable only if one is present in the context in which it is produced, then it will not give rise to universal meanings. Only the participants in the speech act will understand it. Particularism is thus related to context-dependence. It is also related to implicitness. If a speaker relies on the fact that she shares with her hearers knowledge not only of a context of situation but also of a context of culture, she may communicate in elliptical and unelaborated utterances; she won't feel under any compulsion to "spell out" every idea in an explicit way. And the text she produces will not be understood by a universal audience.

What determines whether a family will use a restricted or an elaborated speech variant? According to Bernstein, the determining factor is the form of social relations, including the type of controls used. "Positional" controls foster a restricted code; "personal" controls foster an elaborated code (pp. 152-54). In a family that uses positional controls, "judgments and the decision-making process are a function of the status of the member rather than a quality of the person" (p. 154). In matters of discipline children are not presented with alternatives; there is no discussion of the reason for a rule. Children are told to behave in a certain way because that is the way children are supposed to behave. In a family that uses personal controls, however, the status of the family member is less important than his psychological characteristics. Rules are elaborated and explained and alternatives presented.

Bernstein's causal chain has then the following links: parents brought up under a system of positional controls speak a restricted speech variant in raising their children. Hearing restricted speech in "crucial socializing contexts," these children become oriented toward using this restricted speech variant themselves.

It is easy to see why composition theorists have found Bernstein's work interesting, particularly his distinctions between different kinds of meanings (context-dependent, context-independent, etc.). These can be used by those who reject his sociological theories concerning the origin of the two codes and their correlation with social class. Used to distinguish not speech variants but typical oral texts from typical written texts, they suggest possible explanations for three common errors in the essays of inexperienced writers: coherence gaps, vague pronoun reference, and premature closure on a point. One can hypothesize that these errors are caused by oral language interference, a transfer of communicative strategies that work in most speech situations into writing situations, where they do not work. For example, in searching for an explanation for the use of the pronoun *this* with an unclear antecedent, a common error, we can hypothesize that the student doesn't make the antecedent specific because, accustomed to speaking strategies, he assumes that his readers will know what the *this* refers to—which indeed they might if they were hearers, not readers, and shared with him a context of situation and culture.

According to Bernstein, some people are "oriented toward" context-dependent speech because they have been socialized in a certain way—by parents who use positional controls, for example. Greenfield (1972), however, and other investigators of the consequences of literacy consider context-dependent speech to be evidence of a lack of exposure to written texts. Because writing is "practice in the use of linguistic contexts as independent of immediate reference," Greenfield argues, learning to write will increase a student's capacity to produce context-independent speech (p. 174). Because context-independent speech is, in Greenfield's view, related to context-independent, or abstract, thought, experience with written texts will enhance a learner's ability to think abstractly. Greenfield found that Wolof children in Senegal who had been to school, and thus had been exposed to context-independent texts, performed certain categorization tasks more expertly than unschooled children and used more explicit and elaborated language to explain why they had grouped items the way they did.

For Bernstein the semantic features context-dependent/context-independent, particularistic/universalistic, and implicit/explicit distinguish the speech variants of different social classes in a modern technological society. Greenfield uses these same features to distinguish the typical speech of people in preliterate societies from the typical speech of people in literate societies. And Olson (1977b) uses these features to distinguish the typical speech of children and adults in literate societies. Language acquisition, he says, "is primarily a matter of learning to conventionalize more and more of the meaning in the speech signal" (p. 275). According to Greenfield and Olson, culturally and developmentally there is movement toward texts which are more context-independent, universalistic, and explicit.

These researchers draw on the work of Havelock (1976) who has argued that the Greeks developed their capacity for abstract thought only after they adopted alphabetic writing, a system which enables a writer to represent meaning more explicitly than ideographic scripts or syllabaries. Ong (1971), another scholar interested in the relation of media to thought processes, points out that to send a message in societies with no written language—Homeric Greece, for example—the sender had to fill his text with formulary expressions and other mnemonic devices to ensure that both messenger and receiver could retain it. This dependence on formulary devices made the "highly analytic thought structures we take for granted in certain utterances among literates ... quite simply unthinkable" (p. 290). So much energy was expended in preliterate societies in making sure what was already known wasn't forgotten, none was left to explore the unknown.

Although Ong, Olson, and Greenfield are not, strictly speaking, linguists, their work is relevant here for two reasons. First, they point out another level at which speaking and writing may be contrasted. For Ong, speaking and writing are not simply modes of communication which vary in structure and function; they are different noetic processes representing stages in the "evolution of consciousness" (1977, p. 334). In Ong's scheme there are four stages. The first stage, primary orality, is characterized by the use of formulary devices and the absence of "analytic thought structures"; the second stage, residual orality, exists when people have a writing system but are still dominated by preliterate modes of thought; the third stage is represented by modern literate cultures before the advent of radio, television, and other electronic devices; the fourth stage, secondary orality, emerges as electronic devices transform the old culture of the written word.

Ong and Olson push us toward a new level of awareness concerning approaches to language description. They help us understand, for example, why Malinowski, who did his field work with preliterate people, would insist that the context of situation is indispensible for the understanding of words (1923, p. 467) and why other linguists who take their examples from people who speak a language that is also written assume that the meaning is in the text (see Olson, 1977b). According to Ong, structural linguists insist that spoken language is primary and concentrate on it, but their unconscious "chirographic and typographic bias" leads them to overemphasize the extent to which language is a "closed system" (1977, p. 309).

The work of those investigating the consequences of literacy is also relevant because it has been proposed that courses in writing should recapitulate the stages of evolution described by Ong. According to Farrell (1977), since historically the emphasis was first on fluency, achieved in preliterate cultures by the use of formulary expressions, we should first get students to write fluently and attend to clichés and mistakes in grammar and punctuation later. "Just as the conventions of regularized spelling, punctuation, and grammar were late historical developments," Farrell says, "so too the perfection of these matters should be late in the teaching of the writing process" (p. 454). Farrell also believes that students at different institutions have not all reached the same stage in Ong's scheme of four stages and that teachers should adjust their syllabi to fit their students. He contrasts students at an open admissions school such as The City College of CUNY with students in Berkeley's Subject A remedial course. The open admissions students, he says, because they come from residually oral cultures, need more help with the "detached, analytic forms of thinking fostered by literacy" than do the Berkeley students, who, according to Farrell, come from a secondary oral culture (p. 455).

Farrell's justification for his writing curriculum is unnecessarily esoteric. Surely there are other more compelling and less abstruse reasons for the very sensible sequence of instruction he recommends. Ontogeny recapitulates phylogeny, Farrell believes; the "individual recapitulates the history of communications in the race" (p. 445). But Ong explains that this is true only in a crude sense. The oral stage that children in a technological society pass through only superficially resembles the oral culture of adults in preliterate societies (1977, p. 299). Other researchers, too, have concluded that terms used to describe oral and literate patterns of thought, while significant historically, cannot be applied to adults in any contemporary society (Scribner & Cole, 1978).

## Dialogue and Monologue

Having summarized the different ways speaking and writing can be compared and contrasted, I'd now like to argue that it is more useful for teachers of composition to ponder another dichotomy—the opposition between dialogue and monologue. Many composition theorists don't agree. Emig (1977) stresses the importance of the opposition between speech and writing. Writing is a more valuable mode of learning than talk, she says, because writing, like a good learning strategy is "self-rhythmed," represents "a powerful instance of self-provided feedback," and "establishes explicit and systematic conceptual groupings" (p. 128). But an oral monologue also has all these attributes, excluding perhaps an oral monologue that arises when one speaker seizes the floor in a conversation and keeps talking. These monologues may not be very self-rhythmed or explicit; there may be intermittent audience feedback in the form of "continuers"—"mmhmm" or "yeah," or "right"—and an occasional request for clarification. But even the extemporaneous oral monologue contains, in embryonic form, the attributes Emig mentions. When during a conversation one person takes over the floor, audience feedback drops off dramatically and the speaker has to come up with some logic to hold his text together.

An oral monologue does differ from writing in that it does not force one to transform verbal symbols into a graphic product; nor does an oral monologue become a reskannable record of the development of one's thought. According to Emig, these are other attributes of writing that make it a good mode of learning. Only if it is written down before it is spoken in performance does an oral monologue have these attributes, but then it becomes difficult to say whether the oral monologue is writing or talk. Some linguists distinguish channel and medium to make the point that any text in the oral medium can be recorded and written down and any text in the written medium can be read out loud. Perhaps Emig would subsume extemporaneous oral monologues under oral medium and prepared monologues under written medium, but this, in my opinion, is unsatisfactory because it puts the wrong opposition on top. Emphasizing the spoken/written opposition leads to long lists of *all* the differences between talk and writing, lists that obscure the crucial difference: the unilaterial vs. collaborative production of a text. "The most critical adjustment one makes" in learning to write, Moffett (1968) says, "is to relinquish collaborative discourse, with its reciprocal prompting and cognitive cooperation, and to go it alone" (p. 87). The dialogue/monologue opposition highlights this critical adjustment.

Unfortunately there are few linguistic studies of dialogue and monologue. Moffett's treatment is still the most useful for teach-

ers. Joos' *The Five Clocks* (1961) is another insightful work. He
doesn't use the terms dialogue and monologue, but his five
styles—intimate, casual, consultative, formal, and frozen—can be
viewed as different points on a continuum from dialogue to
monologue. His consultative style is what I have referred to as an
extemporaneous oral monologue: consultative speakers, Joos says,
don't plan "more than the current phrase"; they benefit from listener participation which takes the form of requests for more, or
less, background information (p. 37). Joos' formal style is a
planned oral monologue. This has no audience participation and is
planned in advance. Many people, Joos says, must compose a formal text in writing before they deliver it. Joos' frozen style is a
written monologue: it is "defined by the absence of authoritative
intonation in the text" and by the fact that the audience "is not
permitted to cross-question the author" (p. 39). Joos demonstrates
that the context of situation constrains not only the style (defined
by the presence or absence of certain phonological, grammatical,
and lexical elements) but also the polarity of discourse. He points
out, for example, that when a group gets larger than six people,
dialogue usually ceases and one person addresses the group in a
monologue.

A group of researchers usually referred to as conversation
analysts have demonstrated in rich detail how in dialogue text is
developed as a cooperative enterprise. This cooperation is
exemplified in "sentence completion": a speaker starts an utterance and her partner completes it. According to Duncan (1973),
sentence completion functions as a "back channel cue": it is one
way an auditor can indicate to a speaker that she realizes some
unit (topic or story) is in progress and that she wishes the speaker
would continue (p. 38). Other back channel cues are the expression "m-hm," requests for clarification, brief restatements, and
head nods and shakes. The back channel cues of an auditor seem
to be provoked by the "within-turn signals" of the speaker. Duncan found that these take two forms: the speaker's turning of her
head toward the auditor or her completion of a grammatical clause.
Termination of a grammatical clause is also one of many turn signals a speaker may emit. An auditor who mistakes a within-turn
signal for a turn signal and starts to talk may be quieted by a "turn
claim-supressing signal," a gesture using both hands.

Conversation analysts typically analyse small stretches of texts.
Their favored unit of analysis is the speaker turn, but they have
moved beyond the turn to consider openings and closing se-

quences. Closings, Schegloff and Sacks (1973; see also Schegloff, 1978) demonstrate, are thoroughly collaborative affairs. After some talk on a topic one of the participants can fill her turn with a "possible pre-closing," an expression such as "We-ll . . . ," "O.K. . . . ," or "So-oo" (with downward intonation contours). By employing one of these expressions, the speaker passes—decides not to use her turn to provide an utterance coherent with the topic being discussed or to initiate a new topic. These possible pre-closings invite the auditor either to start a new topic or begin a closing sequence. If she wishes to do the latter, the auditor completes the pre-closing sequence by answering "O.K." or "All right." Then the speaker initiates the closing sequence proper with an expression such as "Good-bye," "See you," or "Thank you" and the auditor ends the conversation with an appropriate expression— "Bye," "Goodnight," etc.

In employing a possible pre-closing, then, the speaker is only proposing completion; her auditor may at any time "disallow" it by starting a new topic. Stories, too, by which conversation analysts mean any report of an event, cannot be completed unilaterally by the speaker. A speaker can only propose story completion; the auditor completes it by acknowledging understanding. But the auditor can always disallow completion—usually by asking a question (Schegloff, 1978).

Inexperienced writers have mastered the complex "grammar" of dialogue described by the conversation analysts. They know how to produce a text in cooperation with a partner. But they don't know how to monologue: how to initiate a text, prolong it, and bring it to a close unassisted by an auditor. In the absence of any "disallow completion" signals, they lapse into premature closure. "One of the most notable differences between experienced and inexperienced writers," Shaughnessy (1977) comments

> is the rate at which they reach closure upon a point. The experienced writer characteristically reveals a much greater tolerance for what Dewey called "an attitude of suspended conclusion" than the inexperienced writer, whose thought often seems to halt at the boundary of each sentence rather than move on, by gradations of subsequent comment, to an elaboration of the sentence. (p. 227)

Monologue is thus different from dialogue: in the former, text is produced unilaterally; in the latter, collaboratively. Many monologues, however, have a dialogic quality: questions are asked and then answered, problems are posed and then solved, opposing views are presented and then refuted. Undoubtedly many monologues have a dialogic quality because, as Vygotsky (1934/1962) argues, the inner speech of thought is a conversation with ourselves and we inscribe this inner dialogue when we write.

That all monologues have a dialogic quality (and all dialogues a monologic quality) was the thesis of an article by Mukarovsky (1977) first published in 1940. He argued that the relation between monologue and dialogue is best characterized as a "dynamic polarity in which sometimes dialogue, sometimes monologue gains the upper hand according to the milieu and the time" (p. 85). He defines dialogue as "a special kind of semantic structure oriented toward a maximum number of semantic reversals" (p. 109). By "semantic reversals" Mukarovsky does not mean topic shifts but the changes in attitude towards a topic that one finds most clearly in dialogue because in dialogue the same topic is being considered by different people.

To illustrate the presence of dialogue in monologue Mukarovsky discusses Burian's dramatization of Dyk's short story "The Pied Piper of Hamlin." He shows that it was easy for Burian to rewrite Dyk's narrative monologue as dialogue because like all monologues it contained semantic reversals, and these could be made the boundaries of separate speeches assigned to the different players. For example, in Dyk's monologue there are these lines describing a pub:

> One couldn't drink better wine anywhere else for miles around, and the cook at the tavern, the black Liza, could measure up to any other cook. Neither did the heads of the community spurn the entrance to the vaulted hall of the pub; they had their own table carefully guarded against intruders.

In Burian's dramatization this stretch of monologue is dialogized as follows:

> *First guest:* You can't drink better wine anywhere else for miles around.
> *Second guest:* And the cook, the black Liza, can measure up to any other cook.
> *Roger* (serves them a glass of wine).
> *First guest:* It's true, friend . . . that neither do the heads of the community spurn the entrance to your pub. . . .

Mukarovsky explains that Burian exploited the break between coordinate sections of Dyk's first sentence and the change in "evaluative nuance" signalled by the conjunction *neither* in the second sentence, making these semantic reversals the boundaries for the speeches of his characters. In other words, his dramatization was relatively easy because the monologic text itself was "oscillating between monologue and dialogue" (p. 106). The oscillation is not pronounced, Mukarovsky suggests, because the text is a narrative. There is much more contradictoriness in persuasive essays. In *The Practical Stylist,* a popular freshman rhetoric text, Baker (1977) recommends that students develop the middle section of their papers as a "kind of Punch and Judy show." First present one argument of the opposition; then knock it down. Then present another argument and demolish it, and so on (p. 11). Argumentative essays that employ this tactic are obviously much more dialogic than Dyk's narrative.

If all monologues are dialogic and students are practiced dialogists, why do they have so much trouble writing monologues? Because conversation dialogues are different from the dialogues found in essays. When we converse, at least when we converse with friends, we need not be explicit because we share a great deal of knowledge with our hearers. Hints and code words will suffice to get across our message. According to Vygotsky (1934/ 1962), conversation with friends with whom we share much is like the inner speech of thought in which we converse with ourselves. In inner speech the "mutual perception" is absolute: the two "participants" are in the mind of one individual. In conversation it is not absolute but still significant (p. 145). The monologues students write often have a dialogic quality but to understand the question and answer or statement and elaboration exchanges set up we must be able to read the mind of the writer.

Because writing does have a dialogic quality, conversation is good preparation for it, a point strongly argued by Moffett (1968). Since the conversations which best prepare students for writing are full of requests for clarification and elaboration, a teacher may have to guide the discussion to ensure that such requests are made. The type of conversation that is close to writing is not the dialogue between two friends, in which text is produced for the benefit of only the two co-participants, but the dialogues of a talk-show host with his guest, in which the purpose is to produce text which a third party—the TV audience—will find understandable and interesting. Teachers in writing conferences are like talk-show hosts: they keep trying to get their interviewees to elaborate their statements so they will be understandable to a more universal audience.

## Linguistic Studies and Teaching Strategies

Certain trends in the work surveyed here are clear. One is an emphasis on the grammar of sequence, on linear rather than global coherence. Many of the linguists surveyed have moved beyond the sentence, but they have been more interested in intersentence or interutterance relations than in what makes a text whole. In *Cohesion in English,* for example, Halliday and Hasan concentrate on links between sentences; they mention but do not describe "discourse structure"—"the larger structure that is a property of the forms of discourse themselves: the structure that is inherent in such concepts as narrative, prayer, folk-ballad, formal correspondence . . . and the like" (pp. 326-7). Similarly, conversation analysts usually focus on a short stretch of conversation, not on the structure of a complete conversation. To apply a distinction recommended by Lyons (1977), these researchers more often describe *text* than *a text,* the latter carrying with it "presuppositions of internal organic unity and determinate external boundaries" that the former does not have (p. 631).

Other text linguists have been interested in the structure of a text as well as of text. Van Dijk (1977a) explains that although the following propositions are semantically related and therefore linearly coherent, they lack global coherence:

> I bought this typewriter in New York. New York is a large city
> in the USA. Large cities often have serious financial problems.
> . . . (p. 149)

To account for such cases, he introduces the concept of "macro-structure," which corresponds to a topic of a discourse. For a series of propositions to be acceptable, he says, they must be capable of being subsumed under a macro-proposition. The three propositions just discussed are not acceptable because they don't meet this test. In van Dijk's scheme a macro-structure or a group of macro-structures fulfills certain functions in what he calls "conventional superstructures" (1977b). For example, in the superstructure of a narrative, macro-structures may function to communicate setting, complication, or resolution; in a research report they may function to convey introduction, problem, experiment, and conclusion.

In the introduction to *Text and Context* van Dijk says that "it may be assumed" that "dialogue-discourse" has "textual structure similar to that of (monologue-) discourse" (p. 3). Because he makes this assumption and concentrates on monologue, van Dijk doesn't systematically compare the two polarities of discourse. But his book is sprinkled with insights regarding them. Macro-structures, he says, are found in dialogue as well as monologue. A dialogue is not coherent if the utterances of the two participants cannot be assigned to the same "macro-structural topic" (p. 140). But topic changing follows different rules in the two polarities. In dialogue one can use what Schegloff and Sacks (1973) call a "misplacement marker" ("By the way . . . ," or "Oh") and switch to a new topic that is not coherent with the one previously discussed. In a monologue, however, the speaker-writer must obey stricter conventions regarding topic changing. Although it is not a study of spoken and written language, van Dijk's *Text and Context* is a thorough presentation of an approach to text linguistics.

Besides an interest in the grammar of sequence, another trend evident in the work surveyed here is the influence of behaviorism. Speakers are portrayed as being in the grip of factors in the environment over which they have no control. One gets the impression that in reacting against linguists who would disown context these linguists want to assign it too large a role. By insisting on the importance of context, linguists who have adopted a Firthian view of semantics have appropriated certain aspects of rhetoric. Like rhetoricians they want to make judgments about a text's appropriateness to the situation in which it is produced. In another sense, however, they have purged linguistics of rhetoric. They have done this by leaving the impression that if one knows everything about the context of a speech or text act, one can predict what someone will speak or write. Although it may be possible to predict within certain limits what people will say or write in routine situations in life, it will never be possible to predict what they will say or write when they are realizing their fullest potential as human beings. By suggesting that such prediction is possible, linguists will alienate rhetoricians, who are convinced that the effective use of language is an art not a science.

Recent linguistic studies of spoken and written language do not support the idea that one can predict what people will write. But they may lead us, as teachers of composition, to accept the oral language interference hypothesis as a fact when it is still really only a working hypothesis. In this regard it is interesting to note that similar hypotheses are slipping into disrepute. For many years the contrastive analysis hypothesis, the assumption that the errors students make in learning a second language are caused by interference from their first language, was accepted by teachers of English as a second language. But as anecdotal evidence has given way to research results, second language acquisition experts have reduced the percentage of errors they believe to be caused by language interference from the high sixties or seventies to five percent (see Hakuta & Cancino, 1977). The dialect interference hypothesis that the spoken dialect of some students interferes with, and causes errors in, their writing is also coming under attack. Hartwell (1980) surveys the research and concludes that dialect interference doesn't exist: so-called dialect interference errors and errors for which another explanation is usually offered (the spelling *stomack* for *stomach*, for example) are not dialect interference errors, he says, but are "correlated with reading dysfunction, both reflecting an imperfectly developed neural coding system, the print code" (p. 109).

Bartholomae (1980) agrees with Hartwell. One of his students wrote the phrase "1600 childrens" throughout a paper, but when he asked the student to read his paper out loud he always said "1600 children." When Bartholomae asked him why he put an "s" on the end of children, the student replied, "Because there were 1600 of them." Bartholomae concludes that the student realizes that written language has its own conventions. The error and others like it reflect his struggle to master these conventions, not interference from his spoken language. If there is interference in writing, Bartholomae argues, it is a different type of interference from that described by advocates of the dialect interference hypothesis. When he had the same student who wrote "childrens" read a paper in which he had made many errors in verb endings and noun plurals, the student corrected most of his errors. Bartholomae concludes that many so-called dialect interference errors are errors in transcription, errors "caused by interference from the act of writing itself, from the difficulty of moving a pen across the page quickly enough to keep up with the words in the writer's mind"; they indicate problems of performance, not a lack of grammatical competence (p. 259).

The interference which advocates of the contrastive analysis and dialect interference hypotheses posit as the cause of errors operates at levels of phonology, morphology, and (rarely) syntax. Speakers of Vietnamese and speakers of American Black dialect, a typical argument runs, both write *He kick the ball* because consonant clusters don't exist in Vietnamese and in Black dialect they tend to be simplified. As linguistics has moved beyond the sentence to the text and context of situation, the interference hypothesis has moved along with it, and now the interference is seen as operating at the levels of context or code. And the errors it is presumed to cause are usually semantic errors—incoherence, inexplicitness, etc.—not errors in morphology or syntax.

I have argued that beginning writers quite possibly do suffer from oral language interference at the level of context of situation; I agree, for example, with Hirsch that "the difficulty of writing good prose arises very largely from the linguistic abnormality of addressing a monologue to an unseen and unknown audience" (1977, p. 58). But this will not be the correct explanation for most errors. Most errors probably have multiple causes. If we blind ourselves to other possibilities, and conclude too quickly that they are all dialogue or code interference errors, we may use the wrong strategy to combat these errors.

We should also realize that a particular kind of oral language transference can help, not hurt, writing. Most students would write better if they channeled some of the liveliness that characterizes their conversation into their papers. While consistency of voice is achieved differently in writing than it is in speech, it is a quality of well-formed texts in both modes. We should avoid giving students the impression that talk is in no way a model for good writing, a danger we may fall into if we make too much of Bernstein's distinctions. Emphasizing that statements must be elaborated in writing, for example, can encourage wordiness. Adopting a view diametrically opposed to the interference hypothesis, Zoellner argues that bad writing is caused not by interference but by a disassociation of the two modes; writing teachers, he says, have to help students achieve a "vocal-scribal reweld" (1969, p. 307).

In summary, we need to discuss with students how their experience as talkers prepares and doesn't prepare them for writing. In these discussions we should assume that students are not so much enslaved by habits of speaking as confused by the conventions of written English. Comparing something they already know how to do—talk—with something they are eager to learn how to do—write—is one way to decrease the confusion. In leading such discussions, in analyzing student errors, and in planning our teaching strategies, we will be greatly assisted by linguistic studies of spoken and written texts.

## Notes

1. Code is often used loosely to mean any variety of language that a speaker uses for a particular purpose. Here, however, it refers to Bernstein's (1971) "regulative principle" which, as I explain in the second section, he believes influences the way we speak.

2. Firth takes the concept context of culture from Malinowski. See *Coral gardens and their magic* (Vol. 2). London: George Allen & Unwin, 1935, p. 18 and p. 51.

# 2 Developmental Relationships between Speaking and Writing

Barry M. Kroll
Iowa State University

Are speaking and writing alike or different? Is practice in talking good practice for writing? Answers to such simple questions concerning the relationship of speaking and writing would seem to be central to the teaching of writing, especially in the elementary school. However, opinion appears to vary considerably concerning the relationship between speaking and writing, and the implications of this relationship for educational practice. A number of language arts specialists point to similarities between talking and writing, and emphasize the close relationship of oral and written language:

> Oral language is closely related to written language. Some authorities believe that written expression is simply speech "written down." (Rubin, 1975, p. 219)

> Reading and writing should be taught in a way that maximizes opportunities for observing the intimate connections between oral and written language. (Cramer, 1978, p. 18)

Other authorities point to differences:

> We find that spoken English is often quite a long way removed from written English. (Wilkinson, 1971, p. 47)

> To encourage pupils, as teachers often have done, to "write as you speak" is to ask the impossible. (Harpin, 1976, p. 32)

Such opinions may appear more different than they really are. Talking and writing are multidimensional processes. Thus, whether the modes are viewed as essentially alike or different depends, at least in part, on the dimension one chooses to focus on. Speaking and writing have been compared in many different ways: as linguistic systems, as communicative acts, as cognitive processes, and so on. Even within each of these specific dimensions, speaking and writing can be seen as similar in certain respects but very different in others. Attempts to summarize the relationship between speaking and writing are further complicated by such factors as the function of the discourse (e.g., "expressive," "transactional," or "poetic"; see Britton, Burgess, Martin, McLeod & Rosen, 1975) and the register of the discourse (e.g., deliberative speaking/formal writing vs. casual speaking/information writing; see Gleason, 1965). An "expressive" piece of writing might be considerably closer to oral language than would a "poetic" piece. And a formal talk might be quite similar to a written essay.

But there is yet another complicating factor, for the relationship between speaking and writing seems to change as a person develops as a writer. Thus, the relationship between the two modes of expression for a seven year old will probably not be the same as the relationship for a fourteen year old. This "developmental factor," which is particularly relevant for education, is the focus for my paper. First I explore the developmental factor by examining some elementary-school children's oral and written explanations—focusing on a few of the ways in which these explanations are alike and different at various grade levels. Following this analysis, I propose a general model of how the dominant relationship between speaking and writing changes in the course of developing writing abilities.

## The Developmental Factor

It may seem obvious that the relationships between speaking and writing abilities will change as children gain maturity and experience as language users. Perhaps because it seems so obvious, there has been little research into various dimensions of these changing relationships. There have, of course, been several major studies of oral and written language that focus on linguistic factors, primarily on various syntactic indices (Harrell, 1957; Loban, 1976; O'Donnell, Griffin, & Norris, 1967). But there are other important aspects of children's oral and written discourse that have not been so carefully examined. For example, if we were to give children a specific communication task, when could they accomplish the task equally well in oral and written forms? In what ways would the spoken and written versions be alike and different? Would children use the same "approach" in both versions? Some research I have conducted, although small in scope, begins to explore such questions. One study involved gathering, from the same elementary-school children, both oral and written explanations of how to play a game (Kroll & Lempers, 1981).

In this study, children in grades three, four, and six first learned to play a simple board game and then attempted to explain the game so that another child would know how to play it. Each child explained the game both orally and in writing (with order of speaking and writing counterbalanced). For the oral explanation, children were asked to make a cassette tape recording to accompany the game materials. For the written explanation, children were simply asked to write a set of instructions. By having the children make a tape recording of their spoken explanation, I was able to make the contexts for the oral and written messages more similar than they typically are: for neither explanation was an audience present to share the explainer's frame of reference or to provide a response. This design permitted exploration of those differences in oral and written messages which would persist even when the two modes were made much more alike than is typically the case.

One way to look at the resulting explanations is to consider their content. In brief, the game is a race in which each player tries to be the first to move a rubber bird along a playing board from the starting point to the finish point. A person who hasn't played the game before needs to have information about how to set up the game board properly, how to initiate the game, how to move the bird along the board, how to observe the special restrictions on movement, and so forth. The adequacy of the explanations can thus be assessed by rating each message for specific elements of the game which must be communicated to a new player. The scoring procedure used by Kroll and Lempers involved assigning points according to how adequately a person explained these elements of the game. (In all, there was a maximum of 30 "total" information points.) The mean number of points for spoken and written explanations could then be compared for each grade level and the results would indicate how speaking and writing affect the "informational adequacy" of explanatory messages.

The main finding from this analysis was that the children in grades three and four communicated, on the average, more total information about the game when speaking than when writing, whereas the children in grade six communicated nearly the same average amount of total information in both modes.[1] Thus, in the younger grades, children were generally better at communicating when talking into a tape recorder (even with the artificiality surrounding such a procedure) than when writing out a set of directions (even with the increased ease of review which this afforded). But by grade six, children were equally proficient at speaking and writing the directions. The older children's spoken and written explanations were alike in content. It is this developmental trend toward *similarity* in informational adequacy that I will take up later.

The explanations gathered in this study can be analyzed for features other than content. I want to focus on a feature of the explanations which I'll call "approach," defined as the way a child sets up the message so as to imply whether the explainer, the reader/listener, or two hypothetical players will be involved in playing the game. When the child explains the game as if he or she will actually be involved in play, this reflects a situational orientation to the explanation—one that would be quite appropriate for spoken interaction, but not for writing. I call this approach "subjective," because the explainer projects himself or herself into the situation (e.g., "I move the bird to the blue stripe. Now you roll the die"). However, when the child's explanation implies that the reader/listener and some other player will be involved in the game, this reflects a different approach, which I call "objective" (e.g., "You move the bird to the blue stripe, and then the other person rolls the die"). Finally, if the child's explanation implies that any two people may play the game, this is labeled a "hypothetical" approach (e.g., "One player moves to the blue stripe, and then the other player rolls the die"). Although any of these approaches could be used to convey game information successfully, the "objective" and especially the "hypothetical" approaches are further removed from the context of an actual game in progress, and also tend to be addressed to a less concrete listener/reader—hence they seem more characteristic of written than of spoken discourse.

Only a few of the children used a "subjective" approach. However, the younger children tended to use an "objective" approach for both their oral and written explanations, while the sixth-graders tended to use an "objective" approach for their oral explanations, but a more "hypothetical" approach for their written explanations.[2] The sixth-graders, therefore, made more of a distinction between the approaches used for their oral and written explanations. Thus, when we look at the approach used in these explanations, we find a developmental trend toward *differences* in oral and written discourse. The use of these approaches can perhaps best be illustrated by examining briefly two pairs of explanations. (Spoken explanations are transcriptions from the tape recordings. For the written explanations, spelling and punctuation have been regularized.) The first pair of explanations is from the same fourth-grade boy.

### Fourth-Grader's Spoken Explanation

Well, first you start out and you take the two little birds and you put them behind your back and mix them up, and then you put them in front and the person who you're playing— well, then they pick a hand and then they take the one that they picked, you know, in the hand. And then they put it on the side, like if they have a blue, there's a blue thing, you know, the blue thing down at the end. You put, well, if she has the blue, then you put it in that alley. And then, if you have the yellow, then you put it in that. And then you take the chip and then you throw it, you know, you roll it on the thing and then whose ever color it is, starts. And then you roll the dice, you know, and then you go onto the color. And then, but if you get a white, then you have to stay where you were. And then if you go on the same color as your opponent, you have to—you can't do that—so you have to go back where you were. And then you try to go down to the end. And if, like if, when you get down to the end and you're on green, and then you have to, to get to the dot you have to get a, you know, a blue, to get onto the end.

### Fourth-Grader's Written Explanation

You take the two little birds and you put them behind you. Then you put them in front of you and the person you're playing chooses which hand it's in so the one they choose, you take the other one. Then at end with the dot of the color you go to the other end. And you roll the chip. If it is the blue side the one with the blue bird goes first. Then you roll to see what color you go to. Then the person who rolls next. If it gets on the color that rolled first you have to go back to the color you were at first. But if you roll a white you have to stay where you were.

There are some obvious stylistic differences between the two explanations. But this boy's written explanation is like his spoken explanation in that both entail an "objective" approach (referring to "you" and "the person you're playing with") and both employ a "narrative" organization pattern (the most frequent connective is "then"). However, the following pair of explanations from a sixth-grade boy illustrates much more marked differentiation in approach.

### Sixth-Grader's Spoken Explanation

OK, you start out and you put one bird in each hand, and you hold it behind your back, so the other person can't see. And then you ask them which one they want and then that's the color they get—want—either yellow or blue. So then you put the yellow bird on the black square opposite the yellow circle and you put the blue bird on the black square opposite the blue circle. You flip the chip and whichever side lands up, then that's who gets to go first. So then you put the die into the little shaker thing and you shake it out. And if you get green, you land on green, you know. But if you get white—then there's no white on the board, so you can't go anywhere. You have to stay where you are. And if you land on a color that someone else has already landed on, in the same stripe, you know, across, then you can't do that, so you have to go back to the beginning. And the first person to reach their end place— the circle at the end of the board, wins. But you have to get that color to go on it. Oh, you go to the closest stripe of that color. The closest one to you.

### Sixth-Grader's Written Explanation

1. One person puts a bird in each hand. The other one picks a hand and the bird in the hand he/she picks is his/her color. The other person gets the other color.

2. Put the birds on the black squares, the yellow bird on the black square opposite the yellow circle at the other end; ditto for the blue. (Put it on the other black square.)

3. Flip the chip to see who goes first. Whichever color lands up goes first.

4. Put the die in the shaker and roll it (the person who goes first does this). Go to the nearest band of that same color on the board, moving towards the circles. Then the other person rolls and moves. Continue in this manner until somebody lands on the circle the same color as his/her bird. He or she must have the same color on the die as the circle is to land on the circle. Whoever lands on the circle first wins.

Important: the two birds may not land on the same color strip (going the short way across the board). They may be on two strips of the same color but not the same strip. If the die lands on white, the player doesn't move until his/her next turn. Also the player doesn't move if he/she would land on a strip already with a bird on it, or if there are not strips in front of him/her with the color on them.

The boy's spoken explanation involves an "objective" approach: he addresses the listener as "you." The structure of the explanation is essentially narrative—the story of a game in progress—and many of the connections between elements are chronological: "and then," "so then." However, this sixth-grader's written explanation demonstrates the use of distinctively "written" features: use of numbered elements, several uses of parentheses to set off clarifying information, use of a heading ("Important:"), and the use of "he/she," "his/her" (a formal feature, if not an exclusively written one). The written explanation involves elements of a "hypothetical" approach: "one person" and "the other person." Moreover, the structure of the explanation departs from simple narration. The first four numbered items are in chronological sequence, but the information presented under the heading "Important" includes all three of the exceptions to the general rule for advancing the bird. Thus the overarching structure is (a) general rules, (b) exceptions. Connections between game elements are made by the use of visual devices—the numbers or the heading—rather than by the more oral, narrative devices such as "and then" sequences. The use of imperatives gives this explanation a tone of authority. The writer has captured the form and tone conveyed by "real" explanations printed on the lids of boxed games.

In sum, the analyses suggest that, with age and experience, elementary-school children's oral and written explanations become both increasingly similar in certain respects and increasingly different in others—more similar in content, but more different in approach. Thus, two processes seem to be involved: *differentiation* and *integration*. These two processes are, I believe, important for understanding the developmental relationships between children's oral and written language abilities. In the next part of the paper, I will use these two key processes to build a general model of the changing relationships between children's speaking and writing abilities.

## A Developmental Model

The processes of differentiation and integration appear to be aspects of a fundamental, widely-applicable principle of development, which Werner (1957) summarizes as follows: "wherever development occurs it proceeds from a state of relative globality and lack of differentiation to a state of increasing differentiation, articulation, and hierarchic integration" (p. 126). Thus, the two processes are generally useful in characterizing the relationship among two or more "components" in a developing "system." At certain periods in the course of growth, either differentiation or integration tends to be the *dominant* relationship among a system's components. Thus development, although continuous, can be marked off into identifiable "phases" during which a system's components tend to be related in a particular way. When the components are structurally and functionally discrete, their relationship is in a phase of relative differentiation; when the components are unified into a whole, their relationship is in a phase of integration. Such "phases," while useful for analysis, are somewhat artificial, since the boundaries between phases will be imprecise, and since there will be large individual differences both in the timing and duration of progress through the phases.

Both the concepts of differentiation and integration and the notion of phases of development (during which one of these processes is dominant) are relevant for understanding the changing relationships between speaking and writing as two "components" in a child's productive language "system." The developmental model proposes that speaking and writing progress through four principal relationships: separate, consolidated, differentiated, and integrated. Each principal relationship defines, in turn, a "phase" of development.

The first phase involves *preparation* for writing, during which children learn the technical skills which will enable them to represent in written symbols the words they can effortlessly produce in speech. Speaking and writing are essentially separate processes in this period, since children's writing skills are very minimal. The second phase involves *consolidation* of oral and written language skills. While children's writing does not long remain identical to their talk, nevertheless a child's written utterances during this phase rely heavily on his or her spoken language repertoire. Writing and speaking are relatively integrated, and writing is very nearly "talk written down." The third phase involves *differentiation* of oral and written language resources. Children learn that writing and speaking, in their most typical forms, often differ in structure and style—that writing tends to be formal and explicit, a relatively autonomous "text," while speaking tends to be casual and context-dependent, a conversational "utterance." The fourth phase involves *systematic integration* of speaking and writing. At this point, speaking and writing are both appropriately differentiated and systematically integrated. Thus, for the mature individual, speaking and writing have well-articulated forms and functions, but they also form an integrated system, so that each can serve a diversity of overlapping purposes and employ a wide range of forms, depending on the context, audience, and purpose of communication.

However, this kind of model oversimplifies development by making it appear to be unidimensional and strictly linear. On closer examination, the development of speaking and writing would undoubtedly appear to be cyclical and multidimensional: at any point in time, certain aspects of oral and written language are being differentiated, while other aspects are becoming integrated, as illustrated in the earlier analysis of children's explanations. Consequently, generalizations about *the* trend toward differentiation or integration during a particular period are bound to be oversimplifications. Both processes are often at work. Moreover, trends are quite likely to vary with the nature of the speaking and writing tasks, with the particular features of the oral and written products one chooses to analyze, and, of course, with the developmental level of an individual child. Nevertheless, with the proper tentativeness, I think it is useful to generalize about the sequence of principal developmental relationships between speaking and writing. A general theoretical model is often useful precisely because it does oversimplify. A model's purpose is to enable one to see the broad outlines of development, those generalized "phases" that might be overlooked when focusing on the complexity of individual details.

The model proposes that, in the course of developing writing abilities, an individual progresses through "phases" of preparing, consolidating, differentiating, and systematically integrating his or her oral and written language resources. Of the four phases, the middle two—consolidation and differentiation—are the most significant for language arts instruction. Thus, I will focus my discussion on these two phases, dealing more briefly with the preparation phase and only sketchily with the phase of systematic integration. In elaborating the model, I have drawn generously on two major sources. The first is theoretical accounts of the development of children's language skills (such as James Britton's theory of development as a dissociation from the "expressive" to the "poetic" and "transactional" functions). The second source is practical accounts of how schoolchildren's oral and written language are related. These textbook accounts by language arts specialists are, presumably, based on fairly extensive classroom experience. By drawing on such sources, I hope to demonstrate that the proposed model, if not based on extensive research evidence, is at least consistent with a good deal of informed opinion.

## Preparation

When most children first enter school their written language skills are, at best, minimal. By contrast, their oral language skills are relatively well developed. Thus, a major goal of the earliest stages of school instruction is to *prepare* children to use their oral language resources for "independent" writing development. There are at least three important factors in this preparation. The first factor involves acquisition of the "technical" skills of handwriting and spelling.

> Success in written composition depends on the early acquisition of good handwriting and orderly, as opposed to random, spelling. Only when the writer has these skills well controlled is he able to concentrate on the higher intellectual tasks involved in communication and expression. When they appear together, slow and clumsy handwriting and insecure spelling are likely to ensure that a child will view any writing task with dismay. (Mackay, Thompson, & Schaub, 1978, p. 103)

The point of gaining control over these technical skills should not be lost: mastery of these skills enables the child to draw more freely on his or her oral language competence. Harpin (1976) makes this point cogently.

> When children begin the process of learning to write there is a big gap between their general language competence and their performance. The effort involved in learning the new skill is considerable and attention is, naturally enough, on the mechanics of the business. What is drawn on from those oral language resources is sharply restricted. As the act of writing becomes habitual, so more opportunity is available to bring oral competence and written performance into harmony. (p. 52)

Moreover, the fact that these technical skills are important does not mean that original "composing" should be delayed until such skills are mastered. The second factor in preparation for writing is to give children practice in composing. Taylor (1973) is surely right to recommend simultaneous training in technical skills and in the expression of thoughts in a form suitable for writing: "We begin by giving him activities which are designed to help him to control his pencil and to see how letters and words are formed; and we encourage him to express his thoughts about things he

finds interesting enough to express, and the technical business of
writing them down is done for him until he can do it himself" (p.
88). Many language arts specialists would concur that, "for a child,
*dictation* is the major bridge to writing" (Lundsteen, 1976, p. 233;
cf., Cramer, 1978; DeVries, 1970; Fisher & Terry, 1977; Petty,
Petty, & Becking, 1976). Dictation demonstrates the connection
between oral and written language. As Ferris (1967) notes, when
they enter school "some children will already know that writing is
'talk put down on paper.' Others will have to learn this. The
teacher should create opportunities to write children's sentences
on the chalkboard. Through this, children learn that . . . spoken
language can be translated into written language" (p. 187). Dictation also provides an opportunity for composing experiences. Burrows, Monson, and Stauffer (1972) ask: "How can children experience satisfaction in written composing when they are just
beginning to spell and write? The answer to this question is, 'By
dictating what they want written'" (p. 190). Burns and Broman
(1979) similarly suggest that to "start the written composing process before the children have mastered handwriting and spelling
skills, as well as other technical, written expression skills, the beginning step involves the teacher's recording (writing) the children's oral expression" (p. 234).

The third factor in preparing children for independent writing
involves extending oral communication skills. Tough's (1977a)
work appears to demonstrate that, when children enter school,
they differ considerably in their ability to use oral language to express their ideas clearly. Because of different experiences in using
language in the home, some children are able to employ a wide
range of uses of language, while other children habitually select a
rather restricted set of forms. Tough (1973) notes that for

> some children what has been learnt in the home will be excel-
> lent preparation for life in school, and for talking with the
> teacher; for other children, however, the ways of talking which
> have been learnt in the home may prove to be seriously in-
> adequate for dealing with new experiences, for interpreting
> teachers' talk and for responding in ways expected by teacher.
> (p. 49)

Thus, enhancing children's ability to use talk is crucial for learning and important for literacy, since "reading and writing both
have their basis in talk, and ways of using language for writing and
in reading must first be established through talk" (Tough, 1977b,
p. 7). Tough's important point is that children need to learn to use

oral language for more complex purposes (e.g., to give clear and explicit instructions). Tough (1977a) is open to criticism when she focuses on social class differences in the uses of language (see Wells, 1977, for an empirical and theoretical response to Tough). Nevertheless, it seems likely that children who can use oral language for a variety of communicative purposes will have a stronger basis on which to build written communication skills.

## Consolidation

After children have acquired some of the skills necessary for independent composing, the primary developmental goal is to strengthen writing by drawing on the child's oral langage competence. During this stage of consolidation, writing and speaking are relatively integrated. Children's earliest writing is "often very like written down speech" (Britton et al., 1975, p. 11). Rubin (1975) comments that by age six "children are quite set in their pattern of speech, and their writing is a reflection of this speech" (p. 219). Wilkinson and Swan (1980) find that "young children often write in oral modes, or mix spoken and written" (p. 181). And Rosen and Rosen (1973) ask us to "imagine a line drawn from talk to the language of books, and then place children's writing somewhere along the line. The youngest children's writing is nearest to talk though rarely exactly the same as it" (pp. 110–111). Because of this subtle relationship between talk and writing, young children face the problem of discovering *how* to draw on their oral language capability. Taylor (1973) conceives of early writing development as a "compromise" between talk and writing:

> In expressing himself in writing, the child is likely to go through quite recognizable stages. At first he will make no distinction between spoken and written language. He will try to write exactly as he speaks. This will lead him into difficulty, because in speech we use a great many extra words and phrases which we do not need when we are writing. . . . So he learns to compromise; he writes as he talks, but he leaves out the conversational incidentals. However, it is not easy for him to reorganize his speech into a form of words which is suitable for writing and he needs a great deal of help from his teacher in reaching this compromise. (pp. 92-93)

What teaching practices help children consolidate their oral and written resources? There seem to be at least three important elements in promoting writing development in this early stage.

One element is to continue to promote the development of oral language skills. Smith, Goodman, and Meredith (1976) argue that written language "is founded upon speech development and derived from inner speech. The cultivation of speech is a primary task, for on it all else is built" (p. 209). Despite such strong and sensible claims, there are still unanswered questions concerning "the part that increasingly varied talk might have in the growth of ... written language competence" (Britton et al., 1975, p. 16). Groff (1979) points out that there is little research "to prove the assumption that the oral language of children greatly influences their written language" (p. 35). Nevertheless, if speech provides a resource for writing, then the ability to use speech for a greater variety of purposes will probably benefit writing development. Lundsteen (1976) takes the view that

> oral language is basic to writing, both draw on past experience of organizing speech in appropriate sequences, choosing words properly, and using language patterns. If a child's written composition is poor, the teacher probably needs to help him work on his oral language. Usually a child will not write better than he talks. Whether the aim is effective reading or effective writing, the factor of spoken language skills sets the child's ceiling of performance. (p. 112)

A second element involves providing language activities in which the forms and functions of speech and writing are made as similar as possible. Consolidation of oral and written language resources can be aided in two complementary ways. On the one hand, children can be encouraged to use oral language in ways that are less like conversation and more like sustained written messages. Conversation is typically dialogic, involving interaction between speaker and listener; however, writing is essentially a monologue in which the full responsibility for sustaining the discourse falls on the writer. Thus oral monologues, which Moffett (1968) defines as "the sustained utterance by one speaker who is developing a subject for some purpose" (p. 30), may serve an important function not only in consolidating speaking and writing, but also in providing a basis for differentiation of "utterance" and "text" (a point developed in the next section). Thus Britton et al. (1975) can claim that monologue "forms the best basis for writing, that is to say an uninterrupted utterance able to be sustained in spite of the lack of stimulus from another speaker" (p. 16; cf. Johnson, 1977). On the other hand, children can also be encouraged to use writing in ways that are closer to speech. Some language arts specialists propose "personal writing" (e.g., letters and journals) as the kind of writing which is "the closest to 'talk written down' that exists" (Fisher & Terry, 1977, p. 252). Others propose "sensory" observation as the subject of early compositions. In discussing proposals for early written "themes," Harpin (1976) finds a

> remarkable consensus among many of those who have written about language work in the junior school on starting with exploration of the senses. . . . To use the senses as starting points is to meet the requirements of some general truths of teaching; begin with the child's own experience and understanding, prefer present to absent, concrete to abstract, look for the most direct and accessible ways of enlarging experience. (p. 117)

But perhaps the fullest, the best known, proposal for consolidating children's talking and writing resources is James Britton's claim that language entailing the "expressive" function provides the important bridge from speaking to writing, a claim incorporated into the influential Bullock Report, *A Language for Life* (1975). Britton and his colleagues (1975) became interested in expressive language "both because it represented some overlap between speech and writing, and because, looked at developmentally, it seemed to be the mode in which young children chiefly write" (p. 11).

Expressive language has three major features: (1) it is language "close to the self," with the function of "revealing the speaker, verbalizing his consciousness, and displaying his close relation with a listener or reader"; (2) it is language in which much "is not made explicit, because the speaker/writer relies upon his listener/ reader to interpret what is said in the light of a common understanding . . . and to interpret their immediate situation . . . in a way similar to his own"; and (3) it is language which "submits itself to the free flow of ideas and feelings" and is "relatively unstructured" (p. 90). Because of these features, expressive language represents the "move into writing most likely to preserve a vital link with the spoken mode in which up to this point all a child's linguistic resources have been gathered and stored" (p. 197). Thus, behind "expressive writing lie the resources of speech and the ongoing accomplishment of spontaneous informal talk" (p. 144). This means that writing in the "expressive function" plays an important *consolidating* role in early writing development.

> It is certainly not the case that every child's first attempts at writing are expressive according to our definition of the term, and to suggest that it is a "natural" way to start probably raises

more questions than it answers. But it must be true that until a child does write expressively he is failing to feed into the writing process the fullness of his linguistic resources—the knowledge of words and structures he has built up in speech—and that it will take him longer to arrive at the point where writing can serve a range of his purposes as broad and diverse as the purposes for which he uses speech. (p. 82)

A third element in consolidating talking and writing is the practice of using talk as preparation for writing assignments. Oral preparation for writing is generally endorsed by language arts specialists:

It is seldom wise to simply assign writing chores to children without first providing an oral language experience. (Cramer, 1978, p. 161)

Oral discussion prior to writing is often particularly important. (Petty, Petty, & Becking, 1976, p. 163)

Student talk also plays a crucial role in shaping the language students use in their writing. (Burton, Donelson, Fillion, & Haley, 1975, p. 82)

The most essential factor in helping students make decisions about the content of writing is to let exploratory talk precede writing. (Marcus, 1977, p. 146)

Since oral and written language are closely related, children should have many opportunities to express themselves orally, before being expected to write. (Rubin, 1975, p. 219)

Despite this consensus, such advice may need to be qualified. Groff's (1979) review of the educational research leads him to conclude that it "has not been shown that the oral preplanning of their compositions by children will greatly affect their writing" (p. 36). Perhaps the wisest qualification is offered by Harpin (1976), who acknowledges that the general principle of building writing on a background of talk "seems to be a sound one; beginning writers are likely to be aided by the opportunity to rehearse in speech their own ideas and to overhear the thoughts of others" (p. 135). However, extensive oral preparation should not be adopted as a universal practice. Harpin notes that the "potential danger in the method is that, carried on for too long, it may obstruct the development of individual imagining in much the same way as strongly teacher-directed discussion does" (p. 136). Harpin's research on the writing development of junior-school pupils (approximately ages eight to eleven) showed that, for "factual" writing, there were few differences in "the language resources employed, whether there had been full verbal preparation, or none." For "creative" writing, pieces preceded by verbal preparation were "less mature, judged by the language measures we were examining," than those undertaken without such preparation (p. 136). The results lead Harpin to conclude that

> full verbal preparation for writing should not be an habitual practice. We may, in over-employing this approach, set boundaries for the writer of which we are unaware and inadvertently hinder the development in written language we are trying so hard to promote. In addition, the self-motivating writer is less likely to emerge, if these are the standard conditions for work. (p. 137)

During the consolidation phase of writing development, children's written language resources become progressively strengthened by drawing on the generally more mature oral language resources. Though rarely identical, oral and written expression are often quite similar, and a child's early compositions may appear to be a kind of "talk written down." But the influence is reciprocal. As writing skills develop and begin to be used for conveying full and explicit messages, oral language skills are influenced. Cramer (1978) notes that writing "can foster the growth of oral language" (p. 161) and Lundsteen (1976) acknowledges that when "children have practiced saying exactly what they mean through written language, the clarity of their spoken words improves" (p. 274).

## Differentiation

When oral and written language resources are well on their way to becoming consolidated, emphasis shifts to the process of differentiation—to the key differences between talking and writing—the next phase of development. The transition from consolidation to differentiation is complex, and can be difficult for children. Petty (1978) stresses that children "struggle with the transition from the basically overt language of speech to the essentially covert activity of writing" (p. 76). And Lopate (1978) admits to "circling around that chancy, awkward, difficult moment of the progression from speaking to writing, because in a sense I feel that the ease of transition has been exaggerated" (p. 140). To progress in writing, the child must learn some special skills which, as Bereiter and Scardamalia (in press) show, are not easily developed through oral conversation: children must learn to generate text freely without a respondent, to engage in whole-text planning, to function as the reader of their own writing, and to revise their own texts. Thus, Bereiter and Scardamalia claim that mastering written composition is not just "a matter of incorporating new rules into an intact language production system"; rather, they propose "that the oral language production system cannot be carried over intact into written composition but must in some way be reconstructed so as to function autonomously instead of interactively."

In the next chapter in this book, Kantor and Rubin focus on the differentiation of speaking and writing, taking a comprehensive look at this important process. Their view of differentiation is compatible with mine, though it differs somewhat in focus. For my more general overview, a useful way to discuss the divergence of speaking and writing is to focus on what Olson (1977a, 1977b) has termed the differences between "utterance" and "text."

According to Olson, "utterance" is closely allied with oral conversation, includes mainly informal structures, and performs largely interpersonal functions. Moreover, the meaning of an utterance depends on shared experiences and interpretations—the interaction among speaker, listener, utterance, and context. Thus "conversational speech, especially children's speech, relies for its comprehension on a wide range of information beyond that explicitly marked in the language" (Olson, 1977b, p. 272). On the other hand, "text" is closely connected with writing, and entails predominantly formal structures and ideational functions. The meaning of a text is to be found in the text alone. Text must be autonomous: "all of the information relevant to the communication of intention must be present in the text" (Olson, 1977b, p. 277). Olson's claims need to be qualified by noting that meaning can never reside wholly in the text. Thus, as Wells (1981) notes, "it must be insisted that *all* linguistic communications require an interaction between sender, receiver, and context. In this respect, varieties of spoken and written language differ only in the extent to which they attempt to achieve autonomous and explicit representation of meaning in the form of the message alone" (p. 244). Nevertheless, with this qualification, "utterance" and "text" are useful in defining a major task of this phase of development: the differentiation of written language as relatively autonomous "text."

An important developmental goal associated with differentiation is the ability to produce written "texts" which, on the one hand, are largely free from those features which characterize the language of conversation, and, on the other, incorporate those features which make a text explicit and relatively autonomous in meaning. The compositions of inexperienced writers contain many stylistic features of oral language. A frequently cited example is the use in writing of typically oral "joining methods," particularly the all-purpose "and." Harpin (1976) notes that the "usefulness of 'and' in joining equal units seems to be realized early in speech development. By the time children come to write it is a powerful habit, which gives way only slowly and reluctantly to the very large number of different joining methods provided for in English" (p. 68). Shaughnessy (1977) remarks that

> *and* strings are symptomatic of a style of communicating ... that is customary in speech, where thought seems to be almost simultaneous with speaking and the process of refinement or connection is part of the performance between speaker and interlocutor. As a result, the listener tolerates the use of *and* for a wide range of meanings. But writing begins, in a sense, where speech leaves off—with organizing, expanding, and making more explicit the stuff of dialogue so that the thought that is generated in speech can be given full and independent form. (p. 32)

While consolidation of oral and written language may be functional for a time, children need to learn that written texts differ from everyday spoken utterances. This shift in focus does not mean that consolidation abruptly ceases. There must be a time of transition, during which children continue to consolidate their oral and written resources, yet also begin to differentiate speaking and writing. Moreover, the lessons of consolidation continue to be important, and certain connections between speaking and writing remain significant throughout development.

Differentiation does not mean that children must suddenly abandon their oral language resources, striving for an artificial, "bookish" style that is far removed from their experience and their competence. As Shaughnessy (1977)—dealing with older, but still inexperienced writers—wisely comments,

> this is not to suggest that the inexperienced writer must be expected to make an abrupt transition from writing talk to writing writing, but only that the difference between these two uses of language should be kept in mind, even as the student is engaged in free writing or other expressive exercises that are aimed at getting his writing to the point that it approximates his skill as a talker. (p. 33)

Nevertheless, the processes of "consolidation" and "differentiation" suggest different *emphases* in the approach to the dominant relationship between speaking and writing. While the similarities between speaking and writing should be emphasized in the "consolidation" phase of development, the differences between the two modes should be increasingly stressed in the stage of "differentiation."

One important aspect of differentiation involves helping children discover that writing serves different purposes, employs different forms, and has certain advantages over speaking. Medway (1973) makes the point that, even for young writers, writing must produce "some benefit or satisfaction which he couldn't equally have achieved by the less laborious process of talking" (p. 9). This implies that the pieces children write should become differentiated from the things they ordinarily say. One type of writing which effects a transition from writing which is like speech to writing which differs from oral expression is the composing of stories. In our culture, stories are usually found written down in books, and even young children associate narratives with special kinds of language and distinctive organizational patterns. The writing of narratives requires the child

> to do things which aren't *theoretically* impossible in talk but which social constraints and habitual ways of behaving work against. And here we must record that in infants and junior schools many children are in fact turned on to writing this way—by writing stories, and things about themselves and what they've done and what they've seen, which are quite like the spoken language in their expressiveness and general feel, but which it would perhaps be unusual to find actually spoken by a child. (Medway, 1973, pp. 9-10)

Another type of writing which differs from children's speech is formal transactional writing—exposition and persuasion. In composing formal "texts," a child encounters all the "higher order" difficulties of writing: "organising information effectively, avoiding obscurity and ambiguity, matching manner and matter, interpreting a writing task accurately, acquiring a sense of the varying demands of purpose and audience" (Harpin, 1976, p. 153). Medway (1973) believes that writing which entails "the structuring of complex thought is perhaps unattainable by any but *experienced* writers: you're doing something which hasn't got an equivalent in talk, and you can only get a sense of the possibility of doing it when you're well inside the special world of the written language" (p. 9).

Because of such difficulties, it may be tempting to persist in encouraging kinds of writing which are closer to speaking, avoiding the frustrations inherent in the transition to more "transactional" or "rhetorical" kinds of discourse. The problem with such an approach is that children may get little training or experience in producing more formal "texts" in primary school; yet they are then suddenly expected to display competence in more "academic" kinds of writing at the secondary level. Larson (1971) makes exactly this point:

> whereas the compositions written in elementary school were acknowledged by teachers and parents alike to be "nonrhetorical," the compositions written by the student at this unspecified time later in his school career are expected to display the technical proficiency of utterances designed to affect the thinking of the most fastidious readers. (p. 403)

The answer, for Larson, lies in introducing "rhetorical" writing, alongside the more "expressive" kinds of writing, at the elementary school level. Although non-rhetorical writing is important in elementary school,

> the student's progress toward developing the abilities he will need to carry on the activities of his adult and professional life can be made smoother and easier if he becomes aware of the distinction between writing that has no specific audience or can appeal to any audience ... and writing that is directed toward a particular reader or readers for a specific purpose. Early practice in rhetorical writing ... can be a valuable part of the elementary curriculum in writing, and may even be an essential part that has been substantially neglected. (p. 408)

Finally, it seems likely that reading is a powerful factor in differentiating spoken and written language forms. Britton et al. (1975) maintain that, after some foundation for differentiation has been laid through oral monologue,

> internalized written forms derived from reading feed into the pool of (mainly spoken) linguistic resources on which a writer draws. Probably the first written forms internalized are those of narrative, since anecdotes and stories, spoken or written, are part of a child's social experience from the very beginning. Later, particular interests lead to particular reading, and it is these texts which are internalized, varying very much with the individual. (p. 16)

The Bullock Report (1975) makes the similar point that, in promoting differentiated writing, pupils' "reading interests will be an influential factor, particularly in the early stages. To develop, they must take in written forms of the language and articulate these with their own general language resources, built up by years of listening and speaking" (p. 166).

The failure to have adequately differentiated the forms and functions of oral and written language may continue to plague some students in their college years. Shaughnessy's (1977) account of the problems faced by "basic writers"—college students who have done little formal writing and have minimal writing skills—points to the ways in which these students' failures to differentiate talking and writing lead them into difficulties with "academic" language. Because the basic writer is

> unaware of the ways in which writing is different from speaking, he imposes the conditions of speech upon writing. As an extension of speech, writing does, of course, draw heavily upon a writer's competencies as a speaker ... but it also demands new competencies, namely the skills of the encoding process (handwriting, spelling, punctuation) and the skill of objectifying a statement, of looking at it, changing it by additions, subtractions, substitutions, or inversions, taking the time to get as close a fit as possible between what he means and what he says on paper. (p. 79)

Cayer and Sacks (1979) studied a small number of basic writers enrolled in a community college, to determine whether or not such students are, in fact, "heavily dependent upon their oral strategies and resources when they attempt to communicate in the written mode" (pp. 121–122). Although the findings were tentative, "they do indicate some evidence of the adult basic writer's reliance on the oral repertoire when communicating in the written mode" (p. 127).

While an emphasis on encouraging children to draw on their oral language resources may be functional during the early phases of writing development, enabling children to make a meaningful transition from speaking to writing, during later phases such an emphasis may actually retard the growth of more specialized writing skills. The emphasis in the teaching of writing must shift from consolidation to differentiation, from kinds of writing which draw heavily on oral language competencies to kinds of writing which involve increasingly explicit and autonomous discourse.

### Systematic Integration

Finally, the achievements of the preceding phases seem to come together in a systematic way for the mature writer, resulting in a complex relationship between speaking and writing, a relationship involving elements of both consolidation and differentiation. As in the consolidation phase, aspects of oral language continue to influence writing, perhaps becoming even more important in the later stages of writing development. The expressive qualities most typical of speech (voice, tone, naturalness) are important to advanced writers. Cooper and Odell (1976) found that competent adult writers "were concerned with the oral qualities (volume, speed, inflection) implicit in their writing and with whether those qualities were appropriate for the speaker-audience relationship they were trying to maintain in their writing" (p. 114). Schultz (1978) argues that "writing at its clearest and most effective proceeds from physical voice, from the immediacy, extraordinary precision, and variety of physical voice" (p. 157). Moreover, as speaking and writing abilities mature, they become more extensive, or overlapping, in their potential uses. Mature communicators seem to be able to use speaking and writing for many parallel purposes; indeed, in particular circumstances, they can talk "writing" (creating a relatively explicit and autonomous oral text) and write "talking" (creating a written utterance which is heavily dependent on shared knowledge not explicitly represented in the written product). When oral and written resources are systematically integrated, rather than simply consolidated, a person can make *choices* within a flexible, organized system of voices, registers, and styles—choices which are appropriate for the purpose, audience, and context of communication.

At the same time, it seems clear that, with development, speaking and writing also become better articulated in their dominant forms and functions. Writing *typically* involves the production of texts which are explicit and autonomous, and hence distinct from conversational utterance. Writing comes to serve specialized transactional functions because it is well suited for communicating complex information to distant audiences. And writing seems to serve an important function as a tool for the discovery of thought. Numerous writers insist that writing is a unique way of learning and thinking. To novelist E. M. Forster's oft-quoted "How do I know what I think until I see what I say?" Murray (1978) adds an impressive list of testimonies, from professional writers, concerning the extent to which writing is an act of discovery. And I would add a comment from the eminent developmental psychologist, Jean Piaget, concerning the role of writing in his own intellectual development: "I wrote even if only for myself; I could not think unless I did so" (quoted in Brown, 1980, p. 2).

For the person who is a proficient speaker and writer, the two modes of communication seem to be bound together in a system of subtle and complex relationships: they are both alike and different, both well articulated and interrelated. But such a complex relationship lies at the end of a developmental journey—a long journey through phases marked by shifting emphases on the processes of integration and differentiation. The model I've presented suggests a general sequence for guiding children's development as writers: first consolidating oral and written resources, then differentiating aspects of speaking and writing. By promoting both integration and differentiation, we help children become effective speakers and writers, able to use language flexibly, appropriately, and purposefully.

## Notes

1. As reported in Kroll and Lempers (1981), the total information scores for spoken and written explanations, respectively, were as follows: grade three ($n$ = 16) 18.75, 15.75; grade four ($n$ = 15) 20.40, 17.60; grade six ($n$ = 22) 19.50, 19.68. Mean information scores for spoken explanations were significantly higher ($p < .05$) than mean scores for written explanations for subjects in grades three and four. Mean information scores did not differ significantly for subjects in grade six. An analysis of variance revealed no significant effect for grade level or order of communication for spoken explanations; for written explanations, order was nonsignificant, but grade level approached an acceptable criterion of significance ($p = .06$).

2. These explanations were assigned to one of five possible approach categories: the purely subjective, objective, and hypothetical approaches plus two transitional, or mixed-approach, categories. Two independent raters were able to assign 85 percent of the explanations to the identical categories. Subjects in both grades three and four used virtually the same approach whether speaking or writing, whereas subjects in grade six used the more "hypothetical" approaches significantly more often in their written than their oral explanations (Friedman Two-way ANOVA, $p < .05$).

# 3 Between Speaking and Writing: Processes of Differentiation

Kenneth J. Kantor
University of Georgia

Donald L. Rubin
University of Georgia

The advice, given to students who are having difficulty in writing, is familiar: "Why don't you just write like you talk?" It seems common sensical that if young people have some facility and control in oral language, ability in written language will follow naturally. All they need do is record in written symbols what they can say. Indeed, that principle lies at the heart of the language-experience method of teaching reading, as children are asked to write or dictate to the teacher their spoken thoughts and then use that transcript as material for beginning reading.

Matters become complicated, though, when children begin to attempt to write in forms that are not wholly expressive and self-directed. In effect they encounter certain key distinctions between speaking and writing. As Mallett and Newsome (1977) assert, "it is as though someone who can walk from home to the corner shop has suddenly to travel that same distance pedalling a bicycle he cannot balance through an obstacle course designed to slow him up" (p. 40). Writing, as Britton (1970) and others point out, follows different linguistic and stylistic conventions and is more a "premeditated" act than speaking. It requires acquisition of a complementary set of intellectual processes. Emig (1977) identifies a number of further differences: talk is generally more elaborated, writing selective; talk requires less a commitment to what is said than does writing; talk relies to a great extent on features of the immediate context, while writing must provide much of its own context, specifically the aspects of purpose and audience. Thus have researchers and theorists reminded us of the various tasks of differentiation that individuals must undertake if they are to be successful in writing.

In recognizing those differences, however, we ought not disregard the very real contributions that speaking can make to writing. As Britton (1970) proposes, talk is "the sea on which everything else floats." Indeed, many of the terms we use to describe qualities of effective writing are derived from descriptions of effective speech: for example, personal *voice* and *tone* (writers "speaking" to us through their discourse); a sense of *audience* growing out of our verbal interactions with others. The whole of rhetorical tradition derives from the field of classical oratory and the concerns of the speaker for appealing to and influencing an audience. To negate the benefits of talk for writing would be to dismiss the essential values of that tradition.

Moreover, we ought not forget that writing serves many of the same purposes as does talk. As Martin and associates (1976) contend, talk enables us to communicate basic physiological needs, establish and maintain social relationships, develop our unique identities, understand how and why things happen, predict what will happen in new situations, and simply have fun. Certainly writing can and should fulfill similar functions and as such can profit much from earlier experience in spoken language. Unfortunately writing lacks instrumentality and enjoyment for many individuals in our society. But there is no reason to believe that *must* be the case, as evidenced by the pleasure that many young children take in early nonprescriptive writing experiences. Rejection or dislike of writing may be more environmentally than naturally caused: in school situations, for example, writing is often divorced from speaking.

At the same time, speech is not merely the precursor to writing, since development in oral communication continues beyond the onset of writing, indeed, throughout the entire life span. Repertoires of speech acts expand. Effective speakers learn to select from their repertoires in contextually appropriate and diverse ways. Effective listeners learn to make inferences about speakers' social assumptions. As adults we frequently encounter intense situations which tax our speech communication abilities. Though in many respects writing represents a set of more highly abstract cognitive tasks than oral interaction, the two modes of communication develop concurrently and exert mutual influences.

What members of the Schools Council Research team in England (among them Britton, Martin, Mallett, & Newsome) have asserted is that expressive writing—the free-flowing record of personal thought and feeling—is closest to "inner speech" and at the same time represents the matrix from which differentiated types of writing grow. Specifically, as Britton and associates (1975) have suggested, once individuals establish a foundation in expressive writing, they can then move toward "transactional" writing, in which they act as participants in the business of "getting things done," or toward "poetic" writing in which they act as spectators creating more implicit and evocative statements of meaning. Most writing of elementary and secondary school students will lie somewhere on a continuum between expressive and transactional or expressive and poetic writing (Britton et al., 1975; Martin et al., 1976).

This does not mean, however, that writers need abandon the expressive elements of writing as they mature. The developmental model we wish to suggest proposes that while writing for the sake of differentiation must shed some elements of expressive (or inner speech) discourse, notably redundancy and reliance on external context, its more mature phases also retain aspects of voice and conversationality in order to be effective. The skilled writer, as Britton (1970) held, is one who would "speak" of something that matters to someone who matters.

Additionally, the movement from expressive to transactional or poetic writing is part and parcel of processes of social and cognitive development. Notably, the growth of audience awareness is a manifestation of "decentering"—advancing from an egocentric point of view to one which takes into account the perspectives of others. The theory of Moffett (1968) has suggested a complex of related developmental patterns: the movements from egocentricism to perspectivism, from concrete to abstract, from stereotyping to originality, from talking about present events to talking about past and potential events, from projecting emotion "there-then" to projecting it "here and now," from addressing a small, known audience to addressing a distant, unknown audience.

Growth in speaking and writing ability cannot, however, be viewed solely in terms of maturation. Particularly since writing is a secondary human activity, performed primarily in institutional settings, we cannot disallow the influences of social and cultural context. Moffett (1968) argues that the effects of environment on development are in fact much stronger than those of maturation. The resolution of that question aside, we must at least acknowledge the impact of teaching on growth in writing, since nearly all students from the early grades onward receive some instruction (good or bad) in writing, and thereby formulate attitudes toward writing as well as particular skills. In addition many speech forms, like the oral report, are learned primarily in classrooms. Rather than see those effects of intervention as clouding our conception of development, however, we will instead acknowledge them as important features of the total scenario. We see growth in writing, then, as the result of all the influences upon it, both organic and "man-made." We want to view context, as Mishler (1979) argues, as a resource for understanding rather than the enemy of understanding.

## Facets of Differentiation

We conceptualize communication development—in speech and writing—as progressing simultaneously in three facets: social awareness, coding, and reconstruction of experience. The three facets are also mutually interdependent. Growth in one component promotes growth in the others. When growth is impeded in one component, the others will likewise be affected. Thus our model portrays communication development as propelled by the currents of cognitive development but also as motivated by its own internal dynamics, all within the context of deliberate or casual learning environments.

### Social Awareness

Social awareness is the central component of our developmental model. Communication is first of all a social act, one which involves some kind of intention to affect and be affected by others. In order to successfully realize this intent, individuals must infer information about their audiences: their interests and receptivity, their language processing ability, their beliefs and attitudes, their experience. The process of making such inferences about an audience's covert states is known as role-taking or social perspective-taking. (Delia & Clark, 1977; Flavell, Botkin, Fry, Wright, & Jarvis, 1968). Developmental psychologists have charted the course of growth in this domain beginning with the extreme egocentrism which assumes that others' perspectives are identical with one's own. More mature observers can reconcile seemingly contradictory traits in others ("She's aggressive as a way to cover up her basic fear of being rejected"). Also, cognitively mature individuals can engage in "reflexive" role-taking ("I won't take the last cookie because I don't want my host to think I'm greedy").

Skill in the domain of social awareness is age related, but also affected by other aspects of task difficulty. Young children who perform egocentrically on some tasks may exhibit role-taking when using familiar materials in less complex situations (Maratsos, 1973). In some respects, the task of writing exerts more of a cognitive strain on social awareness than does speaking (Kroll, 1978; Kroll & Lempers, 1981). The transcription process itself poses an intellectual challenge for novice and basic writers, at times requiring such attention that writers lapse into egocentrism just as emotionally overwrought speakers neglect the needs of their audiences. Audience awareness is especially problematic when the audience's identity is ill-defined as in many school-based assignments. Conceptualizing a highly abstract "generalized other" requires cognitive effort (Selman & Byrne, 1974). The writer must, in Ong's (1975) phrase, "fictionalize" an audience. In face-to-face interaction, on the other hand, the audience's concrete presence and on-going exchange of verbal and nonverbal feedback renders the work of inferring audience demands less taxing.

## Coding

The second facet of communicative development, coding, includes not only the "mechanics" of speaking and writing (articulation, enunciation, projection, spelling, penmanship, punctuation), but also organizational control over larger chunks of discourse and knowledge of language pragmatics. Pragmatic competence includes recognition that requests may take the grammatical form of questions ("Do you have the correct time?"), and that stylistic choice compactly expresses constellations of role-related assumptions ("Might I dine with you this evening?" as opposed to, "Wanna grab some chow with me tonight?"). Ability in coding enables communicators to convey a persona and an attitude towards an audience. Along with formal-structural aspects of language development, this knowledge of pragmatics is an ontogenetic phenomenon (Bates, 1976; Western, 1974). Again, one of the more frequently noted differences between oral and written codes is that written language must be context-free while spoken language may capitalize on shared, immediate context. Not only must writers represent the context of communication (including audience) to themselves, but they must also provide necessary context in the text. Writers must acquire a code which renders discourse self-contained, so that all necessary information is included. Formal speech—speech in which speaker and listeners are psychologically remote—shares most of the features of the written code. But informal conversation tolerates implicit meanings, incomplete details, exophoric (outside of text) references, vacuous modification ("really nifty"), digression, and fragmented presentation. (Intimate types of writing like personal journals and letters may approach the conversational code.)

Of the three facets of differentiation, coding has received disproportionate emphasis in American language education. Attempts to improve quality of speaking and writing through didactic instruction in grammar have been as enduring as they have been unfruitful. More recently, and with greater effect, language educators have examined growth in syntactic complexity. Writing and speaking differ little along this dimension of language. Clear age-related trends, however, have been documented. (Hunt, 1970; Loban, 1976; O'Donnell, Griffin, & Norris, 1967). Children move from highly coordinated structures to more frequent subordination and finally exploit sub-clausal syntactic units which package propositions most efficiently. Despite the consistency of this pattern of development, there is little justification for establishing age-related norms of syntactic complexity against which students might be evaluated (Crowhurst, 1979). Syntactic complexity of writing as well as of speech is influenced by the specific purposes and audiences of communication tasks. For example, persuasive writing exhibits greater subordination than narrative, and more remote audiences engender longer clauses than intimate audiences (Crowhurst & Piché, 1979; Perron, 1976; Rubin & Piché, 1979).

### Reconstruction of Experience

Reconstruction of experience, the third facet of communication development, is closely related to the rhetorical canon of invention. The term "reconstruction," however, commits this model to a phenomenological perspective. We perceive the world with greater or lesser degrees of accuracy. More significantly, we construe the world according to our individual systems of personal constructs, with greater or lesser degrees of definition, abstraction, and organization. We sculpt events to conform to our perceptual templates, forcing them into significance. (This notion is similar to Piaget's concept of assimilation. From time to time we must also adjust or acquire new templates in order to accommodate otherwise unmanageable experience.) In this sense, individuals construct their experience. And, in expression, individuals reconstruct experience, imposing yet again new form and meaning.

Conceiving of communication as epistemic—as a way of exploring the world—implies more than that speakers and writers expand their data base through preliminary research or the like. More to the point, the symbol manipulation involved in expressing an idea itself promotes a process of discovery (Bruner, 1966). The common view that communicators conceive a thought and then package it in words for delivery to an audience seems limited. Rather, "languaging" and thinking are simultaneous and not altogether distinguishable processes. Professional writers, looking introspectively at their own composing processes, frequently report that a subject takes on direction and form only in the act of writing (Murray, 1978). British educators have especially stressed the value of speaking and writing as tools for learning about one's self and one's world. Classroom talk and writing can serve as ways of understanding and not merely as vehicles for conveying that understanding.

Speech and writing appear to facilitate cognition in different ways. Literate peoples are disposed to more linear, cause-and-effect thought patterns than nonliterate peoples (Greenfield, 1972; Olson, 1977a). Oral language is less often planned, and because speech is a fast-fading medium, its potential as an adjunct to the cerebrum is limited. Writing, on the other hand, leaves a permanent trace and permits re-vision and ongoing meta-analysis. For some communication tasks, writing's advantage in allowing reflection outweighs its disadvantages in requiring more complex social perspective-taking (Higgins, 1978).

## The Interdependence of the Facets

The interdependence of social awareness, coding, and reconstruction of experience is apparent in a number of respects. Differences between the written and oral codes in terms of context-dependence represent adaptations to respective differences in communicator-audience roles. Vague pronoun reference in writing or predicates without subjects, for example, may be diagnosed as weaknesses in social awareness and not simply as ignorance of the conventions of writing (Shaughnessy, 1977). Coding, we have indicated, is a problem solving technique that facilitates reconstruction of experience. Students endowed with rich linguistic repertoires are likely also to generate insight. Conversely, students who have failed to find a meaningful approach to their subject are likely to use strained, inanimate, and sometimes hypercorrect language. We have also indicated that for beginning writers, lack of social awareness poses a barrier. Conversely, finding an audience may sometimes help students find their way into subject matter. An assignment asking students to describe their school building may be quite difficult until it occurs that such a description might usefully appear in a handbook to be read by transfer students.

For immature communicators, writing and speaking are closely allied in all three components. As Kroll (chapter 2) points out, they are nondifferentiated. Although the strain of graphemic encoding results in reduced fluency, early writing still shows little difference from speech in context-dependency. Young writers are ill-equipped to write for a generalized reader, tending instead to construe such audiences as known individuals (Rubin, 1980). Beginning writers do not often take advantage of the potential cognitive effects of writing, certainly not to the degree of the adult who writes, "Now that I'm writing you about glass recycling I can see that I really should begin a recycling project of my own at home."

During a middle stage of communication development, writing diverges sharply from speech. Often, writing becomes code-centered. Concern with writing mechanics imposed by classroom instruction may become the dominant concern to the detriment of social awareness and reconstruction of experience. The typical audience is "teacher as examiner"; the ideas display little or no evidence of active interaction with experience. At the same time speech patterns retain a high degree of expressiveness and color in the face of the supreme importance of peer interaction and acceptance.

For mature individuals speech and writing reconverge in some respects. More advanced speakers gain control over formal oral discourse and occasionally their conversational speech is inappropriately too booklike. Writers learn to simplify their diction where possible and to introduce a sense of conversationality where appropriate. Tone and voice are qualities of mature writing, representing a realization of the social nature of writing.

Many writers, however, perhaps the majority of high school graduates, remain at a middle level of development, suspended awkwardly between speech and writing. They have acquired, with more or less acumen, the mechanics of speaking and writing. But they have not learned to exploit the interactions of coding, social awareness, and reconstruction of experience in either speech or writing. This pivotal, or "differentiating" stage will be our focus in the remainder of this essay. Our illustrations will reveal transitions between speaking and writing, as children are making various kinds of important distinctions. These "transitional" scripts, primarily in written discourse, will suggest the kinds of growth taking place as individuals move from non-differentiated discourse to mature, integrated expressions of thought and feeling.

Implicit in such an approach is that development of writing ability is not easily defined in chronological terms. Thus, while our illustrations will be taken from the speech and writing of children in grades four through twelve, we do not mean to suggest that productions of older children are always "better" or more mature than those of younger ones. Indeed, in some cases, younger students may demonstrate strengths (for example, greater use of concrete detail) that older ones do not. We want through our selections to identify and illustrate the various patterns of differentiation between speaking and writing, rather than try to assign those patterns to any given stages of development. And in doing so, we wish to demonstrate the interplay between code, social awareness, and reconstruction of experience that highlights those patterns of development.

### Differentiating Audiences

Britton et al. (1975) distinguish between two transactional functions of discourse—"informative," that which has the intent of explanation, and "conative," that which seeks to regulate or persuade. We can see the movement from expressive to informative and persuasive discourse reflected in the following discussion of television shows by a fourth-grade student:

> I like "Happy Days." It is funny and all kinds of funny things happen. Once Fonzie went outside to go to work and his motorcycle which Fonzie calls it his prices dimond he found that his motorcycle was in pieces just plan pieces and Fonzie screamed caused it was torup. It makes me laught and it is a real good show. And Thier's a family of four and their names are Howard Conntingham Marine Conntingham Richar, and Jonie. Witch Fonzie call them Mr. and Mrs. C. I thing everybody would like the show very, very, much because my two sisters my brother, and my mother and I like it "to." I saw it when Fonzie jumped 14 trashcans and ended up in the Hospital with a bad leg and a few scraches to. Well it is a good show so watch sometimes and you'll laugh to.

While this writer clearly has some difficulties with the written code, notably in spelling and syntactic structure, he also shows an emerging social sense: he is reconstructing an experience not only for himself but also his readers, whom he eventually seeks to persuade that they will like the show too. The style is relatively expressive and not much differentiated from speech ("just plain pieces," "torup") but the intent is at least partially transactional, both in the informative and persuasive sense.

We should note, however, that at any age there is wide variation in children's sensitivity to audience. Also, we should not assume that all beginning writers have consolidated their skill in adapting to audiences in speech. Like the author of the previous essay, this next speaker is also in grade four. After listening to a brief dialogue he responds to his teacher's question:

> *Teacher:* Do you think after that that Johnny would let Mike play with his ball?
>
> *Student:* Well if that guy was looking at the ball they might switch and then that guy would play with the game and that guy would probably play with the ball.
>
> *Teacher:* Can you think of another reason why Johnny might let Mike play with the ball?
>
> *Student:* Well like another reason the guy would probably be bugging him and he didn't want anyone to bug him so he would probably give him the ball.

The student's tense switching in his second response suggests that he is having difficulty projecting into the hypothetical situation. He is likely reasoning his way as he speaks. His discourse is referentially confused, but the student appears unconcerned with the listener's effort to keep straight the "guys'" identities.

A more successful adaptation for an audience may result in a more imaginative or divergent response, as in the following writing by an eighth-grader on the various uses of tin cans:

> There are so many different things you can do with a tin can for enstance you can cut out the bottom of it and make coasters or you can make holes in it and put a plant in it so the viens and leaves can grow out the holes. You can really do almost anything with a can. Cut it in half long ways and make it up so it will look like a cradle. And you can put a doll in it. Cut it in half and put a potted plant in it. Cut off the top and you can keep pencils, pens, tooth brushes etc. in it, twist it in the middle and you can make just a little statue. It depends on how you smash it up cut pices out of it and you can put it on a hat to make it look good. When you get mad you can also have one to hit. Or cut it up in little shreds so it would be sharp and we

> can make knifes out of them. Make a boat out of it so you can
> go sail it. Paint it up and give to a friend for a present and let
> her do whatever you want to with them you can take the
> plug-er-uper of it and make necklaces or braclets out of it.
> Thats all I can think of.

Here the writer addresses the audience directly, using the imperative as if she were giving a recipe or helpful hints. Rather than
recounting what she and the reader might already know (as in the
TV writing cited earlier) she is creating "new" knowledge. The
direct address to the audience allows her to brainstorm her list of
uses; we can almost sense these ideas coming to her as she goes
along. When she can't quickly think of a name for something, she
calls it a "plug-er-uper"; when she runs out of ideas, she simply
writes (as one would in conversation) "That's all I can think of."

The "you"-audience in this last essay is not any specific individual reader. Rather, the second person personal pronoun is a
primitive form of reference to a generalized other. In the following
speech sample, a sophomore uses a similar device in explaining
free-style wrestling to a teacher uninformed about the subject:

> It's wrestling. It's a different kind. It's a open class. They've
> got three different classes. They've got kids and they've got
> juniors and open. I'm in o-; I'm in junior, not open. See open
> is about the toughest. It's a; Really you don't start down. Like
> wrestling you'll start down second period. Free-style you start
> up everytime. If you go off the mat you come back on. You
> start up. You get down like if you take the guy down. You've
> got 15 seconds to pin him. If you don't pin him they stop the
> watch and you start up. So it's a lot more physical.

Notice that the speaker adopts the "you"-reference first when he
runs into difficulty in his explication. ("It's a; Really you don't
start down.") The "you"-reference here, and perhaps in the essay
above, is a technique which renders the generalized other more
concrete and thereby simplifies the conceptualization. This
speech sample also illustrates the characteristic redundancy and
nonlinear organization of oral language. Essentially this is a comparison and contrast discourse, but the sequencing of points is
spontaneous and therefore confusing at first listening. A major task
in differentiating speech and writing is to acquire the more linear
patterns of writing.

During this differentiating stage, speakers or writers may be
thinking of an audience of their peers, as well as that of their
teachers. The peer-group audience, as McLeod (1969) and Britton
et al. (1975) reveal, becomes important for writers as they de-

center, especially in contrast to the "teacher-as-examiner," for whom students must often sacrifice personal expressions for the sake of meeting certain formal standards.

To illustrate some of the features of "peer audience" writing, we would like to cite a few examples of eighth-graders writing in "Dear Abby" fashion to seventh-graders worried about the next-grade year. Students doing this task adopted a variety of rhetorical stances: some were condescending, others empathetic, still others simply informative. Many were subjective, generalizing from their own experience, while a few considered that their reader might be different from them.

The first example shows a number of these features:

> Dear Worried,
>
> Its good that you know you have this problem. First of all let me tell you some things that will be expected of you next year. You will be expected to work hard in class and not fool around. The section I was in, Section 5, had a lot of problems as far as behavior in class is concerned. We needed to improve a lot on this.
>
> Classes like Science, Health, Ga. History, and sometimes Language Arts require a project. These projects aren't usually hard but it does involve a little work, such as reading a book and writing a report. The eighth grade teachers are all very nice and you should respect them.
>
> About cutting up in class. Just work hard and don't talk. And don't fight! That's all you have to do to stay out of the office.
>
> The teachers rarely give homework—or at least last year they hardly did. I noticed if we cooperated with them, they were nicer to us. And if they do give homework, do it! Avoid the T.V. set or the hot, sunny days and do your work first. Remember, work always comes first—then recreation.
>
> My biggest and only problem this past year was when I did have homework, I would take it home and forget it. Because I didn't do it first. I would go somewhere to play softball or basketball. Sometimes I would just sit around and watch television all evening and then wait until the very next day the project was due and then do it at the very last minute.
>
> There is no reason to be afraid of the eighth grade, Sure you'll have a few butterflies the first day or two, but after a while you get used to it. Once again, I recommend 2 things for you to do next year.
>
> 1. study hard
> 2. behave yourself
>
> If you do both of these, you should get along just fine.

Admittedly, this writer assumes a somewhat parental, older and wiser stance, that suggests he does not strictly have a peer audience in mind. On the other hand, he does show empathy by confessing his own shortcomings and self-realizations. This shows the writer is making judgments about appropriate distances between himself and his audience. The letter also reflects some powers of organization, with distinct paragraphing and a summary of the two main points—clearly the student has some command over forms of written language that distinguish it from speech. At the same time the writing occasionally takes on a conversational tone: "First of all, let me tell you. . ." "About cutting up in class," "Sure you'll have a few butterflies."

Indeed, in performing this writing task, a number of students employed conversational language, ostensibly to make contact with their audience in a way they might not have done with a typical teacher (or adult) audience. One girl, for example, asked "rhetorical" questions of her reader: "Seventh grade wasn't that hard, now was it?" and "let me know how it turns out, OK?" Another student, a boy, used nonstandard forms to get his message across: "It ain't much work, especially in Language Arts, so you don't have to worry about that. Coach ain't never given anything you cain't handle. . . ." We suspect his usage here is deliberate since in an earlier sentence (and others) he used the standard forms: ". . . most people whose grades aren't so good don't really care." Still another student used "street talk": "So play it cool cause I ain't got no time for jive." Again, it seems to us that as developing writers identify their audience as having more or less equal status (clearly not the case with the teacher-as-examiner), they begin to include patterns of everyday spoken language with the written forms they are presently acquiring, so as to maintain contact with that audience.

Fluency is often enhanced with peer audiences, but problems occur when students are asked to write to audiences and for purposes for which they are not developmentally ready (Kantor, 1978). The following is one of a number of awkward essays by eighth-graders in response to the task of writing a ten-minute television message to the United States:

> If I could get on t.v. for ten minutes and tell the United States what I thought I really don't know what I'd say, I would probably have a list like 1, 2, 3, . . .; The first one would be: 1. Why can't crime be stopped. Everyday I hear of some getting

killed, a bank being robbed, and so, on. 2. The kids who don't
have parents or anyone to turn to, I think ya'll should have a
real fantastic place for those kids and they'll be happy and
want have to think about their parents. 3. I would tell the
United States that I like this country alot and that I would
never leave it. 4. I would probably tell all my family hello.
Then all of my friends hi, and last of all I would tell Ronnie
hello. I would tell Ronnie that I miss him and I can't wait till
August when he comes back to Athens.

So that's probably what I'd say cause I've already wrote a
letter to the president about the first three I just said. I haven't
got a letter back from him lately, but I don't care because at
least I said what I thought.

Well I really guess I better go. I hope this is enough.

Although the writer proceeds in a systematic fashion, enumerating the topics she would discuss, she doesn't appear yet to have
norms for the occasion or type of social awareness needed to address the unknown audience successfully. Actually, the piece is
more an example of prewriting, revealing the author's process of
invention; as such it gives us insight into a way in which a child
might initially approach such an assignment. Her chattiness and
unsupported assertions are appropriate for this stage of finding her
arguments. But an actual television speech she might eventually
write would, we think, need to have a more specific focus and
familiar audience to make it a worthwhile experience for her or to
have a strong impact on that audience.

## Differentiating Contexts

As developing writers move from expressive toward transactional
discourse, they begin to supply the context which is present in
oral communication and absent in written language. Dramatic evidence of this process can be found in the following two pieces:

*Seventh-Grader:*

When you watch T.V. you get hungry and wants something
to eat. By eating a lot that is how I gained my wait. When
something comes on I just keep running to get something to
eat or drink. My mother always is fussing about how much I
eat and fat I am getting and she always say if I keep it I am not
going to have a nice shape. But now I have stop eating so
much.

*Twelfth-Grader:*

Another problem I encounter which causes me to watch a
limited amount of T.V. is the fact I eat so much while I watch
it. It's a terrible habit I got into when I was quite small. We

were not allowed to watch much television, except on weekends. The only real shows I watched, excluding my cartoons, were on Friday nights. I can remember so well how we'd all sit down on the floor in front of the T.V. and eat. It didn't much matter what, nuts, ice cream, popsicles, cookies or any other edible object we could find in the kitchen. So, until this day, when I watch T.V., I have accessive cravings. The problem of that is, now that I'm not a hyper 6 year old the calories add up and I get fat. I've found that staying away from T.V., helps me stay away from food!

While each student is making essentially the same statement, the twelfth-grader fills in the context—the specific situation in which she would eat too much and the kinds of foods she would eat. Thus she is rendering her experience explicit, whereas it remains implicit in the first student's writing. At the same time she is selective, choosing the most salient details to support her point. She also uses a more sophisticated vocabulary ("encounter," "limited," "excluding," "excessive") and in general anticipates the needs of her readers, knowing that they cannot be expected to fully understand the context without her help. This is not to diminish the effort of the seventh-grader, however, who also provides some pertinent information (especially in the reference to her mother's warnings) and seems to sense that she too cannot rely solely on features that may be present in an oral language situation. It seems we can tell a great deal about perception of audience from what writers include "without being asked," and conversely what they choose *not* to include.

Differentiation between speaking and writing contexts is a function of growth in cognitive capacity, especially as students progress from egocentric, concrete operations to more abstract and generalized thinking. The mix of concrete details and generalized conclusions is always a matter of delicate balance. Speakers can rely on their listeners to demand additional elaboration or clarification. The effective speaker, however, anticipates listeners' needs. The following conversational turn is extracted from a mock job interview conducted by tenth-graders:

*Interviewer:* How would you say you get along with your teachers?

*Job Applicant:* Ahm, very good. I'm always teasing with them and joking with them and they're always (minor pause) As a matter of fact, when I was in the eighth-grade my social studies teacher, my history teacher, we used to cut each other down during like we were talking about the American Revolution. Talking, starting to cut each other down, you know. I get along with them easy.

This student recognizes—rather abruptly—his listener's need for concrete detail. This sensitivity is a first step. Later, he will learn to select and craft his illustrations more informatively.

As further illustration of this process consider the following discussions of soap operas written by a seventh-, ninth-, and twelfth-grade student, respectively:

*Seventh-Grader:*

I like to watch soapoperas when we don't have to go to school. I think they are fun to watch. They show people breaking up. Hubands and wives getting back together. Couples going to exspensive restarants and place you go to dance and eat. I like to watch as the world turns, The Young and the Restless, the Guilding light and some others ones. Some soapoperas come on about 11:30–5:00.

*Ninth-Grader:*

I like to watch soap operas. I think they are educational to watch. You can learn how other people solve their problems. I like to watch all my children and Guilding Light. Sometimes you find out other people are worse off than you are. Even though the soap operas on television are not real that does not mean it could not happen in real life. They are trying to get you ready incase it happens to you. This is example of what could happen: On Guilding Light Ed is getting on drinking again. Rita a close friend tries to help him through this difficult period. He does not want her to be with him through this period. He wants to work it out by himself without Rita helping. This situation could happen to someone and it may help them know how to deal with it.

*Twelfth-Grader:*

Cartoons and soap operas are just great! I love them, they're my favorite kind of shows.

These two types of shows are quite similar because neither of them displays true reality. Cartoons just skip over reality and on to the fantasy world. Soap operas always overplay real situations. In cartoons there is always a hero that comes to the rescue at just the right time or some character that thinks he's the star of the show. These are just fun shows that help the mind to relax and enjoy a world of fantasy.

Soap operas do the opposite, they somehow manage to twist the mind until you're so involved that you just can't wait until the next day to tune in. Even if you only watch for five minutes, you're hooked and will want to find out if Marcia really is pregnant and if Brad really does have a brain tumor or if George really will make it through the critical operation.

The shows make you really appreciate your own life a lot more because you aren't the one with all of those terrible problems.

> So to get away from it all with a T.V. set, cartoons and soaps
> are the way to do it.

The first writing points out some features of soap operas without relating them in any particular way. In the second piece, the writer identifies a value for soap operas (learning how others solve problems) and cites a specific example to support her point. The twelfth-grade writer does not mention any particular show, but instead uses generalized characters (Marcia, Brad, and George) to suggest the sameness of soap operas. This represents, we think, a sophisticated mental operation, one which the act of writing perhaps enables the author to demonstrate more readily than conversational speech (Kirby & Kantor, 1979).

Another aspect of cognitive development is reflected in differences in style as it conveys emotionality, especially in persuasive discourse. Since transactional writing is generally a more reflective act than speaking or expressive writing, we would expect it to be more tempered and less spontaneous. Writers just developing, though, may be quite reactive and even "irrational." Such is the case in the following essay by a twelfth-grader, in response to a film *(The End of One)* depicting the death of a seagull:

> The garbage dump in the film the End of One was made by man, just like the other dumps all over the world. Something like what we saw probably happens everyday at each dump. I think that man is responsible for the bird's death.
>
> Man is responsible because he created all of that garbage in the dump. Man and his supposedly fantastic technology created it all. I'm not saying that it is absolutely the pits, but it's not exactly the greatest. If man is so brilliant, why can't he work on saving his own planet, its people, and its animals instead of trying to see who can get their man on Mars first, and who can make and use the most weapons. We, the People of Earth and other living things, deserve the attention and concern first.
>
> Take for instance the poor and hungry people of the world. They require more attention than the little green men on Mars. The little birds deserve more attention than the big, noisy rockets.
>
> If man would pay attention to his own world, everyone and everything would probably be alot better off. The little bird would still be alive.

While the argument is highly subjective and unsupported by factual evidence, we need to recognize it as the writer's attempt to work out his own convictions on the subject and to persuade his audience as to his ideas and feelings. As such it provides a dra-

matic contrast to another twelfth-grader's essay, in which the
writer assumes a highly "objective" pose:

> The movie which we have just seen illustrates a sea gull's
> death. There could have been many causes pertaining to it's
> death. In this paper I hope to suggest and reason with several
> possibilities. Of course the choice is yours for I truly do not
> know what lead to the gull's death.
>
> The garbage dump, which appeared throughout the movie
> seemed to be a harbor for an unlimited number of diseases
> and brutal infections. Since the sea gulls constantly gathered
> and ate trash which was deposited at the garbage dump there
> would be an increasing chance for the spread of an infectious
> disease. This disease could have been harmful to the gull's
> body chemistry in some way. I believe a disease of some type
> appeared to have caused the gull's death because the dying
> process of the gull was unusually slow. The movie shows the
> gull not flying at all, therefore the disease could have been
> retained within the gull for quite a long period of time. Be-
> cause of the perceivably high rate of disease incubation the
> dump should definitely be closed and relocated.
>
> Another possible link to the gull's death could have been
> old age. The bird appeared wearily old-looking. Therefore old
> age should be also considered.
>
> Several times throughout the movie a body of water ap-
> peared. It seemed polluted to a high degree. Again the possi-
> bility of the gull eating a fish or drinking some of the water
> would lend reason to it's death. Perhaps the water was con-
> taminated and contained a chemical harmful to the gull's body
> chemistry. The area near the seashore seemed very industrial
> and of course with industry comes pollution which was proba-
> bly deposited directly into the water. This is another link to
> the gull's death.
>
> In conclusion the choice of the gull's causes of death are all
> good but no one solution is for certain.

We sense that the use of formal structure and impersonal style of
the five-paragraph theme helps the writer disguise his own feelings and avoid the risk of taking a stand. A more effective essay
would perhaps reconcile the "passion" and personal voice of the
first with the concrete illustrations and reflectiveness (if not the
scientific detachment) of the second. As the classical rhetoricians
held, an orator could appeal to emotion as well as to reason (Corbett, 1965).

In balancing detail and generalization, concrete and abstract,
and emotion and reason, students seem to be most in their element in using the narrative mode. Since storytelling is a natural
and comfortable activity for most children, narratives represent a
logical first step in venturing out from expressive toward

audience-directed discourse. Students who have not yet mastered new modes of expression, though, will frequently revert to the expressive when an assignment taxes their discourse competence. Here a fourth-grade girl loses the narrative thread apparently because a psychic need of her own has been jarred in the act of writing:

> One day an old women who went to buy tomatoes and She was a picky one who wanted the best of every thing. She looked here and there and She put them on the top and kept looking for the best. Her name was jane her friends teased her about her name alot they said jane your a jerk and accours that She was little at that time She was about 8 a the least.

Even when children are comfortable in narration, they will frequently use storytelling as an opportunity to reconstruct and explore their own feelings. This story, told to a visitor by a suburban fourth-grader, obviously serves a personal function for the writer:

> There once was a family and their last name was um Schrucke, and they, well they don't look it, but they were poor. And so they lived in this room. And they only lived like Indian people, but they weren't. And they wanted a new house because they didn't like this house. And it was all made out of wood. And um they hadda sleep on trunks and stuff on the floor. And they had very little to eat. So one day they looked at their house. And so the father had to get a job. And he did. And he got just a little job that he gets paid about $325 for. And um this might be about my dad. I just wanted to tell about this. And he was a field rep at _____. And they had a sales meeting one day. And his friend told him that he might be put in a higher store manager. And he was happy because he might get more money. But his mother and the three boys didn't want to move away. They were fond of the place they were living in. But the father said if he does get paid that we must move. And they were all sad. And um he didn't get picked. So they were glad that he didn't get picked. And they still lived in the old house. They now do. And um they lived happily ever after.

The beginning of the story hints that the speaker is privy to more information about this family than she is revealing ("they only lived like Indian people, but they weren't"). Midway through, however, she blurts out her closeness to the events in the story. The story's conclusion, finally, allows the speaker to create a satisfactory outcome for her own very real predicament.

Narrative also serves as a vehicle for children's imagination, as in the following account of a trip to Mars written by a fifth-grader:

On the way I went and saw no trees or ponds when it
landed it seemed to be going down. All of the sudden I saw
red green & blue beside me. It said, "What on Mars are you,"
I am a earthling, I said. He said, We are Marslings. Very interesting you look one color, we turn colors to the temprature I
brought a friend which is called a ring and it changes the same
as you. They almost roasted me but the rope burnt and let me
free. Well I climbed on the ship and I started and something
started pulling me down I got away and something seemed to
be following me. When I got to the feeling that something was
driving for me. Then I saw him. It was the martion. He moved
out of my way and vanished. I made it to earth and no one
believed me. I guess that's how the ball rolls.

We can see in this writing some aspects of oral storytelling, for
example the use of "well" and "then" as connectives, but we can
also see a number of accommodations to written forms, as the
writer varies her sentence structure and vocabulary choices. It also
seems to reveal a sense for "fashioning" a story, for using language
and images that will entertain her readers ("What on Mars are
you?") as well as herself. We suspect too that the remote setting
and imaginative aspects of this kind of task allow children to step
back from their own experience and thereby adopt the spectator
stance to a greater extent.

Narrative serves other purposes for developing writers as well,
especially in helping them cope with demands of more cognitively
challenging tasks. For example, many eighth-grade students faced
with the task of theorizing about what they would do if lost in the
woods began or lapsed quickly into the narrative mode (Kantor,
1978):

### The Ugly Woods

I was walking one day in the woods and then I found myself lost. I hadn't the slightest idea where I was.

All I had with me was a knife and a match. And the clothes
I was wearing. It was during the day about 3 o'clock.

Still others used the present tense to dramatize their narrative:

### Lost

Now I'm lost and I only have a pocket knife, and one match
I'm lost and I need water and in a couple of hour's its going to
be night time.

I am going to go and find a clear area. I need anof wood to
spell out help. Its getting darker and I'm begging to not be
able to see were I'm going. I can't use my match because I
don't need it yet. I just think I'll go to sleep under some bush.

Only a few of the students maintained a hypothetical approach throughout, using the subjunctive:

> Well, if I were lost in the woods, there's no telling what I would do. First of all, I've always heard that if you lost you should stay in one place. But since I have a pocket knife I'd probably go wandering around in the direction I thought I'd come in.

But most students, despite the mode in which they were writing, solved the problem for themselves, either by saving themselves through their own ingenuity or being rescued by others (a few left their endings ambiguous). Our speculation is that when students face a problematic writing task they use the forms (frequently narratives) most comfortable to them, and discover or create their solutions in the process. This is writing to make the world understandable to oneself.

One further device is worth noting: dialogue. Even in oral storytelling children frequently find it easiest to present details in the form of dialogue. In this fourth-grader's story, dialogue permits the student to increase the immediacy and concreteness of the events.

> One day this girl, she was waiting. There was a call she was waiting for. And she waited for hours and hours. And it still didn't, it still didn't come in. But finally it was night time. So she, so she went to bed. And the next morning there was knocking at the door. And she ran to see who it was. And it was her uncle. And it was her birthday today. And he forgot about it yesterday. So then she came and said, "Why didn't you come yesterday?" And he said, "Well I forgot. I was down at the store." And then he closed the door. And the policeman said, "What are you doing, breaking into this little girl's house? Is her parents home?" And the little girl said, "No. They're staying overnight. And I'm the only one here." And the policeman said, "Who is this guy?" And the little girl said, "This is my uncle. And he came to bring me a gift." And so, and then the policeman said, "If I ever see you do that again he's going to be put in jail." And the little girl said, "It's my birthday today. So why should he be put in jail?" And the policeman said, "I didn't say he had to go to jail today. I said the next time I see you doing that again he'll have to go to jail." And then the little girl said, "You wanna come to my birthday party?" And the policeman said, "yeah, sure." So then there's a party and everything. And then there's a telephone call. And it was the police department looking for this policeman cause he'd been gone all day.

Despite the repetitious "He saids" and "She saids," the dialogue form obviously provides this child with fluency in oral composition. In the first several lines, not written in dialogue, the speaker was simply stalling. Once she discovered her plot, she was able to soar with the help of the dialogic form. Notice that the policeman's voice mimics the kind of argumentative, arbitrary authoritarianisms with which children frequently control their peers ("I didn't say . . . I said . . ."). The epilogue, encapsulated in the final three sentences, returns to nondialogic form as if the storyteller, her tale seemingly resolved in her mind, no longer had need for the fluent torrent of dialogue which had enabled her to develop her plot.

Dialogue helps speakers and writers make their context more understandable. For example, one student in her "Lost in the Woods" paper uses an interior dialogue:

### What Should I Do

Oh my goodness I'm lost in these spooky looking woods. How am I going to find my way back? What am I going to do? Should I start a fire? If I won't to start a fire I probably can't cause I've got only 1 match. I need that to start a fire to keep warm. But then again I might better start a forest fire so some one can see it then they might find me.

This is a type of stream-of-consciousness technique which allows the writer to work through the problematic situation. As Moffett (1968) states:

In interior dialogue we have subjective, spontaneous, inchoate beginnings of drama (what happens), narrative (what happened), exposition (what happens), and argumentation (what may happen). As it bears on curriculum this means that students would tap, successively, their inner stream of sensations, memories, and ideas, as raw material for recordings, narrative reports, and essays of generalization and theory. (p. 40)

In other writings, we can see some uses of conversational dialogue, as in this ending to a lengthy story:

The next day I heard someone calling it was momma she said—Paula are you there—(about out of breath) I called and said Yes, I'm over here. Beside this big tree She found me and said Susan called. I said—thank god for that and then momma said why didn't you tell me that it was Susan's house that you were going over. I thought you said Sandra. I did mom but you known that Susan lives near the woods and you wouldn't of let me go if you found out.

Note that in this process the writer decides she no longer has to identify each speaker; thus she has discovered an important literary device. Interestingly, as writers approach mature poetic discourse, they create more implicit meanings and allow the context to explain what is missing, much as occurs in oral language situations. In producing a poem, for example, the writer becomes highly selective, providing hints and gestures of meaning and calling on the reader to fill in the gaps.

## Implications for Teaching and Learning

From the model of speaking-writing differentiation we have suggested and the foregoing illustrations, we would like to suggest some implications for teaching. We propose these not as specific recommendations for classroom practices, but as principles and attitudes that might guide teachers toward more effective practices.

It seems clear that as students "decenter" and gain social awareness, they have a greater desire to engage in transactions with audiences outside the self, particularly to explain or persuade. Teachers can foster this development by providing opportunities for students to talk with each other on topics of common interest, especially in small groups, and by devising writing tasks which require students to consider the potential responses of wider audiences. At the same time, teachers should be aware of children's needs to approach those audiences through an expressive, speech-like mode, even though that method may result in some awkwardness and inconsistency of style.

More specifically, we think that teachers might make greater use of the peer group as audience than they traditionally have. Approaches to composition instruction like Macrorie's (1976) "helping circle" and Moffett's (1968) "writing workshop" have great merit in this respect. The peer group offers possibilities for empathy, identification, and support that the teacher-as-examiner does not. On the other hand, we ought not dismiss the importance of teacher as "trusted adult"; many students may feel more comfortable writing to their teacher than to their peers, since the teacher may be more sensitive to their feelings. Gaining students' trust, however, requires that teachers act as readers, responders, and fellow writers rather than as judges, and in particular recognize students' use of expressive and even colloquial language as essential to their growth in audience awareness.

In related fashion, teachers should understand that too vaguely defined or abstract an audience can create "stage fright" in students and result in strained and artificial expressions. Just as with effective speech communication classes, where informal small group conversation precedes formal speeches or debates, expressive writing for a familiar known audience should provide the foundation for expository writing addressed to wider unknown audiences. While the patterns of oral language eventually need to be differentiated from those of written discourse, they serve initially as an important means for developing writers to make contact with audiences beyond themselves.

Another very significant function of expressive discourse is that of helping students discover what they have to say and how to shape their discourse for an audience. Mallett and Newsome (1977) provide two striking examples of class discussions: in one, the teacher closes off possibilities for discovery by leading students toward predetermined answers, and in another, the teacher enhances the creative process by allowing students to pursue their own instincts and exchange ideas with each other. Clearly, the second approach results in more meaningful learning, as students make things understandable to themselves. Exploratory talk is often helpful as a prewriting activity in which students can generate ideas for their writing. At the same time, teachers need to recognize the moment of "ripeness" for writing (Lopate, 1978) at which further discussion might deflate inspiration.

We find especially that the narrative mode serves a variety of purposes for developing writers. It offers a "home base" from which to operate in dealing with a challenging task, particularly in writing expository and argumentative prose (Kantor & Perron, 1977). We see growth in writing as a process both of venturing out and experimenting with new forms and ideas, and of returning to the familiar and comfortable to "regroup" and plan for further forays into the unknown. A narrative or storytelling mode provides a safe haven for reconstructing experience and shaping one's writing to meet the demands of purpose and audience. Thus teachers ought to view the use of personal narrative and dialogue not as a sign of immaturity but as an indication of writers sorting out ideas and working through problems for themselves, that is, "writing to learn" as well as learning to write.

This means too that teachers should be tolerant of expressions of emotion, even though they may detract from presenting a cogent, reasoned argument. The use of connotative language helps students develop a sense of their own voice, and conveys to their reader a sense of the thinking and feeling person who has done the writing. Conversational language provides students with the qualities of spontaneity and affect necessary to personal voice. The act of writing provides the balancing factors of reflection, distance, and perspective. With Emig (1977), who discusses how writing enhances cognition in ways that speaking generally does not, we think that journal writing in particular offers opportunities for students (or mature writers for that matter) to make things understandable (or known) to themselves.

Many American educators assume that the best approach to improving students' speaking and writing proficiency is a frontal assault on coding skills. Elementary and secondary language arts curricula emphasize vocabulary, word usage, standard syntax, and organizational concerns like outlining, topic sentences, introductions, and conclusions. If text book publishing can be taken as an indicator of classroom practice, it appears that much of students' learning about coding takes place in isolation from the matrix of rhetorical communication. Worksheets, error identification exercises, and a-rhetorical sentence combining remain as standard fare of public school instruction in the written code. Much instruction in oral communication features a public speaking model highlighting research skills, elocution, and organization (though concern with audience, purpose, and responsible communication is happily retained in speech curricula). This emphasis is understandable. Coding is the most tangible aspect of communication development. It is susceptible to atomistic analysis. And in this age of accountability, it is also the most readily testable.

In contrast to these practices, our developmental model asserts that advances in coding skill proceed hand-in-hand with growth in social awareness and reconstruction of experience. Typically, discourse functions to help make sense of the world or to make contact with others. Most often code is the hand-servant and not the master. Moreover, we have pointed out that differences between oral and written language are rooted in the differing demands of communicative contexts, and that coding not only conveys thought but also guides it.

Our critique of code-centered instruction is by no means unique. But the critique rings hollow in the face of teachers' frustration with large numbers of students who seem to lack sufficient foundation in coding skills to sustain extended forms of discourse. "Forget about language skills instruction. It's demeaning. It's not that important. Besides, it no longer holds theoretical interest for us," preach the professors of education. "But our kids can't write sentences or explain themselves in speech," respond the practitioners in honest desperation.

Perhaps we have here a chicken-and-egg controversy. Which should come first, the sentence or the interaction? Clearly both are present, simultaneously and under mutually beneficial conditions, in the successful classroom. Students will internalize the conventions of written and oral codes when, in the course of reading, writing, speaking, or listening, those students experience communicative failure for lack of those conventions or communicative success through their presence. Students will become effective speakers and writers in increasingly extended, formal, complex, or extraordinary discourse types when they have the opportunity to practice new code forms in genuine social situations.

Here we wish to avoid over-simplification. We do not want to suggest that all this learning comes about inductively, that the teacher's only job is to engineer appropriate communication tasks. Young children are not especially adept at recognizing when they are misunderstood and older students will not spontaneously evolve a vocabulary for critically examining their language performances. Teachers need to be like master woodcarvers introducing their apprentices to new types of chisels and mallets that will facilitate their tasks. They need to point out peculiarities of the wood grain in which the apprentices are working. And they need to put the apprentices' products to the test, to see if the bowls will hold water and the candlesticks will please customers. The instruction is didactic, but always in the context of a meaningful task.

Along the road to helping students differentiate spoken and written forms, teachers can build upon the kinds of coding skills with which students are already confident. We have seen that in speech dialogue promotes fluency and can be especially useful in helping speakers leap cognitive stumbling blocks. Dialogue is familiar, immediate, and concrete, and it maintains the element of social awareness. As such, composing and performing dialogues can help students bridge the transition from talk to writing. Extended monologue is a logical next step after dialogue. In writing monologues which record "what is happening," students continue to make use of the oral code, but without the benefits of a respondent. At a later point, writers might again have need of a conversational partner in order to anticipate readers' needs. "Talk-write" is one such method of composing (Wixon & Stone, 1977). But at this more advanced stage, the writer would be expected to set on paper a code more clearly differentiated from that of speech.

In poetic discourse students may learn to intentionally mimic or accentuate the oral code. Language play including rhyming, rhythming, punning, and riddling is a pastime which children enjoy long before they enter school. The poetic mode permits writers to focus on the sounds and feelings and meanings of words with the same attentiveness. Students writing in the poetic mode may experiment with violating conventions of the written code, for impact or fun.

Given these processes of differentiating audiences and contexts for speaking and writing, what kinds of approaches might teachers use to promote growth in making such distinctions? In closing, we offer two suggestions. Consider for example the problem of insufficient context in writing. Beginning writers are familiar with the context-dependent code of conversation. Even their oral performances require amplification in many cases. One way to teach about context-independence would be to mimeograph worksheets asking students to circle pronouns with ambiguous or absent antecedents, and to hand out a list of forms of support (example, anecdote, analogy, statistic). Another way to teach about supplying context in writing would be to ask students to write a shopping list for themselves and compare it to one they would write to enable a stranger to do their marketing, or to allow peers to tell writers what questions were raised but not answered in a personal anecdote, or to assign students the task of describing how to buy lunch at the cafeteria to a literal-minded robot. In this second approach students would use their own writings as laboratory experiments and teachers could help them explain their results by introducing the same principles (but in a reductionistic fashion) in a worksheet/handout class. The second approach would also permit students to revise their work in accordance with their newly found knowledge of context-independence. And this process would be repeated throughout students' careers so that they might assimilate and refine their sensitivity to the need for context and the resources of language for constructing it.

# 4 Oral and Written Relationships: A Reading Perspective

Brian Cambourne
Riverina College of Advanced Education (Australia)

The orthopaedic surgeon, the chiropractor, and the acupuncturist all treat the same painful back injury differently—their behavior directed by their theory of the causes of back-aches. In a similar way, teachers are influenced by their theories concerning the problems students have in learning particular skills. In particular, reading teachers are guided, either consciously or unconsciously, in their classroom behavior and choice of methods by a theory of teaching and learning reading.

Much of the interest and controversy that from time to time surround the teaching of reading can be traced to two divergent theoretical views about how oral and written language relate to each other. One of these views emphasizes the similarities between the two modes of language and de-emphasizes the differences. The other view emphasizes the differences and de-emphasizes the similarities. The first view I shall label the "More-Similar-than-Different" (or MSD) view, and the second the "More-Different-than-Similar" or MDS view. The MSD view is that, because differences are minimal, learning to use written language ought not to be significantly different from learning to use oral language. The implications of this view for a pedagogy of reading are far-reaching, for it strongly suggests that learning to read ought not to be any more difficult than learning to talk and listen. On the other hand, the alternate view, MDS, asserts that the differences between the two forms of language are so obvious, numerous, and significant that they entail quite different learning procedures. One obvious difference, according to this view, is that the written mode of the language is a more abstract, secondary form of the language than the oral mode; written language is more difficult to learn and requires special learning conditions.

When it comes to reading education, these points of view spawn significantly different teaching behaviors and materials. The MDS view is characterized by carefully structured sequences of sytematically controlled material, with an emphasis on progressive mastery of carefully analyzed subskills. The intention of such an approach is to ease the learning task by breaking down the complexity of language into simpler learning tasks, using well-researched principles from learning theory. The MSD view is characterized by quite different teaching behavior. When compared to the MDS view it seems to lack the same degree of structure and sequence. The emphasis, instead, is on replicating the conditions that occurred when the oral mode of language was learned: meaningful immersion in the medium (print), acceptance of approximations to the mature version of language, and little or no *systematic* teaching of carefully worked out subskills.

Of the two views the MDS view has the most currency in reading education. It is predominant in the research literatures: it dominates the published materials that teachers buy and use in classrooms; and it underpins the most frequently used diagnostic procedures. At the college level the majority of specialist courses offered in reading are based on a philosophy of instruction and a style of clinical practice that have their origins in an MDS point of view. However, the popularity of the MDS approach does not necessarily indicate its validity. I want to suggest that the apparent cogency of the MDS view is merely an artifact of the techniques used by most researchers in the field when they explore the relationships between oral and written language. In what follows I will elaborate my reasons for this judgment.

## Exploring the Relationship between Oral and Written Language

In a recent paper Samuels (1980) compares the acquisition of reading and the acquisition of speech by listing their similarities and their differences. There are two inherent flaws in this approach to exploring relationships. First, the approach tends to favor differences rather than similarities; inevitably the two entities being compared appear to be more different than similar. Second, in this case where oral and written language are the basis of the comparison, those similarities and differences that are *obvious* are hardly distinguished from those that are *relevant* to learning to read.

Let me illustrate. Oral and written language can be contrasted from a variety of different perspectives. One obvious point of contrast is that of "physical attributes." The spoken form of the language is manifested in sound waves and involves the ear, whereas the written form of the language is manifested in light waves and engages the eye exclusively. These are *obvious* differences, easily confirmed by observation. It is also obvious that in some respects they are differences of great moment. However, the question that reading educators must address is how *relevant* these *obvious* differences are for a pedagogy of reading. Too often the relevance is assumed but never explained.

The illustration can be extended by showing how oral and written language can be viewed from another perspective, namely, that of "function." Spoken language, as explained by Halliday (1973), has an "interpersonal" function which can be contrasted with the "ideational" function of the written mode. The interpersonal and ideational functions are similar in that both are concerned with "communication," and this appears to be the extent of their similarity. The differences between these functions are numerous. First, the oral mode functions mainly as a channel of social action and is manifested in forms such as conversations, storytelling, verse, and song, whereas the written mode functions mainly as a repository of ideas and information and assumes such forms as statement, argument, and detailed explanation. Second, the oral mode is immediate, transient, and improvised, whereas, by contrast, the written mode is distant, permanent, and planned. Third, the oral mode is accompanied by many contextual supports of a paralinguistic nature (gesture, intonation) which serve to clarify and assist the listener. The written mode, however, because it lacks such contextual support, has to use different controls in order to avoid confusion. This in turn results in different stylistic characteristics which become obvious when one mode is transferred to the other (e.g., oral speech is written down or written prose is read as if it were conversation).

One can use the technique of listing of characteristics to explore similarities too. For example both written and oral language are similar in that both obviously employ the same basic rules of grammar and vocabulary; both are obviously concerned with communication; both are used in a wide variety of every day activities; both are taken for granted by those who use them. There appear, however, to be a few similarities beyond this list. From a number of perspectives, dissimilarities are more numerous and more obvious than the similarities. Thus the MDS viewpoint seems supported by the sheer weight of the evidence.

There is some truth to that conclusion. When analyzed from a number of different perspectives the two modes are obviously more different than they are similar. But what does this mean for those of us concerned with a pedagogy of reading? Are the differences relevant (or trivial) for our purpose—in this case the teaching of reading? Does the greater number of points of difference demonstrate that the two modes require different learning procedures? To maintain this would be to assume some kind of additive and linear relationship between sheer quantity of randomly perceived differences and modes of learning.

A more relevant and meaningful perspective for reading educators is that of comprehension, the perspective concerned with how the brain goes about the task of making sense of each of the two modes of language.

## The Rationale for Taking a Comprehension Perspective

Why restrict the exploration of the relationships between oral and written language to a comprehension perspective? The reasons behind such a decision are straightforward and simple. In the first place the aim of any act of listening to speech or of reading print includes comprehension of what the speaker or author says. Of course comprehension is not always successfully achieved, but unless one is caught up in a Catch-22, Helleresque kind of world, comprehension is always the underlying, primal purpose to any act of listening or reading. Secondly, comprehension is observable in diverse forms and these can be assessed. Comprehension does not necessarily involve verbatim repetition of what has been listened to or errorless reproduction of what is printed on the page; neither of these two behaviors automatically guarantees that comprehension has occurred. Rather, a listener can demonstrate that comprehension has taken place by reporting on, say, a story that has been told. It does not matter that the report uses different terms from those of the storyteller, nor is it important that the listener accurately reconstruct every detail of the storyteller's utterance. Furthermore, the demonstration does not necessarily have to involve language. If a listener can perform a task after listening to an explanation of how to do it, then comprehension is manifest. Similarly, readers can be said to have "comprehended" what has been written if they can reconstruct in their minds, or orally, *most* of the meaning intended by the author. As with listeners, it does not matter whether readers produce exactly the words that were on the page or whether they substitute and/or omit words. The reader who reads and/or remembers that "The cowboy mounted his *mustang* and rode off into the sunset," when in actual fact the text word was "horse" (and not "mustang"), has "comprehended." Conversely, the reader (or listener) who can reproduce verbatim what was on the page or what was said (either orally or in written form), yet cannot comprehend it, cannot be said to have "read" or "listened." The reader (or listener) has mouthed words, or has perhaps performed a transcribing task, but neither reading nor listening as I wish to define it has taken place because comprehension is absent.

In reading education, exploring the relationship between the comprehension of oral and written language has significant consequences. If it can be shown that the brain goes about the task of comprehending these two modes of language differently, then it can be argued not only that they are different, but also that they are different in a way that is highly relevant to pedagogy. If, on the other hand, it can be shown that the brain processes which culminate in comprehension are identical or at least very similar, then, despite the many differences that exist between them, there is one way in which the two are related that is very relevant to reading instruction. In what follows, the nature of the processes that underlie the comprehension of both modes of language will be explored. Finally some conclusions about how each relates to the other will be drawn.

## Comprehending Oral Language—Some Research Findings

For at least fifty years researchers have been interested in explaining the nature of the processes which underlie a listener's ability to comprehend spoken language. An increase in research in this area began in the fifties and burgeoned through the sixties. The changes that Noam Chomsky had wrought in linguistics spilled over into psychology, and a new discipline known as "psycholinguistics" emerged and became a vigorous research era. During this period there was a great deal of interest in developing a theory which would explain how listeners comprehend spoken sentences. Wanner (1973) exemplifies this interest:

... suppose that you and I have just attended a lecture on a difficult subject. Suppose further that it has been delivered in barely audible tones, and that the acoustics of the hall are poor. If as we leave I ask you whether you understood the lecture, it is plausible that you might respond, not without exasperation

1. Understand it? I couldn't even hear it.

But suppose I had asked you whether you'd been able to hear the lecture. It seems unlikely that you would answer

2. Hear it? I couldn't even understand it.

Why is (1) plausible where (2) is not? Presumably because we believe that understanding a sentence or discourse is contingent upon hearing it, that is, upon recognizing the component speech sounds. Hence a failure to hear entails a failure to understand as in (1). But we apparently do not believe that our ability to recognize speech sounds depends upon our ability to understand meanings, so (2) sounds quite bizarre. (p. 164)

Wanner's juxtaposition of "hearing" and "understanding" highlights one of the fundamental issues that researchers into sentence comprehension faced. Did the comprehension process involve a "passive" kind of pattern recognition—an analysis which relied wholly on the physical characteristics of the incoming speech wave-form to carry all the cues that were necessary and sufficient for comprehension? Or was there more to sentence comprehension than a simple correlation between the physical properties of the acoustic signal and subsequent comprehension? The research carried out at the time seemed to favor the latter explanation. For example, in an experiment which was later to become a classic, Miller, Heise, and Lichten (1951) compared the intelligibility of words in two conditions. In one condition the words were part of well-formed sentences, and in the other they were spoken in isolation. By introducing background noise and systematically varying the signal to noise ratio over both conditions, Miller et al. showed that sentential context made words easier to identify. Their conclusion was that information in the form of context, and thus outside the region of the sound wave that is local and specific to any individual word, played a significant role in the word's identification (and subsequent comprehension). In other words, acoustic information had to be supplemented by nonacoustic information for recognition and comprehension to occur. In a related experiment the same researchers demonstrated that listeners' abilities to recognize a word in isolation could be improved by letting them know beforehand details of the set from which the test words could be drawn. This result supports the conclusion that the more we know, the more we will hear, and the less attention we need to pay to the signal (or the less effect "noise" will have).

In a different (but conceptually related) experiment of the same era, Pollack and Pickett (1964) arrived at similar conclusions concerning the nature of the comprehension process. They recorded conversations in a chamber totally free from ambient noise so that their tapes would be of high fidelity. Selections of varying lengths from the taped conversational material were systematically chosen and played to listeners who knew nothing of the context of the recorded conversations. Each selection was scored in terms of words correctly identified by the listeners. Despite the fact that the listeners were permitted repeated exposure to the recordings, performances were relatively poor. Why? The conclusion reached was that conversational speech simply is not clear enough to permit the listener to recognize one word at a time using only the specific sounds in the acoustic signal.

Other lines of research concerning the comprehension process during this period included the work of Ladefoged and Broadbent (1960). Wanner (1973) sums up the particular importance of their work thus:

> Ladefoged and Broadbent made tape recordings of sentences and of sequences of digits. At some point in each recording a brief electronic click sound was superimposed on the speech. These stimuli were played to listeners who were simply asked to indicate the point in the speech sequence at which the click sound occurred. Most people find it difficult to believe that they can make errors on such a simple test; but the task is by no means as easy as it seems. On the average, Ladefoged and Broadbent's subjects mistakenly located those clicks which occurred during sentences about two positions prior to their true location (here each word and each interword boundary was counted as a position). For the digit sequences, performance was somewhat better, but hardly perfect: on the average, clicks were perceived .7 positions prior to their actual location.
>
> As Ladefoged and Broadbent point out, the very existence of these errors indicates that "items do not pass along sensory paths in rigid succession." In other words, if we imagine the flow of auditory information through the nervous system as a sort of parade passing from the ear to the mechanism in the brain which recognizes speech sounds, then our inability to perceive the true location of a superimposed click suggests that the marchers in this parade may not maintain a rigid order. (pp. 171-2)

Fodor and Bever (1965) and Garrett, Bever, and Fodor (1966) explored the "click migration" phenomenon further. Fodor and Bever hypothesized that the click locations noted by Ladefoged and Broadbent could be accounted for by the listener's tendency to recognize sentences a phrase at a time. In a series of experiments, Fodor and Bever (and later Garrett, Bever, and Fodor) attempted to disentangle the questions surrounding the phenomenon of click mislocation. Assuming that their original hypothesis that clicks migrate to phrase boundaries of sentences was valid, they asked, "Are the phrases which appear to displace the clicks determined by the listener on the basis of syntactic knowledge, or are there physical cues which determine the phrasing and attract the click to boundaries?" Taking into account the fact that any number of physical attributes (pauses, temporal junctures, stress, intonation, word length) could cue phrase boundaries, Garrett et al. managed, in an ingenious way, to control all these possibilities. They demonstrated that click migration will change direction when the phrase boundary shifts, even though the shift changes none of the cues which are local to the boundary. This kind of research revealed the unconscious and not directly observable processes underlying listeners' abilities to understand the spoken sentences of their language. It upset some widely-held "commonsense" notions about both the way language is used and the nature of the language user.

One implication of this research is that understanding a sentence or discourse is not entirely contingent upon the recognition of the component sounds which made up the acoustic sound wave. Understanding is not entirely an "outside-in" process. The research indicates that listeners make an active contribution to what they hear, and that this ability to understand speech depends, to a large extent, on the ability to understand meanings first of all, rather than vice versa. In other words, in the act of comprehension of spoken discourse there is a major "inside-out" flow of information; listeners bring to bear their knowledge of the regularities of their language (i.e., syntax) and their background conceptual knowledge of the topic of discourse. In this way they build up a set of expectations of what is going to be said next by their interlocutors before it is actually said. The speech sounds that follow are merely sampled in order to either confirm or reject these expectations.

The notion that comprehension involves an extra source of information that is not to be found in the actual physical signal has been reinforced by insights from a new discipline known as "Artificial Intelligence." Artificial Intelligence researchers aim to simulate human comprehension with computers. In the course of their efforts to design programs that can "comprehend" language, they have been forced to view language and comprehension from new perspectives, often leading to the development of insights into the language process. It soon became obvious to those who were trying to construct language "understanding"[1] programs that computers had to have huge data banks of information, not only concerning linguistic rules, but about real world knowledge of how things operated and related to each other. It was only when computers failed to comprehend language that programmers became acutely aware of the enormous amount of information that one must bring to understanding language. This is illustrated by the following sentences (Dilena, 1975).

1. BECAUSE *IT* WAS SLANTED THE CAT FELL OFF THE ROOF
2. BECAUSE *IT* WAS INJURED, THE CAT FELL OFF THE ROOF

In these sentences "IT" refers to different entities, but on the surface, the syntax is the same. In both cases we know what "IT" refers to, not only because of syntactic rules, but because we have real world knowledge about roofs and cats. This knowledge involves a whole "scenario" or "script" of real world relationships involving the notion of "slanting" and "roofs" and "cats" that goes beyond the meaning of words in isolation (or as they appear in dictionaries). Put simply, Artificial Intelligence workers are suggesting that there is an aspect of language understanding that goes beyond syntax and dictionary-like definitions. To account for comprehension, they argue, we must recognize that comprehension involves knowledge of the world and the way that things relate to each other in the world. Otherwise we cannot explain fully how comprehension of speech and/or print occurs, even at the simplest levels.

Another example from Dilena (1976) illustrates this point:

LION          MAN
THUMB          BIT

Even without word order, inflections and function words we
can guess what the intended meaning is (p. 15).

The example shows that in the absence of linear word order and some syntactic markers, we can comprehend language by using those expectations that arise from the possible roles that the concepts referred to by the four words can take, when they occur together. In the example above, because of our real world knowledge we know men, not lions, have thumbs; that lions typically bite men and not vice versa; and that in a scenario involving a circus or a zoo setting, it is quite possible for a lion to bite a man on his thumb.

The work in Artificial Intelligence also strongly suggests that in comprehending language we also make wide use of contextual information provided by the situation in which the utterance takes place. For example, imagine you have just heard

I'M WAITING ON THE TABLE

If the speaker is dressed appropriately with black trousers and cummerbund, has a menu, wine-list and so on, you interpret this message quite differently from a situation in which the speaker is unloading furniture, dressed in overalls, or one in which he is standing next to a computer waiting for a table to be printed on the printout typewriter. This construction of meaning, which goes beyond the information given by the linguistic cues, is even more obvious when the phenomenon of inference is considered. If one considers the utterances below, it becomes obvious that in order to make the required inferences, certain scenarios of background knowledge are needed.

1. A BURNING CIGARETTE WAS CARELESSLY DISCARDED. THE FIRE DESTROYED MANY ACRES OF FOREST. (Inference: What caused the fire?)
2. JANET OPENED THE WINDOW. SOON THE ROOM WAS FILLED WITH FLIES. (Inference: How did the flies get in?) (Dilena, 1975, p. 47)

A whole set of experiences about cigarettes, flammable undergrowth in forests, smoldering debris bursting into flame, winds fanning these flames, and so on, is necessary for the inference to be made. In fact one must imagine a whole bushfire scenario in order to make the inference. Otherwise, there is not enough in the surface features of the linguistic cues to make the inference (and therefore comprehension) possible. The same point can be made with the second example.

The message from Artificial Intelligence appears to be that the utterance never provides all the information that one needs for understanding. Neither the computer nor the human being, it seems, can be merely a language parser, sorting out information in the incoming signal. Both also need to be constructors of meaning. Understanding is a constructive process which involves using the linguistic cues provided by other speakers as a basis on which to build up a more elaborate and informative meaning representation. This construction can only take place if the appropriate scenarios and linguistic patterns are already part of the comprehender's knowledge.

Thus, the comprehension process involves using one's knowledge of topic, context, and syntax to anticipate what a speaker is most likely to say, and then testing these anticipations against what is actually said. When listeners are familiar with the topic and the syntactic structures, they need to attend to only a limited portion of the acoustic signal. If, however, the topic is not part of the listeners' background knowledge, or if the style of communication is not familiar, or if there is any other kind of "noise" in the system, predicting becomes more difficult and more of the acoustic information must be attended to.

There are times, however, when even more careful attention to the acoustic information is not enough to ensure that comprehension will occur. Sometimes even mature speakers of the same language use such divergent styles of communication within their language that they cannot achieve comprehension, even when given more and more of the acoustic information (for example, when speakers repeat their utterances because it is obvious that their listeners have not comprehended them). In other words, when the conventions of conversational style, register, dialect, rhetorical devices, vocabulary usage, and so on are not shared by interlocutors, then comprehension becomes more and more difficult, even impossible. There are many examples of this phenomenon: Children who are not familiar with the conventions of classroom language typically fail to comprehend much of what is said to them in that particular register (Bernstein, 1961). Patients who are unfamiliar with the patterns of language used by doctors frequently fail to comprehend the advice given them and the questions asked of them (Shuy, 1976). These instances of inadequate or faulty comprehension can be explained as follows: Without shared knowledge of the conventions of a particular style of talking, listeners either look for meaning in the wrong places, or use the cues which are available in inappropriate ways, making predictions that lead them away from the intended meaning, rather than toward what was intended.

## Comprehending the Written Form of the Language

What kinds of processes underlie the reader's ability to understand the written form of the language? Do they correspond to those involved in comprehending oral language? Or does the written form of the language require a different set of processing strategies? The evidence which is available strongly supports the view that in terms of comprehension, the two modes of language are subject to identical processes.

As with effective listening, effective reading is characterized by a predominantly "inside-out" flow of information. The physical signal alone (the print) never provides all the information that is needed for comprehension to take place. Supportive evidence comes from a number of different sources. A paper by Miller (1956), which is now a classic in psycholinguistic research, provides unequivocal evidence that the human mind can process only about seven pieces of random information (a string of seven digits or letters) at any one time. Another piece of research (also now a classic) by Kolers and Katzman (1966) demonstrates that the recognition of a single letter requires between a quarter and a third of a second. If one assumes that readers deal with each and every letter while reading, then the act of reading becomes a "mathematical paradox" (Wolf, 1977). The paradox lies in the observable fact that average readers can read and comprehend at speeds that range from 250-350 words per minute. If one assumes a mean word length of four or five letters, then 250-350 words should contain about 1500 letters, which according to Kolers and Katzman's (1966) work should take five minutes to read. Fluent readers achieve even higher speeds, a fact which Neisser (1967) drew attention to over a decade ago when he stated: "For the present, rapid reading represents an achievement as impossible in theory as it is commonplace in practice" (p. 37). Even if one assumes cluster-by-cluster or phrase-by-phrase decoding, the speeds achieved by fluent readers are difficult to account for if one assumes that *all* of the graphic display must be processed. Smith has gone so far as to state that once the processing rate drops below approximately 200 words per minute, comprehension is severely hampered (Smith, 1980). Obviously, in the act of reading the physical signal cannot by itself supply all the information that is needed for comprehension to occur, simply because the reader does not take the time to look at it all. It follows that if the print does not (indeed *cannot*) supply all the information, then there must be an extra source of information somewhere which is available to the reader. I want to argue that it comes from what is already inside the reader's head, just as is the case for oral language comprehension.

There are many other areas of reading research which identify further correspondences between the ways in which oral and written language are processed. For example, there are literally hundreds of research projects based on the error analysis (or "miscue") paradigm pioneered by Clay (1972) and Goodman and Burke (1973) which show that, like listeners, readers make predictions about the meaning and grammatical structures that are likely to be encountered in the material being read. These projects have studied beginning and mature readers, readers at different grade levels, readers with special learning difficulties (Rousch & Cambourne, 1979), readers who speak different languages (Hodes, 1976), readers who speak dialects of English (Sims, 1972), readers who use sign language instead of oral language (Ewoldt, 1977), and readers reading silently (Cambourne, 1980). In all cases the conclusions are similar: prediction on the basis of familiarity with topic, syntax, and context is common to all effective reading and, conversely, is absent from or wrongly used in all ineffective reading.

Another finding that emerges from research of this kind is the interactive nature of the process of reading, or what Smith (1975) refers to as the "trade-off" between visual and nonvisual information. In fact Smith's (1975) statement about listening, "The more you already know, the less closely you have to listen, but the more you will hear" (p. 61) can be also applied to the reading process. The opposite also applies: the less you know the more attention you pay to the graphic signal, and this too is a common finding of miscue research (Williams, 1980; Irvine, 1979).

One can even find evidence of failure to comprehend print which parallels those problems exemplified by the children who fail to comprehend classroom language and the patients who misunderstand their doctors. As I stated earlier, written language is differently structured from spoken language; in fact all "book language" differs in a number of significant structural aspects from spoken language (Olson, 1977c). Unless one is familiar with the structures of book language, it cannot be comprehended with the same degree of ease and efficiency as one's familiar spoken language would be comprehended, were it to be written down (as it is in the "language experience approach" to reading). The reasons for this inability to handle unfamiliar book language are the same as those offered to account for the failure of some children to comprehend classroom language or the failure of some patients to understand doctors, namely, one cannot predict structures and vocabulary in discourse if one is unfamiliar with the conventions of that kind of language. Even the structural parameters of so-called "book language" differ from genre to genre. There are many readers who can comprehend narrative storybook prose but who find textbook prose extraordinarily difficult, even impossible. These cases are not restricted to the less educated sectors of the community; students at the college level manifest the same problems (Cambourne, 1977a, 1977b).

The difficulties that some readers have in comprehending book language (especially textbook language) have led some theorists to argue that because written language requires different and unique processing skills, it cannot be merely a parallel form of oral language. Smith (1977) agrees that with respect to written language some "different" skills may be needed, but questions the notion that they are "unique." He identifies the issue as:

> how we make sense of language in the first place. The question concerns how language is verified—how we confirm that the information we are receiving is true, that it makes sense, or indeed that we understand the message correctly. For everyday spoken language the matter of verification is simple: look around. An utterance is usually related to the situation in which it occurs. (p. 392)

Smith goes on to argue that a reader's only recourse to "verify," to resolve ambiguity, and to avoid error is back to the text itself. He suggests that the specific skills necessary to do this are "following an argument, looking for internal consistencies, and thinking abstractly" (p. 392). While some may consider these skills "unique" (Olson, 1977b), Smith argues that spoken language is often just as abstract, argumentative, and unrelated to context, implying that for certain modes of spoken discourse (e.g., academic debate) these skills are also necessary and must be learned.

How they are learned is the point at issue. I want to suggest that learning to follow abstract argument such as an academic debate in the oral mode is not significantly different from learning to follow it in the written mode. The more familiar that one is with these particular conventions of vocabulary and sentence structure, the easier it will be for one to predict and confirm (or reject) the propositions at hand. The converse, of course, also holds.

This problem can be approached from another perspective. One can ask, how do speakers learn a new and unfamiliar mode of discourse (such as the language of cattle or sheep auctions)? There can only be one answer: by hearing it often, by being immersed in it, and by trying to make sense out of it. The answer is the same when the question involves learning to comprehend written language. When written language is heard (and/or read) often enough in meaningful situations, implicit understandings of the particular characteristics of written language will develop. It seems that, just as we internalize the language patterns of many registers of oral language in order to understand the spoken form, so we also internalize the patterns of the various kinds of written language. Science textbooks become easier to understand if we have the patterns of "science-ese" firmly established in long-term memory; "legal-ese" is comprehensible to lawyers because they have become fluent in the technical register of their professional language. Conversely, many freshmen in their first psychology course find their prescribed textbooks incomprehensible because they are not familar with "psychology-ese."

One could continue to list the correspondences that exist between the ways in which each mode of language is comprehended. Psycholinguistic research clearly shows that everything which has been claimed about comprehending spoken language also applies to the comprehension of written language. Clearly, the brain tries to make sense of spoken and written language in the same way. From the point of view of developing a pedagogy of reading, this is probably the single most important and relevant relationship that there is between the two modes of language. Few other relationships have so many implications for teachers.

**Implications of the Oral and Written Language Relationship**

The most obvious implication is one which was alluded to earlier: that the successful reader learns to process print in almost the same way that speech is processed. This means learning to sample only the salient bits of the physical signal (the print); it means learning how to make sensible predictions on the basis of both real-world knowledge and language patterns; it means being able to check one's predictions for truth, logic, meaningfulness; it means learning to trade-off visual for nonvisual information in the interests of efficiency. In short, it means learning how to operate on print in what Wanner (1973) refers to as an "inside-out" manner.

A second implication emerges from the first. Because the two modes of language are processed in similar ways, the principles that apply to learning to use one form also apply to learning to use the other. Most children learn to comprehend the spoken form of their language; in fact, it is probably the most startlingly successful learning that a child ever does. Not only is it successful, but it is learned when, from a cognitive point of view, the learner is extremely immature. What if the same principles could be applied to learning to comprehend the written form of the language? Could learning it then be as successful? The research into language acquisition has identified three necessary conditions for successful language-learning to occur. These are:

> Frequent opportunity to hear the oral language used in meaningful situations.
>
> A strongly felt need by learners to make sense out of the oral language that surrounds them; they are encouraged in many subtle and devious ways to learn their culture's tongue.
>
> Warm, friendly, supportive, mature users of oral language who serve two main functions. First, they accept the young learner's approximations to the mature form; errorless adult forms are not expected. Second, they give feedback about the *meanings* that the learners are involved with, not the *forms*.

The degree to which these conditions can be replicated in learning to comprehend the written form of language will determine how natural and uncomplicated this learning will be for beginning readers, assuming of course that one subscribes to the philosophy that learning to read ought to be as uncomplicated as possible. Many programs currently being implemented are not based on this philosophy, for they seem to be intolerant of any meaningful approximations made by children and they deal in bits and pieces of language that are syntactic and semantic nonsense.

Finally, the kind of relationship that exists between oral and written language implies a natural and logical set of experiences which should facilitate learning to read. These experiences should co-occur with one supporting and nourishing the other.

> *Experience 1:* Reading the spoken language that one is most familiar with, that is, one's own speech which has been written down.

*Experience 2:* Hearing the written language of books, that other more mature users of the written mode have produced.

*Experience 3:* Reading the written language that other more mature users of the written mode have produced.

Although all three experiences are important, the second is the least often cultivated. This is a pity, because this experience prepares readers for the transfer to reading material which other people write. It should not be thought that the second of the experiences described above applies only to young children learning to read. High school and college students who are confronted with the technical prose of textbooks can be assisted by "hearing the written language of books that other more mature users of the written mode have produced." This does not necessarily mean having textbook prose read to them in storybook fashion (although I have successfully done this with some fifteen-year-old high school students), but it does mean becoming familiar with the unique stylistic, rhetorical, syntactic, and graphemic characteristics of some textbooks, perhaps through discussion and observation.

To sum up: If the relationship between comprehending spoken and written language is as it has been described above, then readers need to have internalized some of the syntactic and semantic features of the language the author writes in. The same principles should apply to learning to read specialized texts at secondary and college levels. The hackneyed slogan "Every teacher a teacher of reading" really means "Teachers should teach the vocabulary, plus the stylistic characteristics of the register in which their subject is typically expressed, as well as the content and meanings." If this were accepted, then fluent, efficient, and effective reading could be attained with a minimum of difficulty for the learner.

## Note

1. Although some may find the notion of a computer actually "understanding" language strange, "understanding" is the term that workers in Artificial Intelligence use, and for this reason I've maintained the metaphor in this paper.

# 5 Writing: The Divorce of the Author from the Text[1]

David R. Olson
Ontario Institute for Studies in Education (Canada)

Language in its various forms stands at the center of our conception of ourselves as civilized human beings. Speech, the mastery of oral language, is taken as critical in distinguishing ourselves from other animals and from abnormal, that is, retarded or disturbed, human beings. Literacy, the mastery of written language, is taken as critical in distinguishing us from the uncivilized or "savages," the uneducated or "ignorant," and the young or undeveloped. These rough, commonsensical categories serve not only as basic to our picture of ourselves, they also underlie aspects of our social policies such as the right to vote, access to jobs, and to positions of authority, and they underlie one of our most entrenched institutions, compulsory schooling. It is important therefore to articulate, elaborate, define, and criticize these basic assumptions both for the purposes of creating more just policies and institutions and for improving the practice of the existing ones.

We may begin by noting that written language and literacy skills have at least two major components. First, writing may be used as an alternative to speaking; we may discuss this dimension in terms of the communicational functions of oral and written language. But second, writing is used as a predominant archival resource in a literate society, as the means by which important cultural information is preserved and transmitted intergenerationally; we may discuss this dimension in terms of the archival functions of written language. These dimensions are laid out in Figure 1. Both of these dimensions are important in understanding the development of children in a literate society and I shall consider them in turn.

## Communicative Functions of Written Language

The communicative dimension is particularly important because in the past an emphasis on literacy led linguists, psychologists, and educators to underestimate the power and subtlety of natural language and oral language competence. De Saussure (1916/1959), the father of modern linguistics, was the first to attack "the tyranny of writing," the tendency to use literature unreflectively as the model for language, to construct rules of grammar on the basis of written texts, and to study word meaning exclusively through the analysis of written records.

A by-product of this attention to the written word was a serious underestimation of oral language and oral language competence. Psychologists and educators, for example, on the basis of children's performance on standardized written tests and on their poor performance with high status teacher/interviewers, were led to believe that many children had extremely limited linguistic resources, that they did not know "grammar," and that they had limited "vocabulary" and powers of expression. More recent linguistic, psychological, and educational research has greatly enhanced our understanding of the power and subtlety of oral language competence of the native speakers of any oral language, including that of quite young children. It is now well known that all speakers "know" a grammar by means of which they generate a set of permissible sentences of a language using the lexical options available in the relevant contexts of their cultural group. Some children, however, may not know the "standard" grammar or the

| Function | Oral Mode | Written Mode |
|---|---|---|
| Archival | Formulaic<br>Poetized speech<br>Verse, Song<br>Ritual | Encyclopedia<br>Textbooks<br>Essays |
| Communicational | Conversation<br>Argumentation | Letters<br>Notes<br>Student papers(?) |

Figure 1. Archival and communication functions are displayed for both the oral and the written language modes.

vocabulary relevant to specialized activities such as schooling, banking, concerts, or fine art which may be quite divorced from their immediate experience. All children know about social roles, but for some children these roles may interfere with the productive use of language. For example, all children must defer to the status advantage of teachers in a classroom—the teachers do most of the talking, ask most of the questions, and give most of the commands. But some children, assigning themselves low status in school contexts, may remain silent, answer only when spoken to and even then in expressionless one word answers (Goody, 1978; Olson & Nickerson, 1978; Sinclair & Coulthard, 1975).

Let me illustrate the sophistication of oral competence in even quite young children, in this case a pair of four year olds named Jamie and Lisa, in a pre-kindergarten class. These children had some difficulty arriving at an equitable distribution of a limited resource, namely some dominoes. Let us see how they negotiate this social problem.

> L: Let's make a domino house out of these.
> J: Okay.

First, by grabs.

> J: Lookit how many I got. . . . You took a couple of mine!
> L: Now *you* took a couple. . . .

Then, by commands.

> L: Now you got to give me three back!
>
> . . . . . . . . . . . . . . . . . . . . . . . . . . . . . . . . . . . . . . . . . . . . . . . . . . . . . .
>
> L: Now give me just one more and then we got the same.

And then by assertions.

> J: Now, you got more than me-e.

And denials.

> L: No-o we got the same.

By fact collecting, and assertions and inferences.

> L: (Begins to count her dominoes) One, two, three, four, . . . twenty-eight, twenty-nine. (Then counts Jamie's dominoes) One, two, three, four, . . . eighteen, nineteen . . . (short pause) twenty-nine.
> J: I got nineteen and you got twenty-nine. . . . You got more than me.
> L: No-o (shouting) I COUNTED. . . . You have the same as me. . . . We got the same.
> J: NO-O-O.

And when negotiations break down again by grasping.

> (There is a shuffle of dominoes across the floor and now Jamie
> has more than Lisa.)

And finally by appeal to authority.

> L: You got much more than me now.
> J: No we got the same.
> (Paul, a volunteer teacher, enters the room.)
> L: Does he have much more than me?
> P: Not too many more!

Note first that almost all of these quite different utterances are
attempts to alter or preserve the social arrangement of two children playing together and sharing the limited supply of dominoes.
"Now you got to give me three back," a command, has the same
pragmatic meaning as "Now, you got more than me," an assertion
standing as an indirect request, spoken by the same person. And
both speakers appear to be aware of the social meaning, namely,
that the listener should hand over one or more of the dominoes,
even if in one case it is the explicit "give me" and in the other the
implicit "you have more." We may more clearly see the meanings
and intentions expressed if we compare them on two dimensions
of meaning, the logical dimension and the social or pragmatic dimension (see Figure 2).

| Sentence | Gloss | Truth Value | Status-Preserving |
|---|---|---|---|
| J: "You got more than me now." | (Give me some) | + | − |
| L: "No, we got the same." | (I don't have to) | − | + |
| P: "Not too many more." | (Yes, it's true he has more but he does not have to give you any.) | + | + |

Figure 2. A partial analysis of the logical and the social dimensions of children's
and teacher's verbal interaction.

For the logical meaning, true may be marked with a "+" and false with a "−". For the pragmatic or social meaning, the categories are less obvious. We let "+" represent the preservation of any current social arrangement, that is, statements not requiring compliance, and "−" represent the realignment of any social relationship, that is, statements which require compliance and call for revolutionary activity, so to speak. Now let us examine some fragments of this dialogue in this framework.

Note that Jamie tells the truth with the hope of realigning the distribution of dominoes. Lisa, technically speaking, tells a lie. (Recall that she was the one who counted them.) But her denial was not merely one of falsehood. She knows that if she agrees to the truth of Jamie's statement, she will have to turn over some of the blocks. She doesn't want to do that, so she denies the truth of the statement. Presumably this is what all lies are—tampering with truth value for social or personal ends. Truth, like falsehood, is often socially motivated.

More than that, however, Lisa is not denying the truth of Jamie's statement simply in the service of social ends. Rather she has limited means for simultaneously meeting the social and logical criteria. Paul, the teacher, is quite able to meet the situation. Note his reply when Lisa appeals to him. The presupposition of his sentence is that Jamie has more. Rather than assert that proposition, he presupposes it and uses his sentence to hold that no redistribution is required, presumably on the premise that possession is nine-tenths of the law. Both children understand and accept his comment.

This modest example, shows that even quite young children have sufficient mastery of their linguistic resources to maintain a conversation, generate assertions, requests, and commands as well as agree/disagree, or comply with/reject those generated by others. They know alternative means of making statements, commands, and requests and they know that if they don't want to comply with a command, they may criticize or reject the truth of the presupposition or challenge the authority of the speaker. By adulthood, the oral language is fully formed, complex, and applicable to a wide variety of tasks and situations.

What contribution does literacy make to this linguistic competence? The imposition of literacy upon oral language competence may have both positive and negative effects, what we may call the "powers of literacy" and the "tyranny of literacy." The latter were assumed earlier in the assertion that language competence *is* literate competence and in the symmetrical inference that if someone is not literate, he is not linguistically competent, well-informed, or intelligent. That assumption has unfortunate political implications if nonliterates are excluded from jobs, rights, and public respect simply because of the false identification of literacy with competence.

The "powers" of literacy spring from the distinctive properties of written language. These include that writing, like the telephone, can be preserved across space; that like the tape-recorder, it can be preserved through time; that it can be revised and edited; and that it separates the producer both from the recipient and from his text. All of these factors permit language to be used for social purposes which are different from those associated with oral language. For example, writing permits both reading and re-reading or study. To refer back to Figure 1, one may simply read friendly letters, but one must study the writings of, say, Hegel and other texts that make up the archival form. Does reading and writing without the use of archival forms have an effect on cognitive development? Scribner and Cole (1978) in their studies of the consequences of literacy among the Vai, a traditional society in Liberia with limited indigenous literacy, found some intellectual outcomes that were directly tied to those literate practices, such as the ability to provide a general topic sentence before elaborating detailed descriptions; but they noted that literacy was not "associated in any way with general competencies such as abstraction, verbal reasoning, or metalinguistic skill" (p. 457).

Our own research on the cognitive consequences of literacy and schooling suggests that the consequences are more substantial in that schooling encourages a somewhat distinctive "mode of thought" associated with the tendency to pay attention to "what was said" rather than to "what was meant" by the speaker. What is "said" and what is "meant" are more or less conflated in ordinary oral language, but they come to be differentiated during the school years. The differentiation may result from either the acquisition of reading and writing skills or from the sustained study of written artifacts including school textbooks. We saw earlier in the Jamie and Lisa episode that a true statement "You have more than me" was not taken simply as an assertion but rather as an indirect means of requesting some dominoes (Olson & Hildyard, 1981). Similarly, with some of our memory studies, in which children heard stories that ended with similar statements, the children recalled the statements as requests: for example, "She said to give him some." By second grade, around eight years, children begin to remember both what was *said* and what the person *meant* by it: "She said you have more but she meant he should give her some." Attending to what was *said* independently of what was *meant* may mark the beginning of an understanding of literal meaning. Reading, writing, and schooling appear to depend upon this competence with the literal meaning of sentences. (Olson & Hildyard, in press).

Comprehension of the literal meaning of sentences is important for some forms of thinking and problem solving. Again I shall provide two examples which show that the literal meaning of "what was said" tends not to be isolated in most oral language contexts. When Jamie says "You have more than me," Lisa could have said "True, but. . . ." What she did in fact was deny the truth of the sentence because she did not want to give up any dominoes. She heard the sentence in terms of a directive, that is, in terms of its implications for action, rather than as the assertion which it literally is. If someone says "I'm hungry" or "Where's the newspaper" or "My sock has a hole in it," adults frequently do just as Jamie and Lisa did and respond in terms of the indirect meanings of those sentences. They take them as indirect commands and reply "I'm too busy to make a snack," "I'll get it," or "Why do you expect me to fix your socks?" But most literate adults are capable of responding to such utterances in terms of their literal meanings, and may reply "Good, supper will soon be ready," "The paper is in the hall," "Oh, do you have some others?" The former meaning, what I have called the "speaker's meaning," tends to be primary in most oral language, but it appears to be the only meaning recovered and remembered by children. The same may be true of nonliterate adults.

Finnegan (1979) reports a similar lack of differentiation in her studies of oral poets of the Limba of Sierra Leone: "I discovered that when I was told that two stories were 'the same,' this statement meant something other than that the exact words were the same. When I asked a Limba assistant to elucidate the words I could not catch fully while trying to transcribe taped stories, he could not be made to understand that I wanted the *exact* words on the tape. As far as he was concerned any comparable phrase with roughly the same meaning would do" (p. 9). That is, there is a lack of differentiation between what was said and what was meant. To repeat, since writing provides a means of separating a speaker/writer from "text," it encourages the differentiation of intention (what was meant) from the expression (what was said) and an emphasis on the latter. (Olson, 1977b).

The ability to separate what was said from what was meant is important in some additional ways. First, it is important to some intellectual tasks. Consider Piaget's famous problem in which a child is shown two ducks and three rabbits and is asked: "Are there more rabbits or more animals?" The younger child replies: "There are more rabbits" (but should have replied, "more animals"). When asked why, the child says "Because there are only two ducks." What the child has yet to learn to do for such intellectual tasks is to pay attention to the literal meaning of the given sentence—if it is unusual—and compare the two classes mentioned. Such items are common on IQ tests, which therefore can be considered as tests of literacy or preliteracy. Here is a difficult item even for adults: "I have two coins. Together they add up to fifty-five cents. One of them is not a nickel. What are they?" The answer relies upon close attention to the sentence, "One of them is not a nickel." If that sentence is glossed as "Neither of them is a nickel," the problem is insoluble. If it is literally interpreted, one of them is not a nickel does not preclude that the other coin may be a nickel and the problem is solved. Whether they are merely trick questions, or tap an important and general mental resource remains to be seen, but the ability to solve them appears to be general to schooling and to the acquisition of literacy (Bereiter, Hidi, & Dimitroff, 1979). Writing is not merely speech written down, nor is reading merely listening with the eyes. It involves a substantially different, more specialized language code tied to a more specialized knowledge system. A form of language specialized in this way is no longer simply an ordinary oral language, or "mother tongue." It is the language of schooling, and the archival language of the culture.

## Archival Functions of Written Language

Written language and literacy may be important not so much because of the uses of writing as an alternative to speaking as because the archival resources of our society are in written form, stored in papers, books, and libraries. The acquisition of literacy provides the means whereby children are given access to these resources. Furthermore, these resources are sufficiently important that children are required not simply to read them but to interpret, study, and criticize them. Literacy, therefore, provides an archival form—a form for the preservation of significant meanings across generations. That archival form has been extremely important to the evolution of our society. The role of literacy in the evolution of "modernity" seems to be well established. On the basis of cultural, historical, and literary-critical evidence, Havelock (1976), Parry (1971), Goody and Watt (1963/1968), Innis (1951), and McLuhan (1962) have argued that the use of written records has altered the structure of knowledge which is stored for reuse, and by implication, has altered the cognitive processes of the people who rely on that knowledge. Simply put, in an oral society culturally significant information is stored by means of the mnemonic devices of oral memory: rhyme, rhythm, and hence verse, song, formulaic expressions, and imagery. On the other hand, the use of written records for preserving important cultural information, both relaxes the constraints imposed by oral memory and encourages the development of other forms, including the extended expository prose commonly found in encyclopedias and textbooks. Although there are many forms and functions for written language, I shall confine my attention to textbooks.

We may approach the structure and consequences of essayist prose texts by considering the importance of "sentence meaning" in certain contexts. As I mentioned earlier, attention to sentence meaning is important in differentiating indirect requests from simple assertions. Assertions are statements that are advanced as true independently of their use for making requests. School textbooks are full of such assertions. If children have a bias to treat assertions as indirect commands, as they would, for example, to understand that the teacher's "I hear talking" means "Be quiet," they may have difficulty seeing any point in reading and studying assertions which have no pragmatic implications. The things taught in schools may seem "meaningless." Hence, depending upon whether children assumed language was primarily suitable for making assertions and conjectures or primarily for making direct or indirect commands, they will find school texts either easy or difficult.

In this connection, recall that writing permits the differentiation of the speaker/writer from the text. Not only does that encourage the awareness of the difference between "what was said" and "what was meant" but more importantly, that separation permits the editing and revision of a text in the attempt to make "what was said" an appropriate representation of "what was meant." This attempt gives rise to the explicit, logical prose that is taken as standard in a literate society.

Textbooks, I suggest, constitute a distinctive linguistic register in that they employ a form of language particularly appropriate to a set of contexts of use. These include schools and universities; a particular form of interpersonal relations, author/authority and reader/student; and a particular linguistic form, explicit logical prose. Let us consider each of these briefly in turn.

As to the distinctive context of use, it may be interesting to point out the degree of dependency of schooling upon books. According to Black (1967), 75 percent of children's time in the classroom and 90 percent of their homework time is focused on textbooks. Nor is the reliance on textbooks waning. It has been reported that 90 percent of teachers of precollege science have abandoned a "lab" approach in favor of the traditional textbook.

As to the linguistic form specialized for the purposes of expository written texts, there appears to be, first, an emphasis on definitions of terms, that is, on meanings formalized through a specification of criterial features and strict word boundaries, rather than upon typically encountered instances. Second, there appears to be an emphasis on complete and unmarked grammatical forms, typically well-formed declarative sentences rather than, say, imperatives and/or single subordinate clauses. Third, there appears to be an emphasis on explicit logical structure relating clauses and sentences—numbering points, marking assumptions as assumptions, conclusions as conclusions, and so on. The focus upon these aspects of explicitness of meaning reflect the more general attempt to create texts which, like Popeye,. *say* what they *mean* and *mean* precisely, neither more nor less, than, what they *say*. This effort to create language that is autonomous contrasts with uses that are simply the expression of the current speaker.

As to the social relations expressed and maintained by written texts, we may begin by noting that texts have authority; they are taken as the authorized version of the society's valid knowledge. The students' responsibility toward them is primarily that of mastery of this knowledge. The text as the repository of cultural tradition is closely tied to the teacher's use of the "recitation" method, in which children who have studied the text are given a variety of oral questions that serve the function of holding the children responsible for the information "in the text." In this setting, there is a status difference between writer and reader just as there is between teacher and child in the oral language of the classroom.

But how is that authority created and maintained through texts? Durkheim (1954) stressed that through participation in rituals, *representation collectives* were made to appear as powerful, sacred, and originating somewhere other than the current speaker. Bloch (1975), an anthropologist, found that in religious ritual conditions, in traditional society, the speakers speak not their own words but the "words of the elders" and signal these sacred words by the adoption of a special "voice." Both of these features endow the speech with an authority it would not have if it originated simply with the current speaker. This authority is based on the differentiation of the speaker from the speech. As long as the speech originates with the current speaker, the listeners know that it is just a view or opinion that is being expressed and that it is, therefore, eligible for criticism. When it originates elsewhere, particularly if that source is sacred or of high status, it is "above criticism" and believers therefore recite rather than critcize or doubt those expressions. Let us apply this principle to written text.

Written texts, because they are devices which separate speech from the speaker, permit attention to literal meaning and permit elaboration and expression. The separation of speech from the speaker helps to put the words "above criticism." When a child reads a text or when a teacher teaches what a text says, the language appears to originate in a transcendental source just as does ritualized speech—it is not ordinary speech and so it seems above criticism.

Like other forms of language, then, texts have both an intellectual function and a normative, social function. When so viewed, ritualized speech in a traditional society and written texts in a literate society turn out to have much in common. Both serve an important archival function which is to specify what the society takes to be the "true" and "valid" knowledge from which norms of thought and action may be derived. They both help to preserve the social order by minimizing dispute. They do this, however, in quite different ways depending upon, as Havelock (1976) had pointed out, the form in which knowledge is stored for reuse. If stored orally, it takes the form of the memorable-clear exemplars, pithy sayings, ritualized speech, and condensed symbols. But, perhaps more important, the knowledge so stored carries great authority because it appears to originate in a transcendental source, at least, in a source other than a current speaker. If stored in written form, this knowledge takes the form of arguments and conclusions sufficiently explicit and qualified as to be above suspicion.

That explicitness, I have argued, derives in part from an increased awareness of the words themselves and of their conventionalized literal meaning, but it may also depend upon other factors such as the relaxation of the constraints imposed by memory. As with ritualized speech, written, archival texts have an enhanced authority partly because of the split between the speaker and his words and the tendency to take the words, not as the expression of an ordinary person, but as an authoritative "objective" description. The child's growing competence with this distinctive register of language, in which both the meaning and the authority are displaced from the intentions of a speaker and lodged "in the text," may contribute to the similarly specialized and distinctive mode of thought we have come to associate with literacy and formal education.

## Note

1. This paper was presented at the Modern Language Association Convention, San Francisco, December, 1979. I am indebted to the Social Science and Humanities Research Council of Canada and to the Spencer Foundation for their financial support.

# 6 A Cultural Perspective on Talking and Writing

Anne Ruggles Gere
University of Washington

Other chapters in this book describe speaking and writing in linguistic, psychological, and neurophysiological terms. These are all important aspects of spoken and written prose, but they emphasize the individual rather than the group. Because language is social we need to think about speaking and writing in social as well as individual terms. Discussing speech and writing in social or in cultural terms requires consideration of evidence from fields such as anthropology, ethnography, and sociology. This discussion also requires a willing suspension of cultural assumptions; applying unexamined categories can obfuscate our definitions of speech and writing in an unfamiliar culture.

For example, consider the term "literacy." In general, we define literacy as the ability to read and write, but that definition tells us little about what or how much is to be read or written. One's name? The constitution of the United States? A telephone message? At least three definitions of literacy operate concurrently in the United States today: successful completion of the Harris Adult Performance Level test; completion of a specified number of grades in school; and skills sufficient to function in society. Later I will discuss each of these definitions in more detail, but here I want to note that categorizing people as "literate" may obscure reality unless the term is questioned. Yet the word "literacy" is essential to discussion of groups speaking and writing. At first glance literacy, which includes reading as well as writing, may not seem to be the best way to describe cultural dimensions of talking and writing. However, research demonstrates reading's integral role in the act of writing, and current terminology does not permit an effective division of the two. Accordingly, I will use the terms "literate" and "oral" to refer to the cultural manifestations of writing and speaking, respectively.

We know that writing evolved from humans' recognition of the limitations of ephemeral speech. Public economy and administration, in particular, required external means of recording information. Emblem-bearing tags developed by the Sumerians about 3000 B.C. were attached to market goods to remind both "writer" and "reader" of ownership. Does the encoding and decoding required for inscribing and reading these tags constitute literacy? What about the accounting tablets or ledgers which replaced the emblem-bearing tags? What about the lexical lists enumerating categories of flora and fauna; were the encoders and decoders of these literate? Materials for mneumonic devices have varied from one culture to another. Stone monuments, intricate systems of tied knots, wood carvings, and stained glass windows are among the media used to help a culture remember. Can we apply the term literate to the Incas who administrated large empires by means of *quipu* or tied knots? Can we, with our current concern for "visual literacy," describe as illiterate European peasants who constructed or learned biblical stories from stained glass windows? If literacy is defined as encoding and decoding information, can we limit the term to written language exclusively?

Unexamined categories, then, have no place in discussions of speech and writing from a cultural perspective. Further, such discussions raise complex questions such as: Can we assume a monolithic definition for all oral and all literate cultures? Does writing have inherent value? What influence does literacy or lack of it have upon the thought and behavior of individuals within a culture? Is literacy that exists apart from formal schooling qualitatively different from school-fostered literacy? And finally the practical question: How can a cultural perspective on talking and writing inform our work as English teachers? This chapter will explore these questions.

## Literacy as a Cultural Phenomenon

Categorization frequently helps us distinguish one group from another. Differences of race, color or ethnic background, boundaries of class or religious heritage help us to sort people into identifiable groups. Global, as opposed to national, delineations are even more pronounced. We identify our culture as advanced and scientific as compared with the primitive and mythbound societies elsewhere in the world. We base our knowledge on empirical findings while they rely on magic or intuition. Our logical thought and capacity to abstract give us a genuine sense of history while their prelogical and concrete means of conceptualizing bind them to a-temporal repetitions. We foster individuality while they subsume persons in group solidarity. These are not unschooled responses; they reflect the scholarship of philosophers, anthropologists, and sociologists such as Ernst Cassirer, Claude Levi-Strauss, and Emil Durkheim. More recently theorists from several disciplines have isolated literacy as the most effective means for marking cultural differences.

These investigators point to literacy's influence on disparate areas of life as evidence that literate and nonliterate cultures occupy separate categories. Religion, politics, education, economics, literature, and characteristic modes of thinking are among the cultural dimensions literacy touches. Religion's capacity for indoctrination increases with literacy because access to a written code influences adherents' behavior (Bloch, 1968; Schofield, 1968). Likewise the functional dichotomy between priests and rulers may be possible only in literate societies because literacy permits complex laws and precise social distinctions (Gough, 1968). In addition to facilitating more clear role definition, literacy enables the development of large political units; administrative functions in large empires rely upon the communication and record-keeping permitted by literacy (Gough, 1968). In fact some historians argue that human chronicles can be most effectively portrayed by tracing literacy's development (Carter & Muir, 1967; Einsenstein, 1968). Investigations of indigenous education in African societies suggest that education in an oral culture is much more contextbound than that in a literate culture (Cole et al., 1971; Gay & Cole, 1967; Greenfield, 1972). Children watch what they are to learn and, in contrast to education in European cultures where what is discussed is not usually present, they imitate concrete behaviors to demonstrate their knowledge. Literacy influences a culture's economics in several ways. Collection and recording of taxes, long distance trade arrangements, and highly rationalized division of labor often accompany literacy (Gough, 1968; Horton & Finnegan, 1973; Wilks, 1968). Because it offers an alternative to inherited status in many societies, and because it invests readers and writers with special powers, literacy frequently increases individuals' economic gain (Goody, 1968; Meggitt, 1968). Although the similarities between oral and written literatures may outnumber the differences (Finnegan, 1970), research shows that literacy changed the nature of literature (Havelock, 1976; Lord, 1960).

Characteristic thought patterns are more difficult to discuss or document than economic or political structures, but investigators from several disciplines have examined literacy's effect on human thought. Crosscultural studies of problem-solving suggest that individuals from nonliterate cultures lack capacity for abstract thought and do not progress easily to higher cognitive processes, such as the formal operations described by Jean Piaget (Bruner et al., 1966; Dasen, 1972; Greenfield, 1972; Olson, 1977a).

As this summary makes clear, real and important differences do mark the boundaries between literate and nonliterate people. Methods of governing, business practices, literature, education systems, and religious observances shift as members of a culture learn to read and write. However, generalizations about thought patterns cannot, I think, be accepted without question. Since we have at least three operating definitions for literacy in our own country, how can we accept at face value the conclusion that Kpelle villagers think less abstractly than we do because they belong to a nonliterate culture? Which of our definitions of literacy do they lack? And how can we generalize from Kpelle to Limba villagers or to any other of the world's nonliterate groups? Since our "literate" culture (which contains from 10 to 20 percent adult illiterates depending upon which definition of literacy is used) contains so many variations, how can we make literacy a blanket term to be applied across cultures?

Ironically, literacy itself contributes to the tendency to ascribe monolithic definitions. You who can read this book are, of course, members of a literate society, and, in the opinion of scholars such as Bruner, Eisenstein, and Havelock, your ability to read and write renders your mental processes significantly different from someone who is illiterate. Among other things, your literacy allows, perhaps even forces, you to classify what you know, to create categories for knowledge. You appreciate the divisions created by philosophers, anthropologists, and sociologists, divisions which allow you to separate the world into "we" and "they." And, according to Goody (1977), you may be very comfortable describing human events in terms of columns and lines on a page:

> ... this standardization, especially as epitomised in the Table consisting of K columns and R rows, is essentially the result of applying graphic techniques to oral material. The result is often to freeze a contextual statement into a system of permanent oppositions, an outcome that may simplify reality for the observer but often at the expense of a real understanding of the actor's frame of reference. (pp. 71-72)

In other words, your ability to read and write social scientists' tables and other forms of graphic representation may obstruct your vision. Being literate enables you to classify information about the world, a process which may distort the reality of that world. In the first paragraph of this chapter I mentioned the need for a willing suspension of cultural assumptions, and resisting easy generalizations is part of this suspension, even though literacy dictates such classifications.

### Literacy as an Historical Phenomenon

Discussing literacy in historical terms requires as much caution as defining it in contemporary cultures. Technologies of writing—ranging from alphabetic script to paper and printing press—have changed the meaning of literacy over time. Cultures whose writing predates that of the Greeks employed syllabic scripts such as hieroglyph or cuneiform which fixed a one-to-one correspondence between signs and speech sounds. The hundreds of distinct syllables in any language dictated that the syllabic languages employ hundreds of symbols or assign multiple sounds to a single sign. In either event, the task of reading involved excessive memorization and considerable ambiguity. These difficulties led to selectivity and simplification in order to minimize the idiosyncratic element in writing. The archtypal quality of, say, the Old Testament illustrates the kind of writing produced with syllabic scripts. By determining that a sign could represent a consonant rather than an actual unit of speech the Greeks developed an alphabetic system where only one acoustic value could be attached to a given shape. This technological shift redefined literacy in terms of the ease of reading and the content of writing. (For further discussion of the technology of writing see Havelock, 1976.)

Likewise, shifting from vellum to paper writing surface changed the nature of literacy. Expensive and relatively scarce, vellum books were used for oral reading at public gatherings. Few people could own their own books, and reading was largely a communal, not individual, activity. As Howard (1976) explains, the introduction of paper changed the nature as well as the audience of reading: "the book is available, controllable, instrumental, in part disposable. The solitary reader can, more than ever before, choose books, select passages, bring his private thoughts to the book, pick thoughts from it, and neglect what he wishes" (p. 65). The introduction of the printing press added strength to the changing concept of literacy by offering mass production of texts on relatively inexpensive paper. Prior to the use of paper and printing, literate and nonliterate cultures shared a communal quality; just as members of an oral culture could not avoid hearing stories told by the fire, so public reading ensured common knowledge among the general population. The introduction of paper and printing, then, transformed writing's audience from public group to private individual. Literacy, like society itself, has changed through time and continues to change today; its use, value, and nature shift with cultural evolution.

## Literacy as a Socio-Economic Phenomenon

As scholars such as Meggitt (1968) and Goody have noted, literacy is frequently tied to economic gain, and this correlation has existed throughout much of history. Cipolla's (1969) study reveals that children of wealthy urban elite groups in nineteenth-century Europe were much more likely to be literate than were children of poor rural lower class families. Class and region determined who would and would not learn to read and write. Contemporary critics of education (Freire, 1970; Kozol, 1975; Phillips, 1978) argue that this pattern has not changed substantially, that children of poor minority stock have much less chance of becoming literate than do their wealthier white peers. Furthermore, they claim, this relative lack of access to education is fostered by Western governments which need a corps of unskilled workers to take society's mental tasks. Whether or not one accepts literacy statistics as evidence of government design, the fact remains that ability to read and write is linked with money and power. According to Porter (1851), when Joseph Lancaster opened a free school in 1804 his critics claimed that if he succeeded in teaching his students to read and write, "there would be no more servants who would clean shoes or attend upon horses" (p. 694). Well over a hundred years ago people were aware that literacy implied access to higher rungs on the socio-economic ladder.

In informal conversations modern psychometricians will sometimes claim, "Tell me the number of bathrooms in students' homes, and I will tell you within fifty points the SAT scores they will achieve." This assertion (boast?) trivializes the complexities of their literacy-economics equation, an equation whose unknowns include most important dimensions of our culture. It isn't simply that children from comfortable homes become better at writing and reading than youngsters who grow up in less privileged circumstances, although that is often the case. The point is that access to literacy is available almost exclusively through our culture's schools, and all the consequences of literacy or lack of it radiate out from formal education. Today's highly charged educational issues—issues such as achieving desegregation through busing, relying upon property taxes for school funding, defining competency in state-mandated tests—and our society's institutionalized efforts to increase its number of readers and writers—Headstart Programs, Title II funding, adult literacy and GED programs, for example—all testify to the interrelationship of schooling, literacy, and economics. Joseph Lancaster's free school did more than threaten the established class structure of his day, it bonded writing to formal education. Children would, as they always had, learn to speak under their parents' tutelage, but instruction in writing became the province of the school.

To be sure, a few societies separate literacy from formal education. Research among the Vai (Scribner & Cole, 1978) suggests that ability to read and write, of itself, may not carry the generalized cognitive psychological or social benefits commonly ascribed to it. Within a narrow range of transfer to similar literate tasks, literate subjects demonstrated ability to apply their abilities to new problems. However, and this is the important part, literates did no better than nonliterates with tasks calling for generalized competencies such as abstraction, verbal reasoning, or metalinguistic skills. The idea that literacy may not represent any comprehensive benefits to its possessor goes against the tide of thought and research on the question (Bruner et al., 1966; Goody, 1977; Greenfield, 1972; Olson, 1977a). One reason for the weight of opinion on one side of the issue may be Western society's automatic linking of literacy with schooling. Because we rarely encounter or think about literacy instruction outside formal education, we assign the results of schooling to literacy rather than to the more generalized effects of formal education. Furthermore, we begin to equate literacy with intelligence.

## Literacy's Link with Intelligence

As Olson (1977c) has observed, our schools make literacy synonymous with intelligence by emphasizing literacy skills to the exclusion of all other kinds. Commonsense knowledge, which is coded for action, deals with concrete and particular situations, reflects the variability and inconsistency of events, emphasizes values and authority, and expresses itself in illustration and example, receives little attention in our educational institutions. Scientific or philosophical knowledge, which seeks universal truths, strives to minimize contradictions, deemphasizes values in a disinterested search for truth, and speaks to reflection rather than action, has become the primary concern of most formal education. Literacy, especially the ability to decode the written text, is essential to this kind of knowledge and the result, as Olson describes it, is:

> We have come to define knowledge as 'prose statements known to be true.' That is, knowledge comes to be defined as that picture of reality appropriate to the requirements of a particular technology, explicit written text. The means has become the end. The acquisition of knowledge has become nothing other than the construction of a particular view of reality appropriate to the requirements of explicit logical text. That assumption is unsound both epistemologically and pedagogically. It is unsound epistemologically in that it assumes that the translation can be complete. ... It is unsound pedagogically because the exclusive reliance upon text may lead to the undervaluation of practical knowledge and of the mother tongue. Coding all knowledge in terms of text may make that knowledge inaccessible to people with lesser literacy skills. (pp. 86-87)

Perhaps the most telling support for Olson's objections to equating literacy with intelligence comes in finding that academic achievement correlates very poorly with worldly success (Houts, 1977). This work suggests that commonsense knowledge, not literacy-based philosophical knowledge, provides the basis for success in the world beyond school.

Not only does the assumption that intelligence equals literacy impose limits on members of our culture and diminish the effectiveness of our educational system, it blinds us to the accomplishments of other cultures. Until very recently cultures which relied upon oral transmission of history were assumed to have no history, and techniques for eliciting and recording that history remained undeveloped. The historian Vansina (1965) has demonstrated the efficacy and importance of attending to oral history, of listening to the bards and griots who tell us of the past. While it is true that writing works against the transience of speech and preserves words for posterity, it is also true that writing is no guarantee of permanence. The availability of printed material contributes to its disposibility; Howard (1976) estimates that three-quarters of the manuscripts produced in the fifteenth century have been lost. Libraries' current struggle to preserve books printed on acidic paper demonstrates, once again, that the written word can be ephemeral. Even as books disintegrate around us we continue to claim the superiority of writing. In the introduction to her collection of oral literature, Finnegan (1970) feels constrained to argue vehemently for assigning the term "literature" to orally transmitted poetry and prose. Students of oral history and oral literature may present incontrovertible evidence of speech's power to reflect upon experience, but many of us reserve our real respect for the written word. The journalist's old story about telling his landlady that the price of potatoes would go up, her disbelieving, his printing the same statement in the local newspaper, and her greeting him the same evening with confirmation of his morning statement—because she had read it in the paper—illustrates the authority we ascribe to print.

## The Value of Literacy Reconsidered

Perhaps because literacy so frequently accompanies money, power, and status; perhaps because we cannot separate literacy from schooling and inadvertently ascribe the effects of one to the other; perhaps because our Judeo-Christian tradition emphasizes the authority of the written word; perhaps because we are English teachers, we accept it as axiomatic that literacy is a good thing. We believe psychologists (Bruner, 1966; Olson, 1977a) who claim that cognitive growth is slower and less extensive without literacy. We join national and global social service agencies designed to accelerate literacy programs. And we do this in the belief that literacy will liberate "those who remain fettered in their inescapable poverty and the darkness of ignorance," and help them join the literates "who master nature, share out the world's riches among themselves, and set out for the stars" (Maheu, 1966).

To question the inherent value of literacy may be a form of heresy. Yet beginning with Plato some intellectuals have cast doubt on its value. In his *Phaedrus,* Plato creates a myth in which the god Theuth claims that ability to read and write will make Egyptians wiser and more able to preserve things in memory. The Egyptian king counters this argument by claiming that people will become forgetful when they put their confidence in external marks rather than relying on themselves from within. He denounces writing as substituting remoration for reminiscence, the resemblance of reality for reality, and the appearance of wisdom for wisdom itself. Socrates likewise attacks writing as generating nonliving beings which exhibit sterile sameness, silence in the face of inquisition, and indifference to what they arouse in their readers. Rousseau (1761) attributes separation, tyranny, and inequality to writing. According to him writing separates people just as property separates owners, the tyranny of lexicon and grammar equals that of laws of exchange crystallized in money, and substitutes domination of the learned and the priesthood for the Word of God. Bergson (1911) holds that writing lacks the intellectual effort of searching for appropriate expression because it represents only the deposit of this search and has cut its ties with the feeling, effort, and dynamism of thought.

Illiterates themselves have also questioned the value of the literacy offered them. Contemporary Africans often distinguish between "book learning" and "wisdom" and do not always welcome efforts to foster literacy among their children (Jahn, 1961). Recognizing intuitively the tyranny, separation, and inequality which accompany literacy, many illiterates prefer to maintain the inner link of community. Doubts about the value of literacy flourish among cultural groups within U.S. borders. Blacks, for whom speaking well reinforces social ties and who attain community status by playing the dozens and developing finesse in oral repartee, may see little value in the more solitary and alienating activity of writing (Abrahams, 1970). Native Americans whose sense of community derives from knowing everyone in their village have little use for literacy exemplified in billboards and signs, and they sometimes resist government literacy programs because reading and writing threaten the kinship they value (Philips, 1975).

So far this chapter has consisted of warnings and attempts to puncture comfortable assumptions. To summarize I will return to the questions raised in the opening pages. Can we assume a monolithic definition for all oral or all literate cultures? Examination of literacy's development over the time and within different cultures shows the inadequacy of such a definition. Although reading a contemporary insurance policy and writing a Sumerian-style lexical list both fall under the general category of literacy, they represent different dimensions of the term. Does writing have inherent value? Literacy serves both mneumonic and expressive functions and it facilitates societal transactions, but liabilities accompany its benefits. Ability to conduct long-distance trade negotiations and to defend individual property rights may not be adequate compensation for declining powers of memory and broken community ties. Therefore, we cannot assume an absolute inherent value for literacy. What influence does literacy or lack of it have upon the thought and behavior of individuals within a culture? We can point to specific differences in behavior of literate and oral cultures: British judges write opinions after a court case has been presented and in their writing refer to earlier written documents which provide the precedents for their decisions; judges among the Idoma of Nigeria rely on pretrial personal encounter to make their decisions and court proceedings function to publicize the judges' decisions and rationales (Armstrong, 1954). American schoolchildren study fractions as part of a mathematics unit while Kpelle children learn to estimate quantities of rice through daily tasks of storing and cooking it (Cole et al., 1971). Adherents of Christian faith rely upon the authority of written scriptures while the Yoruba of West Africa invest natural phenomena with spiritual authority. These specific differences do not, however, provide the basis for conclusions about the thought processes of whole populations. Cross-cultural research on cognitive operations remains too primitive to support sweeping generalizations. Is literacy which exists apart from formal schooling qualitatively different from school-sponsored literacy? While it is true that unschooled Wolof children of Senegal have difficulty explaining the abstract principles which enable them to sort similar colors and shapes (Greenfield, 1972), we cannot, without further investigation, assume the same to be true for all unschooled children. Further, since unschooled does not always mean illiterate, we cannot attribute characteristics of the unschooled to the illiterate. Cultural groups within this country ascribe varying degrees of importance to literacy, and while limited ability to read and write may exclude them from the social mainstream, values of the immediate culture often prevail over those of the larger one.

## Towards a More Adequate Conception of Literacy

From a cultural perspective, then, the lines between oral and literate groups, between speaking and writing, are irregular and imprecise. We can demonstrate certain concrete differences between cultural groups, but generalizations and neat divisions belie reality. Still, the more practical question remains: How can a cultural perspective on talking and writing inform our work as English

teachers? We face classrooms full of students whose experience
with the desire for literacy vary widely. Likewise, although they
all—except where pathology has intervened—have mastered spoken language, they carry different assumptions about how it
should be used. The Asian student's reticence and the Black student's eloquence reflect their cultural values.

To begin, I will return to the three operational definitions of
literacy current in this country: successful completion of a
specified number of grades, skills sufficient to function in society,
and the Harris Adult Performance Level test. For many years
completion of the fifth grade was considered evidence of literacy.
This definition began to fall into disuse with the discovery that 13
percent of high school graduates are functional illiterates. If completion of twelve grades does not assure literacy, completion of
grade five proves an even less accurate measure. In 1977 the U.S.
Office of Education, defining literacy as reading and writing skills
sufficient to function in society, calculated that 23 million people
or 10.5 percent of the adult population are functional illiterates.
This attention to functioning in society rather than simple
literacy—ability to read and write a simple message—represents
an important shift in thinking about literacy. The Adult Performance Level test administered by Harris in 1975 extends this
thinking into an even more stringent definition of functional literacy. Based on adults' ability to complete communication and reasoning tasks for occupation and community resources, this measure defined 20 percent of the adult population as functionally illiterate. These three definitions of literacy provide a metaphor for
discussing the English teacher's task. Completion of a specified
number of school grades defines literacy inadequately because it
avoids consideration of language itself. Likewise ability to read
and write simple messages or to pass a competency test does not
define literacy because these measures attend to linguistic features exclusively. Defining literacy as ability to function in society
or to complete community-related tasks assumes an appropriately
broad definition of literacy, one that includes social and cognitive
factors as well as linguistic ones. The English teacher's task, then,
involves much more than helping students learn to manipulate
language; it involves facilitating the transition from a relatively
simple to a much more complex world. Moving eyes across the
page and shaping letters with a pencil manifest, outwardly at least,
the behaviors of literacy, but literacy in the 1980s implies much
more than these behaviors.

While the cultural perspective on literacy shows the fallacies of assuming clear-cut divisions between literate and nonliterate groups, it also demonstrates many specific differences between the two. Literate societies have different procedures than do nonliterate ones. The English teacher's task is to facilitate students' transition from nonliterate to literate culture. Although, as I noted earlier, students have varying degrees of experience with literacy (books, personal letters, observing parents writing), they all come to school essentially illiterate. In many ways the student's individual transition from illiteracy to literacy, if that transition is accomplished, reenacts much of the cultural shift. Gumperz and Gumperz (1979) describe pictographs and lists as early features in children's writing and point to the "ly" phenomenon (he said *quickly,* she spoke *loudly*) common in children's books which, in their view, helps children transfer knowledge of intonation to lexical symbols. While I do not want to push the "ontogeny recapitulates phylogeny" argument too far, I do see parallels between children's pictographs and Phonecian identification tags, between lists and the lexical categories of the Sumerians. Likewise, children's decreasing reliance on intonation as they master lexical and syntactic elements compares with writing's development from syllabic to alphabetic representation.

If we can avoid thinking of literacy in narrow behavioral terms and instead recognize it as a cultural phenomenon, one which has implications for many areas of society, we can, I think, do a better job of helping students move from speaking to writing. In taking this view we will give credence to our culture's many uses for literacy; we will show students that ability to complete simple reading and writing tasks does not constitute literacy in this society. If we cast writing instruction in cultural terms we will inevitably begin to pay more attention to the culture students bring to the classroom with them. We will recognize the commonsense knowledge and the oral facility which complement and enrich literacy.

# 7 Writing/Speaking: A Descriptive Phenomenological View

Loren Barritt
University of Michigan

The conduct of social science research in the United States has proceeded from a narrow philosophical base. It has been presumed that experimental procedures involving measures are better than descriptive procedures because the former are used by natural scientists—and their work, it is assumed, represents an ideal for all science. Most psychologists have been trained to believe that the "harder" (meaning the more statistical), more controlled, more "basic" their research, the more "scientific" and more prestigious it is. Educational researchers have followed the positivistic path blazed by psychologists.

However, the "psycholinguistic revolution"—initiated by Chomsky's (1964) review of Skinner's (1957) work, *Verbal Behavior*—marked the beginning of a change in psychology. After that paper, descriptive research with limited numbers of human subjects became more respectable. The way was then opened to question previously held dogmas about how psychology, and by implication all the social sciences, should conduct research. In the intervening years there has been a stream of articles questioning the belief in psychology as a quasi-natural science (for example, Deese, 1969; Koch, 1976; Levine, 1974; Riegel, 1976). Unfortunately, these newer, broader conceptions of the social sciences have made their way too slowly into fields like education, where many academics are, at heart, teachers, who have been converted, at times reluctantly, to the academic research enterprise. Thus, professional educators tend to be uncertain about philosophies of social science research, and therefore readily take the advice of the "experts" when it comes to the business of conducting research. That expert advice, however, is too often one-sided, based on previously unchallenged dogmas about the necessity for control and measurement in social-science research.

I would argue that a "softer" approach to research can be extremely useful in the area of educational studies—particularly the approach represented by the descriptive phenomenological perspective. I do not want to go so far as to suggest, as Giorgi (1976) has done, that the phenomenological view should become the new center for all social science research; rather, I want to point out that the descriptive phenomenological approach is an important, respectable, and defensible way to conduct research into educational matters. This may be especially true for the study of a complex phenomenon, such as writing. Descriptive methods have already provided the basis for some of the most revealing studies of the writing process, such as studies by Emig (1971) and Graves (1979a, b, c). While such research may not be phenomenological in any strict sense, it does focus quite centrally on the *description of experience*.

Phenomenology means the study of phenomena, or experiences. The philosophy which gave birth to the movement was developed by Edmund Husserl early in this century. In the years since Husserl's work began the phenomenological viewpoint has been elaborated and changed in the hands of followers: in philosophy by Husserl's most famous pupil, Heidegger (1927/ 1962) and Heidegger's pupil Gadamer (1975), as well as by Sartre (1956) and Merleau-Ponty (1962); in biology by Buytendijk (1959); in contemporary American psychology by Giorgi (1970); and in education by Langeveld, who founded a "school" based on the phenomenological view in Utrecht, Holland (Van Mannen, 1978). For a historical overview of these developments, see Spiegelberg (1972).

The phenomenological view is difficult to summarize, but in general it proposes that ordinary everyday experience is the fundamental component of all knowing. It is therefore necessary to "return to the things themselves"—the ordinary experiences of life—in order to learn from them. Experience can be accurately studied if one tries to be true to it. That means describing events in the way they present themselves to consciousness, attempting—as far as possible—to prevent prior commitments from intervening. For example, in a phenomenological study, one would not use prior concepts of language rules to guide research into speech, because such prior concepts or theories strongly influence what one will see. The goal is "naive" looking, which is achieved by "bracketing" prior beliefs, be they doubts or theories. Merleau-Ponty has described this attitude more simply as "a re-

write since I switched. The yellow paper isn't quite right, but it is soft and the pen doesn't scratch—it glides. Some paper is hard and scratchy, diminishing the feeling of pleasure from writing on it. For typists an analogous situation exists. It must be the right machine. It must feel right.

There is an aesthetic pleasure in the look of clean writing. If you could see the state of this manuscript, with sections scratched out, loose sheets of paper, arrows, inserts and other messiness, you would perhaps share my feeling of impatience to see it typed. It will look better. I will be able to judge it when I see it "clean." I could copy it over to achieve the same result, but I've learned that copying takes too long—and the copy would still not be as pleasing as a typed manuscript. I envy those who can write by typing. They seem always a step ahead.

Finally, in order to write, I must be in a "writing place" (reminds me of B'rer Rabbit). I can't write just anywhere, and some places are better than others. I've been writing this manuscript on a card table in our summer cabin. The table moves under my hand. The work area is small and cramped. I prefer to write on a large, solid surface, where I can spread out and lean over. A sense of place is often important to those who write. Whether the place is a special one or not, writing has to be done where there is a table and a chair—or at least a chair and some backing for the paper.

*When I write, I have some idea what I intend to say.* Writing asks for plans. I can recall being taught, first in junior high school, and again in high school, and again in college, that one had to make an outline before writing a paper. Sometimes the teacher wouldn't accept a paper without first seeing the outline. Sometimes, if you were lucky, the outline could be turned in with the paper. In the latter case I always wrote the outline after the paper was done. The only problem I had then was that "for every *I* there had to be a *II*, for every *A*, a *B*"; I had a precocious ability to write outlines that did not conform to that pattern.

My experience with outlining is an example of a truth gone bad in its pedagogical application. Writing does involve plans, but not necessarily the kind of specific, detailed plans that comprise formal outlines. I'm sure there are wide differences among people in the degree to which they make plans. I recall being shocked when a writer friend told me of the elaborate plans he had drawn for his novel. In my naivete I had presumed it was the height of artistry to be spontaneous. There was probably also a desire on my part to put the best face on my own inadequacies, which I did by considering them artistic.

Planning a piece is frustrating and difficult. There is always the sense that there may be a better way to do it. There seem to be so many alternatives and no way to choose among them until they are enacted. Frequently, after making one choice and embarking on it, I'm later plagued by a doubt that this was the best choice; I suspect the alternative had to be better. I'm tempted to start over, lured by the hope that the other path will be easier to tread than my present direction. But such hopes are usually, for me, illusory. Doubt waits to ambush every written undertaking, trying to make me turn back, start over on that "better" path. This has happened so frequently that I've learned to override the feeling of uncertainty, ignoring the lure of a new start. "There it is again," I think to myself. The temptation no longer surprises me.

*I write for someone, with a purpose in mind.* It is seldom far from my mind that I am addressing an audience. This audience isn't very specific; no one person or single group of people is clearly in view, but there is a sense of how "they" will react to what I say. This disembodied "they" is not a friendly group. "They" sit in critical judgment. "They" are tough-minded and unforgiving. "They" are looking for the weak spot in every argument. Obviously, "they" are my own sense of an audience. Others may have a different sense, but I know from my conversations with graduate students that this foreboding sense of a negative critical judgment is not mine alone. This negative sense of audience may be the result of the training we get as writers—training which occurs almost exclusively in school, where papers are criticized, corrected, and graded. I remember, quite vividly, being told by one of my undergraduate professors, after she finished criticizing one of my papers, that I would always be a "B" student. Thank God for grade inflation.

But this sense of audience is more than the sum total of encounters with English teachers, as striking as these experiences may be. It includes, as well, one's sense of what a good paper should look like, a sense acquired from one's experience as a reader. I write to please myself, but that self is influenced—perhaps partially created—by my previous encounters with the printed page.

*When I write, my thoughts tumble over one another. I have trouble moving my pen to keep up with my thoughts.* Writing is frustrating because it takes so long to turn ideas into physical representations that the ideas are gone before they can be captured. They come too fast; one idea ignites another and often the last idea doesn't belong in this section of the paper, so it must be held for a better time. Often when that time comes, the idea is gone. This problem leads to a search for techniques to avoid loss: lists, rough outlines, notes, etc. Most writers probably develop techniques to overcome the problem of lost ideas.

*You are alone when you write.* Because writing is a solitary—and physically passive—activity, I find it easy to avoid getting started on a writing task. Writing means going off somewhere to be alone with my thoughts and plans. It requires an act of will to get going. This paper has been a prime example. Each morning I've looked for ways to keep from going upstairs to write. I can always find some "enjoyable" job like taking out the garbage or doing the dishes. Most people I've talked with agree that they avoid writing, although I'm sure there must be exceptions. Writing is a struggle. It is difficult to realize one's thoughts on the page, partly because ideas usually seem better in the mind than in print.

Although you are alone when you write, this "you" often refracts into several "personalities." Because a paper is often written over several days, you have to go back and re-read previously written sections, trying to "become again" the personality which produced the earlier material. Sometimes there are surprises—did I write that? In any case, going back over previous material is essential for stepping back into the role of writer in a way that keeps the paper coherent.

Re-reading a "finished piece of writing means taking on a somewhat different personality role—that of sympathetic editor. As editor, one has the chance to see oneself as others will, to judge the effect of the writing. When the effect isn't the desired one, you can change the text. This "second chance" is a unique advantage of the written word, but it is an advantage which exacts a price: other readers are unlikely to forgive indiscretions, poor style, unclarity, ambiguity, mispunctuation, or poor spelling. A text is expected to be "perfect." In fact, published pages, at least in English, are often so doctored that there is some question whether they reflect the author's or the editor's style. I recently became aware that this attention to editing does not exist in all countries in the western world. There are countries where a published manuscript appears in print exactly as the publisher received it.

## Writing Contrasted with Speaking

From what I have already said about writing, it should be clear that there are important differences between the experiences of writing and speaking. Speaking is spontaneous and direct. I say what I mean without plans or thoughts or tools of any sort. My thoughts are alive in speech. Talking is usually pleasant. I do it mostly when I'm with other people. We talk about a large variety of subjects, usually understanding one another without effort. Of course, not all speaking is like that. Giving a speech is different. That experience is more like writing, because language choices as well as meanings become the focus of attention. But if we think about the ordinary speaking that occurs in everyday conversations, then it is clear that the two experiences are not similar.

In speaking there is often little or no awareness of a tool (language) or a message (the meaning or intent) or even a plan. There are occasions, of course, when, in the act of speaking, we suddenly become aware of where our discourse is leading us. I can recall this happening to me in embarrassing circumstances. I had embarked on the telling of a joke to a group of new acquaintances, all older, distinguished academics. In the middle of the joke—too late to halt my narration—I realized that the punch line required that I use the colloquial term for the male organ. Although this term was a ready part of my everyday vocabulary, I realized it might offend them. I chose the ignominy of a failed punch line by using the clinical term. It was no joke. But I shall always recall my discomfiture as I proceeded inexorably toward that moment in the narrative when I would have to choose. Editing of speech happens, but not usually. Most often we just talk and the words fit our circumstances.

The spontaneity of speaking is aided by context. Usually we talk to someone who can see us, and thus gestures and objects can be used. Brown (1973) has concluded that young children begin speaking by talking about their surroundings. Their speech is a natural outgrowth of their actions in the world. They use language to comment on happenings around them. This spontaneous growth of speech occurs in a social world of adults who talk. But there is no history of tutorship in speech as there is with writing. It is one of the class of what Piaget calls spontaneous concepts. A very good case has been made by Fodor (1975) that speaking (he calls it language) isn't learned at all, but is "known" in some nascent way in the genetic heritage of the human species. Children unfold their speech much as a tulip unfolds its predestined shape and color. It takes only the right conditions in both cases.

Our physical involvement in speaking differs from that in writing. We can speak while standing, sitting, walking, or even while chewing gum (some of us anyway). We are free to move when we talk. Speaking can even serve as a guide to physical action. Vygotsky (1934/1962) pointed out quite a while ago that children use speech as an aid to activity. The same is true for adults when doing a complicated task. It helps to label actions before or while doing them, for example, when building a piece of equipment from a plan. It helps to say: "This one goes here, that one there, and the whole thing will stand up like that," etc.

To sum up, speaking is social, easy, automatic, and natural, while writing is solitary, difficult, controlled, and learned. Writing and speaking are quite different experiences. They are made to appear translations of one another only by overlooking the ordinary facts and focusing on the extraordinary. It is possible to see both writing and speech as language events—if one views them from a linguistic perspective. But such a view begins with the assumption that language is the primary fact. This may be true for the linguist, but it is not for those doing the talking or writing. If we bracket our linguistic knowledge and focus instead on the experiences themselves, we see that writing and speaking are quite different. From a descriptive-phenomenological view, it seems remarkable that anyone should expect them to be alike.

The phenomenological perspective has an important place in educational research—particularly research on language—because it focuses on human experience in all its complexity. It has been hard to apply so-called "basic" learning research to educational matters because that research overlooked the complex nature of human subjects: that people think, decide, feel, know, and communicate. By adopting the phenomenological viewpoint, these "complexities" are no longer difficulties to be overcome, nor inevitable causes of inadequate research designs. Rather, human complexity becomes the source of interest, the very reason for doing research. Moreover, because the phenomenological approach uses everyday language as a major tool of analysis, it produces research findings which can be understood by all practitioners.

The goal of educational research is, after all, the improvement of the human situation. By adopting a phenomenological view, we put the everyday experiences of those we are trying to help in the forefront, rather than focusing on someone's theories about those experiences. The study of what is going on in the minds of our subjects may bring us closer to practical educational insights than the pursuit of so-called "basic" research questions. In investigating speaking and writing, we need to focus on the meanings which these experiences have for our students. We need a fresh, "naive" look at the process of writing, bracketing our presumptions and prejudices. In advocating a descriptive phenomenological approach, I am arguing, quite simply, for relevance and meaning in educational research.

# 8 Writing, Speaking, and the Production of Discourse

Barbara J. O'Keefe
University of Illinois at Urbana-Champaign

Although language and discourse are intimately related, they are not the same thing. Discourse is language-in-use, not simply linguistic production. However, most treatments of the differences between writing and speaking make the mistake of equating discourse with linguistic production, thereby ignoring important aspects of discourse as language-in-use, and hence confusing more than clarifying the relationships between speaking and writing. For this reason, it is important to explore the ways in which discourse is created in the use of language. In the first part of this paper I will focus on three uses of language—in practical activities, to perform meaningful actions, and for communication—devoting most attention to the last use. Following this discussion I will show how an understanding of discourse as language-in-use offers a framework for investigating the relationships between speaking and writing.

## Discourse as Language-in-Use

Obviously, people speak and write in the process of doing things. In a given context, discourse may be the main activity, a necessary part of another activity, or merely an accompaniment to activity. In any case, discourse is shaped by the *practical activity* of which it is a part. By "practical activity" I mean the various projects engaged in by members of a social group: working, playing, socializing, creating art, conducting scientific discussions, resolving conflicts, and so forth. Such practical activities differ in regard to their purposes, role structures, and histories—and each of these three factors has important consequences for the structure of discourse. First, discourse is shaped by the specific purposes at hand. For example, in the context of an academic department and its affairs, a committee may attempt, through oral discussion, to reach consensus on some important issue; a written memorandum summarizing the results of the committee's deliberations may then serve to institutionalize, through documentation, the committee's decision. Thus the speakings and writings produced by the committee will reflect the various immediate and long-range purposes of the activity in which the committee is engaged. Second, discourse is constrained by norms governing who may say what, in what manner, to whom. For example, some social roles are characterized by restricted rights to speak. In a rigid business concern, a worker may lack the right to argue with a supervisor's decisions. Similarly, children often have limited access to the floor in discussions with adults (Sacks, 1972). Finally, practical activities are part of a history, emerging as part of a continuing series of interactions. Past interactions provide a context of shared knowledge and belief, in terms of which discourse is constructed. Speakers and writers exploit such background knowledge in constructing discourse that is both relevant and informative.

In addition to practical activity, discourse is also associated with *meaningful actions*—a point which has been made in a variety of ways by theorists as diverse as Mead (1934), Searle (1969), and Hymes (1972a). The point is that speaking or writing always accomplishes some specific action: telling a joke, requesting, offering an excuse, asking a question, lecturing, making an argument, storytelling, and so forth. The form that a piece of discourse takes is a function of the act which it performs.

Finally, discourse is also associated with a *process of communication*, and it is shaped by the characteristics of that process. Contrary to popular belief, communication is not a process of transmitting information. Conceptions of communication as the transmission of information by a source, in the form of a message, through some channel, to a receiver, have been rejected by most communication theorists—for a variety of reasons too complex too detail here (Delia, O'Keefe, & O'Keefe, forthcoming a). A more contemporary view is that communication is founded on a process of interpretation, rather than transmission. To a large extent, this more recent view has been based on an "interpretive" conception of human nature (Delia, O'Keefe, & O'Keefe, forthcoming b). According to this conception, human beings never encounter reality directly. Instead, human experience is always a product of both the reality being experienced and the processes by which reality is perceived and cognized. Human beings are active interpreters of their worlds, and thus live in intrinsically subjective realities.

This interpretive view requires a reconceptualization of the nature of messages. Within an interpretive view of communication, messages do not contain or carry meaning. Communicators can only produce "performances" which are given meanings by those who observe them. Communication is thus best conceived as a process in which people try to create shared meanings. The creation of shared meaning is, however, aided by two sets of practices (Cicourel, 1974). First, people interpret messages by attending to surrounding activities, as well as by making a number of simplifying assumptions in the process of interpreting messages. For example, hearers assume that events that are ambiguous will be clarified by later events, and so do not demand continual understanding; they are satisfied to construct partial understandings which are sufficient for the practical purposes at hand. Second, both message producers and message interpreters rely on perspective taking—the imaginative construction of the perspective of the other person—to guide communication (Delia & O'Keefe, 1979). By imagining the perspective of the interpreter, the message *producer* can select expressions on the basis of the interpreter's likely responses. Conversely, by imagining the perspective of the message producer, the *interpreter* can make inferences in terms of what the producer seems to be trying to express.

For both speaker and writer, messages are always discourse acts which take form according to the type of discourse act being performed and the context of practical activity in which the discourse occurs. Thus, a speaker or writer's messages are constrained by the conventional forms that discourse may take in a given social situation. Moreover, messages are shaped by the goal of creating intersubjective meaning. Every discourse act involves an attempt to make meaning available to an interpreter. "Intelligibility" is a function of the fit between the discourse produced and the interpretive frame available to the message receiver—a frame consisting of general world knowledge and specific beliefs about the relations between participants, as well as an understanding of the social, historical, and practical context in which the communication process occurs (Cicourel, 1974). The intelligibility of messages is controlled by adapting them to their receivers' interpretive frames. Finally, discourse is also shaped by the more specific purposes of a message producer. Discourse is often designed to achieve particular effects: to amuse, to teach, to persuade. Discourse structures are adapted to serve these ends. In sum, message producers develop a repertoire of strategies for adapting discourse forms in relation to context, interpreter, and personal objectives.

## Comparisons of Spoken and Written Discourse

In the preceding section of the paper I have argued that the characteristics of any piece of discourse reflect three aspects of language-in-use: the practical activity in which discourse was produced, the particular type of action it represents, and the role it plays in communication in a particular context. The question remains, however, whether mode of production—speaking or writing—is an additional factor which influences the shape of discourse.

Comparisons of spoken and written discourse must deal with concrete instances of speaking and concrete instances of writing. However, in making comparisons, researchers have ignored the complexities of discourse production. Since writing and speaking only occur in an act of discourse production, any instance of writing or speaking is shaped by such discourse factors as context of practical activity, type of discourse act, nature of the interpreter, and the communicator's special objectives. Thus, the discourses being compared frequently vary along several dimensions simultaneously, with modality of production only one of these dimensions. In such cases, differences between particular instances of spoken and written discourse cannot be unambiguously attributed to differences in mode of production.

The fact that discourse used for comparisons varies in ways other than mode of production is sometimes recognized explicitly, as in the case of Barbara Kroll's (1977) study of differences in written and spoken discourse. She asked students to construct narratives in two versions: (1) as an extemporaneous spoken performance addressed to a class, and (2) as a written essay prepared as an out-of-class assignment. Kroll points out, following Ochs (1979), that an *unplanned* spoken form was compared with a *planned* written form of discourse. Despite recognizing this confounding factor, Kroll discusses observed differences between speaking and writing.

Often, however, such confounding factors are not explicitly recognized. Cases in which comparisons of particular discourse forms are presented as generalized comparisons of production mode are common. Consider, for example, Ricoeur's (1976) suggestion that writing produces an autonomous text which transcends the dialogic context of speech. His argument rests on an implicit identification of speaking with dialogue and writing with literary texts. But speaking can take the form of public speech or newscast—both removed from the dialogic model—and writing can take such contextualized forms as personal notes and memos. A contrast of specific spoken and written forms, not general differences in modality, guides Ricoeur's analysis.

Similarly, Olson (1977b) is influenced by an implicit contrast between conversation and scholarly writing. He argues that only in writing can the ideational function of language be realized, asserting that there are difficulties in conducting chained, coherent argument in spoken discourse. While the sequential structure of *conversation* certainly limits a speaker's ability to produce a complex argument (if only because of norms governing floor time and speaker exchange), this problem is not characteristic of speaking in general. Clear examples of the production of chained argument in spoken discourse can be found in many public speeches. The simple fact that, in our culture, the ideational functions of language have, to a large extent, been allocated to written forms should not be taken as evidence that only one modality can serve those functions; neither should comparisons of technical reports and informal conversations be taken as generalized comparisons of writing and speaking. Instead, discussions of the differences between written and spoken discourse should be based on a sensitivity to the variety of forms that discourse can take. Conversation, novels, poems, arguments, essays, stories, and public speeches represent different varieties of human activity which have in common their exploitation of language but differ in many ways in addition to modality of expression.

The most important differences among discourse forms are differences in their culturally-defined structural characteristics. Each form takes shape as what Hymes (1972a) has called a "speech act" or "speech event," governed by specific rules of production/ interpretation. For example, conversation and public speaking are characterized by fundamentally different floor-allocation mechanisms which produce structural and functional differences in these two speech events. Meaningful conclusions about the differences between speaking and writing can be made only within a general classification and structural description of discourse forms. Such a general system would provide a basis for either a more careful analysis of general differences due to mode of production or more specific comparisons of the same act expressed in different modalities (where comparable acts are conventionally performed in both spoken and written modes). Current discussions of spoken and written discourse generally lack such a framework.

Current discussions of speaking and writing also suffer from a failure to see discourse in the context of communication. In addition to the fact that speaking and writing exist only as specific, culturally-defined discourse forms, discourse functions as a message within a process of communication and is designed to serve both practical purposes and needs for intelligibility within the communication context. Researchers have, in general, ignored the ways in which discourse is shaped as communication, and as a result have focused overwhelmingly on differences which are not clearly relevant to the purposes for which the discourse is produced.

For example, it is common to examine differences in lexical selection, syntax, and other linguistic features of discourse. The study by Barbara Kroll (1977), summarized previously, examined just such differences. The selection of such a basis of comparison was arbitrary; it is not clear why these differences should be important for either discourse or communication. Not every difference between spoken and written discourse is important; important differences are tied to the achievement of intelligibility and the practical aims of communication.

What I am suggesting, then, is that study of spoken discourse should be based on the way in which discourse forms perform their communicative functions. Discourse should first be analyzed *as discourse,* with regard to its characteristic form and communicative function. In what follows, I will sketch out a framework for the analysis of verbal messages—a framework which identifies relevant features of discourse and suggests bases for the comparison of discourse forms, including spoken and written discourse forms.

### The Analysis of Discourse

The analysis of discourse should begin with systematic analyses of the *forms* of the various discourse acts employed within a culture—with their distribution and use in practical activities, and their characteristic structures. Such analyses are common in ethnographic studies of communication. Detailed analyses of jokes (Sacks, 1974), stories (Sacks, 1967), requests (Labov & Fanshel, 1977) and other discourse acts have been offered. Some researchers have conducted analyses of the conventional forms of discourse within practical activities. For example, Labov's (1972) analysis of the use of ritual insults, Bauman's (1974) analysis of speaking in Quaker meetings, and Frake's (1972) analysis of Yakan litigation are detailed treatments of discourse events. It is both possible and desirable to give a general description of discourse acts and their forms within practical activities.

Such analyses could form the foundation for systematic studies of writing and speaking. Obviously, a general understanding of the discourse forms employed within a culture would provide a better foundation for conclusions about differences due specifically to mode of production. But such analyses have a more specific utility: they create a systematic comparison procedure. Analysis of discourse forms creates possibilities for examining differences in performance of similar functions within different forms. One could, for example, conduct a study of systematic variations in requests produced in a variety of spoken and written discourse forms based on existing analyses of requests. Comparisons could be made in terms of the translation of the underlying form of requests within different discourse contexts. Thus, one could compare sequentially produced requests and supporting appeals taken from conversation with similar structures within speeches or written persuasive messages. A focus on discourse acts and their characteristics provides a context and a basis for comparison.

Discourse can be analyzed in relation to its functions as well as its structure. Alternative methods of message analysis arise from a focus on the *intelligibility* of messages or on the *practical purposes* which discourse serves. As I argued earlier, the intelligibility of a message is a function of the relationship between the message and its receiver's interpretive frame. Interpretive frames consist of background knowledge derived from several sources, among them knowledge of the practical context of the discourse and knowledge of the discourse form. Thus, one can analyze the intelligibility of a message not only in relation to the interpretive frame employed by the receiver, but also in terms of the relation of the message to the aspects of context incorporated within the interpretive frame or in terms of the relation of the message to abstract discourse form. One could, for example, compare the intelligibility of instructions produced in written and spoken forms in terms of their relation to the context of their production. Production of instructions in face-to-face contexts provides opportunities for visual monitoring and feedback that production in other contexts lacks; it provides a different context for production and interpretation, and thus a different interpretive frame. One could alternatively focus on the completeness or conventionality of discourse forms as they contribute to intelligibility within different production modes.

Messages can be analyzed in terms of their specific purposes as well as their general intelligibility. For example, Clark and Delia (1976) have developed systems for the analysis of persuasive communication. They offer a classification of message strategies in terms of the degree to which the strategy is adapted to the perspective of the persuadee. Such systems judge discourse in terms of the achievement of specific objectives, and provide useful bases for the comparison of discourse produced in alternative modes.

The framework I have proposed has clear consequences for investigating the relationships between speaking and writing. If we are going to compare instances of discourse then we must consider carefully the factors which shape production. By focusing on these factors we should be able to generate dimensions for comparing instances of discourse—dimensions which have more practical and theoretical significance than the arbitrarily-selected dimensions used in much research. It may well be that the kinds of factors I've discussed in this paper—context of practical activity, action performed, communicative purpose—are much more powerful shapers of discourse than is mode of production. But, in any case, we will determine the effect of production mode only if we compare spoken and written discourse in terms of a systematic analysis of discourse forms and in terms of functionally significant aspects of messages.

Finally, the view of discourse I've presented in this chapter has implications for the way we teach oral and written communication skills. Perhaps the main lesson is that we need to sensitize students to the central role of interpretive processes in communication. Too often students in both speech and writing classes view communication narrowly as message construction, focusing their efforts on finding and expressing their own thoughts. But the interpretive view of communication, by emphasizing instead the goal of "intelligibility," asks students to understand the interpreter's perspective. Hence, courses in oral and written communication need to emphasize training in audience analysis—challenging students to move beyond a narrow focus on their own points of view, toward a representation of their audience's interpretive frames.

# 9 Writing as an Integrator of Hemispheric Function

Benjamin M. Glassner
Michigan Technological University

The current outcry for a return to the "basics" in education is ironic coming as it does at the very moment that the neurosciences are on the threshold of illuminating what is truly basic to learning, the operation of the human brain. What the reigning behaviorism of the past decades has dismissed as beyond description is now coming to light as researchers consider input and output in relation to underlying cognitive states. In our own discipline, attention is turning from the products to the processes of composing, processes which bear a striking resemblance to the operations of the brain. It is possible that writing will emerge as perhaps our most fundamental tool of learning.

## Research in Localized Brain Functions

The first empirical interest in the localization of brain functions began with the debate over the early nineteenth-century phrenologist Gall's assertions of a link between particular behaviors and the protuberances of the human cranium, views largely rejected by the scientific community of his day. Dax, in 1836, was the first to associate language with the left cerebral hemisphere. His claim was confirmed in 1861 by Broca's discovery in a post-mortem examination of substantial tissue damage in an area of the left cerebral hemisphere of a patient who had suffered from a disruption of articulate speech. Thirteen years later, Wernicke published results linking receptive aphasia, profound deficits in the comprehension of oral speech without disruption of production, with lesions in an entirely different area of the left cerebral cortex. Such findings encouraged early investigators to attempt to locate specific brain centers responsible for particular behaviors. Although different parts of the brain are now clearly recognized as controlling particular body functions, the search for the neurological foundations of the higher cognitive functions has proved more complex.

The most prominent feature of the human brain is the cerebral cortex, a structure divided into two symmetrical hemispheres which are connected, down in the fissure between them, by the some 200 million nerve fibers comprising the corpus callosum. Of primary interest in the search for the neurological structures responsible for higher psychological behaviors has been the pinkish gray surface structure of the neocortex, a region found exclusively in mammals. Its expansion, particularly in the association areas between the sensory and motor regions, has been the principal development in higher mammalian brains, most strikingly in man. These areas integrate and process information from the different sensory regions and seem to be associated particularly with the uniquely human behaviors. Until quite recently, investigators have paid attention chiefly to the structures of the left, so-called "dominant," hemisphere, owing largely to the assumption that the other higher functions would reside there, as does language. As a result, the right cerebral hemisphere was largely ignored, regarded as merely responsible for directing simple motor activity and capable of only preliminary analysis of sensory input. However, in the past thirty years, reports of specific cognitive deficits resulting from right cerebral injuries have accumulated, and the right hemisphere is increasingly recognized as playing an important role in human cognition. Early studies revealed that such patients suffered deficits in visual perception of spatial relationships. More recent data indicate similar deficiencies with regard to the tactile, kinesthetic, and auditory senses. As a result, the original concept of hemispheric *dominance* is increasingly giving way to one of hemispheric *specialization*.

Although it is the largest nerve tract in the brain, little was known about the function of the corpus callosum, the cerebral commissures which connect the left and the right hemispheres, until the early 1950s. Early examinations of epileptic patients who had had these fibers surgically severed as a means of controlling the spread of seizures revealed no overt changes of behavior. However, the split-brain experiments of Sperry (1961) and Meyers (1956) on cats and monkeys disclosed the presence of two separate spheres of consciousness. Their procedure included not only the severing of the corpus callosum but also of sections of the optic chiasm, restricting the input of the right eye to the right hemisphere and of the left eye to the left hemisphere. When the animal was subsequently trained to respond to a symbol with one eye, the training did not transfer to the other hemisphere; for the animal to perform the task with the other eye, it had to be retrained.

Armed with this knowledge, investigators developed special testing techniques for human split-brain patients which revealed striking evidence of man's two-brained nature (Gazzaniga, 1970). As with the split-brain animals, the transfer of information from one hemisphere to the other was totally disrupted following commissurotomy. All visual, tactual, proprioceptive, auditory, and olfactory information presented to the left hemisphere of right-handed patients could be verbally described and reported; that presented to the right hemisphere could not. (Here and throughout this paper, I will be writing as if the left hemisphere is primarily verbal and analytic in everyone; in most of us it is. However, left-handed adults have different degrees of lateral specialization; some share the pattern of right handers, some show a reversed pattern, and others show evidence of both modes of thought in each hemisphere.) However, tests not requiring a verbal response revealed that the right hemisphere does have a life of its own. For example, when a word was projected to the right hemisphere alone, the subject would deny having seen anything, the verbal hemisphere ignorant of the stimulus; yet the subject would be able to retrieve the object denoted from a series placed out of view with the left hand. The right hand would be incapable of performing the task.

This series of studies has confirmed and expanded earlier clinical findings suggesting that the left hemisphere excels in verbal processing and in calculation, while the right is superior in such tasks as drawing figures, arranging blocks to match a pattern, recognizing faces and performing mazes. However, as these findings, too, come from the study of patients with some form of brain disease, the question still remains whether these phenomena are present in the intact normal brain.

One avenue of inquiry which makes such study possible is the comparison of a normal subject's ability to handle various stimuli presented to the left and right hemispheres through the visual pathways. One study found a quicker reaction time for verbal responses when stimuli were projected in the right rather than the left visual field, thus informing the left hemisphere (Filbey & Gazzaniga, 1969). Others reported a right hemisphere (left visual field) advantage in fundamental perceptual processes (Durnford &

Kimura, 1971; Kimura, 1966, 1969). A similar approach involves dichotic listening tasks in which each ear receives different sounds simultaneously. Such studies have indicated superior recall of verbal material when presented to the right ear (left hemisphere) (Kimura, 1961), and a left ear (right hemisphere) advantage for recalling melodies (Kimura, 1964).

Other approaches have been developed which make possible the study of cerebral asymmetry in normal subjects on a physiological level. One makes use of a radioactive isotope technique for measuring increases in blood flow and hence activation in the different structures of the cerebral cortex (Lassen, Ingvar, & Skinhøj, 1978). Another is that based on the electrocortical measures of the electroencephalograph (EEG) which permits the analysis of the asymmetry between amplitude levels of matched sites in the left and the right hemispheres while keeping intact the chronology of variations. It has been shown that the more active the cortical involvement, the lower the EEG amplitudes, so that when dealing with the right over left ratios, deviations above the overall mean ratio indicate a relatively greater activation of the left, while deviations below correspond to relatively greater activation of the right hemisphere. In normal right-handed adults, the distribution of deviations has been shown to be random. However, during specific cognitive states, there has been shown to be a clustering towards a higher degree of left hemisphere involvement during spatial preoccupations, particularly over the temporal lobes (Goldstein, 1979).

Such findings have tempted investigators to propose various dichotomies characterizing the different capacities of the left and right hemispheres, stressing either the types of response required or stimulus materials presented. Their characterizations include the common distinction between the hemispheres as verbal versus nonverbal and the now popular notion of the left hemisphere as our "scientific" brain, the right as our "artistic brain." But such simplifications may confuse more than they clarify. Critchley (1953), for example, has warned of the dangers in attempts to locate arithmetic processes exclusively in the left hemisphere, pointing out that, despite clinical evidence that links *discalculia* more frequently with left hemisphere disease, arithmetic entails spatial thought as well as analytic, owing to the horizontal and vertical arrangements of numbers. In fact, Dimond and Beaumont (1972) report a right hemisphere superiority in adding and subtracting when the solution does not require a verbal response.

It is becoming increasingly evident that what distinguishes the hemispheres is not so much the materials with which they deal as the ways in which those materials are processed. One study (Levy, Trevarthen, & Sperry, 1972) reports that when the same kind of problem was presented to each hemisphere of a split-brain patient, "the two ... accomplished the same task by characteristically different strategies" (p. 74). One of the pioneers of the split-brain procedure, Bogen (1977), while not denying a certain degree of "modality specificity," proposes that it is far less important than the "process specificity" (p. 138). Such process distinctions have been described as analytic versus holistic (Bever, 1975), propositional versus appositional (Bogen, 1969), and analytic versus gestalt (Levy, 1974). Each implies that the right hemisphere is predisposed to see wholes simultaneously, the left to focus on individual elements within a field and to analyze them in series. According to Bogen (1977), the most important distinction concerns "the extent to which a linear *concept* of time participates in the ordering of thought" (p. 141). Thus both clinical and laboratory evidence suggest that each cerebral hemisphere has capacities for learning, remembering, and perception, each participating in the full range of human behaviors in its own characteristic manner.

### Brain Research and Language Functions

That the left hemisphere is intricately connected with language is undeniable; clinical evidence clearly links gross disruption of language processes far more frequently with left than with right hemisphere disease, observations which are substantially supported by experimental data. Yet as early as 1874, Jackson (1958) suggested that the right hemisphere may play a role in language activity as well. He wrote that "to locate the damage that destroys speech and to locate speech are two different things" (p. 130). Dimond (1972) concluded, in his review of the split-brain research, that although "speech output" may be a left hemisphere function, "antecedent links" appear to be present in both hemispheres (p. 170).

Although rarely indicated in the various forms of aphasia, the right hemisphere does have language of its own, particularly in the realm of comprehension. Studies of split-brain patients (Gazzaniga & Hilljard, 1971; Gazzaniga & Sperry, 1967; Sperry & Gazzaniga, 1967), as well as of patients whose entire left hemisphere was anesthetized in a diagnostic procedure preceeding surgery (Milner, Branch, & Rasmussen, 1964), indicated that the right hemisphere can understand spoken and written nouns, some phrases, and very simple sentences. It was further shown to be capable of decoding even complex verbal cues, for example, responding to the words "shaving instrument" by pointing to a razor and to "dirt remover" by pointing to a bar of soap (both, of course, with the left hand).

These findings proved modest when compared to more recent studies which, making use of a special contact lens, made possible communication with either hemisphere of split-brain patients for considerably longer periods of time (up to two hours of continuous input as opposed to the 0.1 seconds of flash duration in tachistoscopic half-field projections necessary to prevent eye movements from deviating the visual data to the other visual half-field). This advance permits the administration of standardized tests (Zaidel, 1966, 1973). The results of these studies led Sperry to revise his earlier evaluation of a more primitive right hemisphere level of comprehension and to go so far as to suggest that the right hemisphere in right-handed adults has language ability to the extent of having the vocabulary of a fourteen year old and the syntactical ability of a five year old (Rensburger, 1975).

There are also suggestions of a limited right hemisphere capacity for language production. Some studies (Luria, Simernitskaya, & Tubylevich, 1970) report the production of spontaneous speech and writing in otherwise aphasic patients. Bogen (1969) and Gardner (1978) report that aphasics can sometimes sing words; in fact, Boston Veterans Administration Hospital now offers a training program for aphasics which has successfully boosted language output. During the first state of therapy, patients learn to sing simple phrases. The melody is gradually phased out, and patients are reported to be able to produce short but grammatical and appropriate sentences in about three months.

But far more significant than just having language of its own, the right hemisphere does display certain specialized language functions not shared by the left, namely, crucial roles in the modulation of speech sounds (Luria & Simernitskaya, 1977), in the ability to use metaphorical expressions appropriately (Bogen, 1969), and in what Gardner (1975) calls our sense of "emotional appropriateness" in discourse "being related not only to *what* is said, but *how* it is said and to what is not said as well" (p. 372). These findings should explain reports of nonaphasic patients who were creative writers suffering from impairments in their output as a result of right hemisphere disease (Gardner, 1975, p. 369).

Writing is differentially affected by damage to the left and right hemispheres. Defects in the conscious coding of sounds accompanies damage to the left hemisphere while more involuntary writing processes are disrupted by damage to the right hemisphere and/or subcortical structures (Simernitskaya, 1974). Another study (Luria, Simernitskaya, & Tubylevich, 1970) describes aphasic patients unable to write a word by dictation yet able to write when asked to produce their signature as quickly as possible. Similar effects are often observed in the speech of aphasic patients who, although unable to produce a word voluntarily, may do so spontaneously. Luria (1974) cites such examples as: "No, doctor, I can't say 'no'!" and "Oh, I have forgotten how you call this inkstand."

## Thought Processes and Language Production

Luria (1973) has proposed a theory of "dynamic localization of function," asserting that rather than residing in fixed locations, the higher psychological functions are instead complex functional systems combining the workings of different structures within the brain. In light of recent findings (Luria & Simernitskaya, 1977), he has proposed:

> a radical change in our approach to the basic mechanisms of cerebral organization. In place of the sharp distinction between the verbal and the nonverbal, each assigned to its respective cerebral hemisphere, we have to think in terms of a variety of factors involved in the organization of psychological processes and of a heirarchy of functional levels in their cerebral representation. Thus the structure of any given psychological activity may depend on a number of factors, some of which are governed by the activity of the major hemisphere and some by that of the minor hemisphere. (p. 175)

This new line of thought reflects not only the recent findings in the neurosciences but a subsequent shift away from the strict behaviorist's concern with performance to the exclusion of process. As long as we focus on products, it is easy to be misled. Language, for example, is necessarily linear (words must be strung in sequence from left to right), and successful communications are structured and logical. But the language production process is concerned with more than structuring and articulation; it is concerned with thought itself. Though differing in function, thought and language are united, mature thought only developing in the presence of language. The two processes cannot be separated. As Vygotsky (1934/1962) has observed, "Thought is not merely expressed in words; it comes into existence through them" (p. 215).

Obviously one of the crucial elements of thought underlying language processes is memory, and here the left and the right hemispheres meet. Lashley (1951) argues that articulation of thought must be based on the translation of an underlying matrix of a-temporal images into a serial order. Since Simonides (556-468 B.C.) developed a system for teaching students of oratory to use imagery to improve their memories, similar mneumonic devices have been widely used as aids to learning. Recently, psychological investigators have renewed interest in memory processes. Paivio (1971), reviewing a series of studies, concluded that (1) individuals recall lists of words better when instructed to "image" information, particularly if they develop interactive images involving two or more words; (2) concrete words are learned faster than abstract words; and (3) pictures accompanying words facilitate recall. He suggests that thinking consists of two major components, "dual processing systems," which incorporate, respectively, nonverbal imagery and verbal symbolic processes. Bower (1970) notes that the imagery system shares many of the properties of a spatially parallel system, while the verbal system seems better suited for handling sequential, serial information. He suggests that this may reflect the lateral specialization of the left and the right hemispheres.

That higher cognitive thought is dependent on the interplay of different modes of consciousness has long been reflected in the introspections of creative thinkers and writers. Describing the origin of a particular poem, Stephen Spender (1952) wrote:

> Obviously these lines are attempting to sketch out an idea which exists clearly enough on some level of mind where it yet eludes the attempt to state it. At this stage, a poem is like a face which one seems able to visualize clearly in the eye of memory, but when one examines it mentally or tries to think it out, feature by feature, it seems to fade. (p. 116)

Surprisingly, the thought processes of the poet are not unlike those of our most "logical" thinkers. For example, Einstein (1952) described his own thought as follows:

> The physical entities which seem to serve as elements in thought are certain signs and more or less clear images . . . [in] combinatory play. . . . The above mentioned elements are, in my case, of visual and some of the muscular type. (p. 43)

Wallas (1926) described creative thought as a four-staged process, crediting Helmholtz, the German physicist, with describing the first three. Speaking in 1891, Helmholtz described the thought processes that followed his conscious examination of a problem as follows:

> Happy ideas come unexpectedly without effort, like an inspiration. So far as I am concerned, they have never come to me when my mind was fatigued, or when I was at my working table. . . . They came particularly readily during the slow ascent of wooded hills on a sunny day.

From this account, Wallas derived three stages: *preparation, incubation,* and *illumination,* and later added a fourth, *verification,* which includes the testing of the idea and its articulation. Henri Poincaré's (1952) description of mathematical creativity resembles this account, especially in its depiction of largely unconscious creative works framed by deliberate conscious attention:

> Most striking at first is the appearance of sudden illumination, a manifest sign of long unconscious prior work. . . . The role of unconscious work in mathematical invention gives us the result of a somewhat long calculation *all made,* where we have only to apply fixed rules. . . . All one may hope from these inspirations . . . is a point of departure for such calculations. As for the calculations themselves. . . . They require discipline, attention, will, and therefore consciousness. (p. 38)

Einstein (1952) reports that his process, too, ends in a conscious and deliberate stage:

> Conventional words or other signs have to be sought laboriously only in a secondary stage, when the . . . associative play is sufficiently established and can be reproduced at will. (p. 43)

## The Integrative Function of Writing

If language and thought processes represent the combined workings of integrated systems within the left and right hemispheres, it is this final stage of articulation and verification which suggests a distinction between the processes of speaking and writing, singling out writing as a particularly powerful heuristic. Commenting on the crucial difference between animal and human consciousness, Karl Popper (1977) has argued that:

> The basis . . . is human language which makes it possible for us to be not only subjects, centres of action, but also objects of our own critical thought, of our own critical judgment. (p. 144)

But writing, by virtue of its slower pace and of its making a graphical representation, further extends human consciousness. As Popper (1977) also observed:

> As long as we carry intuitive belief without a symbolic representation, we are one with it and cannot criticize it. But once we have formulated it, we can look at it objectively and learn from it, even from its rejection. (p. 108)

Luria (1971) has singled out writing as an especially powerful instrument of thought precisely because of its integrative features, its ability to exist independently of ongoing events which allows for the merging of analysis and synthesis, suggesting that writing's slower process

> makes it possible not only to develop the required thought, but even to revert to its earlier stages, thus transforming the sequential chain of connections in a simultaneous, self-reviewing structure. (p. 118)

Emig (1977) suggests the following distinctions between talking and writing. Writing, she notes, is

> learned . . . artificial . . . technological . . . slower . . . stark, barren, even naked . . . ; (it) must provide its own context . . . audience . . . (and) because there is a product involved . . . (it) tends to be a more responsible and committed act . . . (often with) an aura, an ambiance, a mystique . . . more readily a form and source of learning than talking. (pp. 123-124)

Citing similarities between the writing process and that of learning as described by Dewey (1938), Piaget (1971) and Kelly (1963), who all characterize it as an active process of modification or confirmation of previously established conceptual schemes in light of an experience, Emig (1977) argues for a "unique correspondence between learning and writing" (p. 124). Both proceed by trial and error, by a transaction of analysis and synthesis, incorporating in their processes—exploration, formulation, criticism, modification, retesting and confirmation—a complex and highly personal rhythm.

Unfortunately, much of the writing which goes on in our schools does not seem to be such a powerful instrument of thought and learning. Emig's (1971) case study of the composing of twelfth graders suggests that this is due to school's emphasis on the most superficial kind of writing, the report. Her results are supported by subsequent studies on this continent and abroad (Pianko, 1979; Whale & Robinson, 1978; Britton et al., 1975). Emig's (1971) data suggest that writing occurs in two principal modes, the *extensive,* "the mode that focused upon the writer's conveying a message or a communication to another," and the *reflexive,* "the mode that focuses upon the writer's thoughts and feelings concerning [her] experiences" (p. 4). Writing in the two modes differs in style and pace: *extensive* writing is "assured, impersonal, and often reportorial," more regular in execution, while *reflexive* composing is "tentative, personal, and exploratory," longer, more complex, and recursive in its processes.

*Reflexive* composing suggests the features that Luria (1973) identifies as an integrated functional system. Differences in right hemispheric involvement have been shown in different reading tasks; stories tend to engage the right hemisphere more than technical materials as measured by R/L EEG amplitude ratios (Ornstein, Herron, & Johnstone, 1979). Preliminary findings in an EEG study by this writer (Glassner, 1980) suggest similar differences in writing. Reportorial writing, focused on communicating information already familiar and formulated by the writer, characteristic of extensive composing, is accompanied by greater relative engagement of the left cerebral hemisphere as indicated by lower relative EEG amplitude ratios measured from electrodes placed symmetrically over the left and right temporal areas. Writing which is focused upon discovering meanings, which is tentative and exploratory—characteristic of reflexive composing—is accompanied by greater relative engagement of the right cerebral hemisphere.

## Implications for Writing Instruction

Our failure to stimulate students to utilize writing as a powerful tool of learning reflects our cultural bias towards one way of knowing, as well as the profound influence of behaviorism on educational theory and the "new critical" orientation to the analysis of products which has typified training in the English profession. By mistaking the qualities of products for those of processes, we have been led to characterize composing as a rather neat, orderly, straight-forward, and wholly conscious series of acts. Our overwhelming concern for the surface features of written language has kept students from understanding the true properties of the composing act. In their attempts to adopt our prescriptions for form, students fail to recognize the form inherent in the emergence of their own ideas, in fact, they rarely get that far. The very nature of assignments deprives them of the opportunity to examine their own thoughts and experience, so locked are they into reproducing someone else's—teacher's or text's.

Polanyi (1958) observed that "the aim of a skillful performance is achieved by the observance of a set of rules which are not known, as such, to the person following them" (p. 49). He distinguishes between "focal awareness," which is directed towards the purpose of a behavioral act, and "subsidiary awareness," which refers to the whole complex of feelings which guide the act but are not subject to our direct attention. This distinction, which also suggests a bipartite division of consciousness, resembles a fundamental assertion of current discourse theory. Kinneavy (1971) wrote:

> The aim of a discourse determines everything else in the process of discourse. "What" is talked about, the oral or written medium which is chosen, the words and grammatical patterns used—all of these are largely determined by the purpose of the discourse. (p. 48)

And yet, it is purpose which student's writing most often lacks and to which instruction frequently fails to attend; students are more often concerned with the teacher's purposes than their own.

Clearly our educational system's emphasis on analytical skills is lopsided (we might rather say half-brained). Language predominates in the classroom and in most school-related activities, but it is almost exclusively the language of reporting, not that of discovery or learning. Neither does our curriculum accommodate the various styles of individual learners nor their repertoire of cognitive abilities. Classroom practice too often operates under the assumption that if concepts can be sufficiently ordered, presented simply and repeated often enough so that students can reproduce them in similar words and contexts, then learning has occurred.

While not neglecting the discourse of our own disciplines, we must, as educators, turn to our colleagues in other fields for help. The findings of researchers in the neurosciences should compel us to recognize the need for a radical restructuring of the curriculum. The behaviorist's concern with the input and output of instructional systems can no longer be considered adequate; the "black box" is being opened. While the specifics of this change must await further research and application by classroom teachers, we should recognize that key to this development must be a new orientation towards writing instruction in the classroom as well as its infusion throughout the curriculum.

# 10 Bridging the Gap between Oral and Written Communication in EFL

Roberta J. Vann
Iowa State University

The passage of the Bilingual Education Act, the advent of open admissions policies at many universities, and a new wave of immigrants who need to learn English have made us increasingly aware of the special problems of students who are non-native speakers of English. English teachers, often expected to wear an EFL instructor's hat, have traditionally had to bear the largest share of the responsibility for helping these students. This chapter is addressed principally to those teachers who, though trained in teaching English, feel relatively unprepared to cope with the problems of teaching English, especially composition, to non-native speakers. By suggesting ways in which the foreign language writer resembles and differs from the native speaker/writer, I hope to address some of the concerns of teachers faced with an EFL minority in a traditional composition class. I do so by proposing a model for the relationship between speaking and writing among second/foreign language learners based on similar models for native speakers. The model serves as a basis for suggestions for narrowing the gap between the speaking and writing of EFL students.

EFL students' abilities and attitudes about English result largely from their previous language instruction. Students in our classrooms are products of certain pedagogical traditions. What follows is a brief overview of some of the factors shaping these traditions.

## Our Heritage in Foreign Language Pedagogy

What does it mean to know a language? For the layman, the linguist, or the teacher the answer is obvious—to speak it. An emphasis on oral language dominates recent linguistic theory and has occasionally been criticized. According to F. Householder (1971):

> many linguists . . . imply by their total silence, that writing and written materials (other than linguists' transcriptions, of course) are not of concern to the linguist, that his description of a language is complete if it correctly accounts for every possible spoken utterance. (p. 250)

As Schafer asserts in chapter 1, linguists have supported the notion of oral primacy since approximately the beginning of this century, when structuralists, rebelling against the predominant nineteenth-century focus on written language, argued that it was "an incomplete mummified repository" (Salus, 1969, p. 184). Language teaching theorists espoused the direct method, a language teaching approach that attempted to simulate the conditions of first language acquisition by moving away from the formal teaching of grammar and written language. A few decades later the audio-lingual approach followed suit by placing written language in a decidedly subordinate role. Strongly influenced not only by structuralist linguistics, but by behaviorial psychology as well, proponents of audio-lingual theory specified a carefully sequenced chain of learning: listening, speaking, reading, and writing.

In the foreign language class, this adherence to a tightly imposed learning sequence was intended to simulate patterns of first language acquisition. Because children usually acquire language skills in that order, theorists assumed that this sequence was inherently superior and thus ought to be applied to adult foreign language teaching. The direct method and the audio-lingual approach discouraged literate adults from writing until they had gained competency in listening comprehension and spoken fluency. Advocates argued that by restricting the use of writing as an aid to memory, adult learners had a better chance of acquiring native-like pronunciation, an area where children seemed to have an advantage. Children have this advantage, it was implied, because they are preliterate. By extension, then, we would expect adults who postponed literacy in the target language indefinitely to acquire native-like accents. But this is simply not how it works with adults. If children have an advantage in pronunciation of a foreign language it is the result of inherent biological characteristics (Lenneberg, 1967).

Whether or not children have an advantage in language learning, language teaching methodology is moving away from imposing the learning strategies of children on adults. Writing is becoming increasingly important in the EFL classroom and being recognized not only for its own sake, but for the valuable practice it affords in encoding the language. While the direct and audio-lingual methods stressed oral practice, recent evidence suggests that writing may actually have certain advantages over talk as a form of encoding. One study asserts that a combination of listening and writing (in lieu of speaking) at the early stages of adult language learning may increase the likelihood of native-like pronunciation (Postovsky, 1970). This implies that the best adult language learning strategies may differ from those of children and, specifically, that writing may serve an important need in adult language learning.

The changing focus of EFL methodology is evident in the recent advice given by prominent theorists. Rivers—who a few years earlier, in the height of the audio-lingual movement, minimized the role of writing in foreign language learning—now is a strong advocate of writing in developing fluency. In a recent book, Rivers and Temperly (1978) point out certain advantages of using writing in the foreign language classroom to build oral skills. They state that writing reinforces what has been practiced orally, provides practice in forms that are more fully realized in writing (for example, present perfect forms "lost" in rapid speech), and allows students with physical or emotional difficulties or slow reactions to demonstrate their abilities through a more relaxed medium (pp. 276-277).

In summary, the nineteenth-century view of written language as the proper focus of foreign language study gave way to the dominant twentieth-century view of oral language as the central classroom emphasis. Today we have begun to integrate these views and once again to recognize writing as an essential part of language learning.

## A Model of Speaking and Writing Development for the EFL Learner

If we now recognize the weaknesses in past language teaching approaches, we also recognize the value of research that compares first and second language acquisition. Research in second or foreign language learning has typically followed in the wake of similar research in child language acquisition. Hunt's study (1970) of the syntactic development of children's writing was followed by comparable studies of the writing of adults learning foreign languages (Cooper, 1976; Monroe, 1975). These studies revealed similar kinds of growth in syntactic maturity. Children acquiring English and adults learning German and French moved from shorter to longer T-units. Studies of oral and written syntactic development in children (Loban, 1976; O'Donnell, Griffin, & Norris, 1967) provided models for my work with adult Arabic speakers learning English (Vann, 1979). Loban found that in the lower levels of school, oral skills surpassed written ones, but that after about the fourth grade, written surpassed oral skills among the better students. Writing became more highly elaborated and syntactically more complex. Presumably this growth occurs when children learn to expand syntax to meet the constraints and demands of a communication situation in which increased and explicit information is required. Subjects in my study showed similar trends: those at the lowest level of English proficiency wrote as they spoke, their syntax was unelaborated and the information they attempted to convey vague and unformed.

This trend is illustrated by the perfunctory description of a silent film, written by a subject in the low proficiency group:

> Then they carried him and after they walk a few distanc they saw some solder scaired them. Some of solder run and fall even he dide. Onother solder pulled that person and went on his walking, when he arrived to a small villige he saw that vilige is burn then *he stop and killed that person.*

The subject's abbreviated style seems to assume a great deal of knowledge on the part of the reader and contrasts with the relatively detailed account of the same film provided by a subject in the highest proficiency group:

> They behaved like real human being and took that man with them. While they were going back to the the rest of their group, they found some of their enemis who carried gons with them. One of these two men who carried the enjored man who was their enemy with them went away, the other pulled him back hom. The enemies when they saw that the two men carried thier freind with them went when he reached his home he found that all the houses were burned by the enemy. So he said to himself, "I save their freind and they set fire on our houses." *Then he carried a very big stick and hit the enjored man to death. He killed the man whom he carried an pulled in that long distance and bad weather. He killed him when his people killed.*

Notice how the second writer provides details including quoted inner speech and, for example, uses three sentences to describe the same event the first writer describes in six words (italicized portions). This is very similar to what we find in children's writing: movement from writing that assumes too much from the reader, perfunctory and undetailed, to writing that has expanded to fit the needs of the audience.

After observing writing development in foreign students, I am convinced that it parallels in many respects the writing development of children. This insight is supported by the similar patterns Cayer and Sacks (1979) observed in the oral and written discourse of basic writers. In short, it seems that chronological age may not be the important variable implied in earlier studies (Loban, 1976; O'Donnell, Griffin, & Norris, 1967). In other words, we all follow certain patterns as we acquire a new language, regardless of our age.

If this is the case, we should be able to find correlates for the relationship of speech and writing between first and second language learning. The patterns of development are not necessarily identical, but certain important parallels exist which may prove insightful for teachers.

For years the term "oral interference" has been a catch phrase to describe what happens when the conventions of speech are projected inappropriately onto written discourse. The term thus includes a phenomenon common to children and adults and to native speakers, as well as speakers of other dialects and languages. Oral interference describes all sorts of problems from the orthographic to the rhetorical and implies deficient oral communication (Hartwell, 1980) or simply inappropriate transfer of speech to writing. In addition, oral interference may suggest stasis rather than changing patterns of oral and written relationships. All of this confusion suggests a need for refinement of the term. What follows is an attempt to come to a clearer understanding of oral interference by looking with the aid of a model at the writing development in EFL in relation to oral language.

## Speaking and Writing Development for the EFL Learner

Weaver (1979) described the writing development of children as a process with three stages. In each stage the child reformulates a hypothesis about what writing is. The child's first hypothesis is that "writing means expressing meaning." Weaver suggests that the child's failure to communicate and/or instructional emphasis on "correctness" may result in the child's formulating a second hypothesis: "writing means producing a correct surface structure." The fortunate student either by-passes the second stage altogether or progresses from it to a third stage: "writing means using as many conventions as necessary to convey meaning" (p. 20). Weaver believes that these hypotheses may be more instructionally than developmentally imposed and warns that children may never arrive at the third stage in the process. According to Weaver, this failure to mature may result from teachers who respond to mechanics rather than meaning.

Although Weaver does not explicitly discuss the relationship of speaking to writing, we can infer that if, at stage one, writing conveys only meaning and little attention is paid to the conventions unique to writing, it is undifferentiated from speech. On the other hand, in stage two, the child, focusing on form rather than function, differentiates writing from speech, but neglects the expressive power of writing. At stage three the child has learned the written conventions necessary to convey meaning, including both those which unite and differentiate it from speech. Thus Weaver's model, when extended to focus on speech and writing, is in many respects similar to Kroll's (chapter 2 of this volume) in moving through stages of differentiation and synthesis.

### Level One Writers

Experience with the writing of foreign adults studying English in the United States suggests certain parallels between these models for children learning to write in their native language and the kind of model that would account for adults learning to compose in a foreign language. The writing of adult learners at the earliest stages of English proficiency, like that of children, is relatively undifferentiated from their speech in the target language. Sentences are often short and redundant and use conversational techniques. The writer of the following passage is only beginning to understand the written conventions of English. Notice the frequent use of "and" to connect ideas, a feature characteristic of conversation, especially that of children. His inventive punctuation and spelling also reflect his own speech pattern in English:

> I am whaching the falm about wor. some pepal tak
> clodes some man becos The wather cold and some pepole no
> lave becose the sno and I E C fang nach and some pepel

died some house burn becose the pepol can the at and some
pepel
died by the gan and by the snoe.
and he angry and some peopol angry becos some pepol
died gun.
fanle. and He died fanle sam that.

## Level Two Writers

As with children acquiring their native tongues, some adult second language learners seem to by-pass stage two altogether and go
from stage one, in which writing is *limited* by the patterns of
speech, to stage three, in which writing *incorporates* the patterns
of speech. Others seem to move from stage one to a stage where
they focus on form and avoid the patterns of speech, perhaps to
insure error-free writing. Students with this view of writing are
like the basic writers described by Shaughnessy (1977) for whom
the major question is not how to make a sentence better, but how
to make it right (p. 44). These students have strategies for avoiding
errors, typically by writing a minimum of words in short, simple
sentences:

> The class is calm now. The students are writing the essay, the
> teacher is walking around the room. She is looking at their
> work. Their are thinking how to write a paragraph.

By circumventing problematic lexicon and syntax, the writer has
avoided error with the exception of confusing "their are" for
"they're" in the last sentence. Unfortunately she has also sac-
rificed expression.

This kind of writing is what Macrorie (1970) termed
"Engfish"—writing that is lifeless precisely because it lacks voice.
Its writers, like those basic writers described by Shaughnessy,
may find themselves lost in the gap between their oral and written
communication skills:

> The spoken language, looping back and forth between speak-
> ers, offering chances for groping and backing up and even hid-
> ing, leaving room for the language of hands and faces, of pitch
> and pauses, is generous and inviting. Next to this rich orches-
> tration, writing is but a line that moves haltingly across the
> page, exposing as it goes all that the writer doesn't know, then
> passing into the hands of a stranger who reads it with a
> lawyer's eyes, searching for flaws. (p. 7)

Such students, whose errors may go unnoticed in speech, may approach writing, where errors will be evident, with frustration and

hesitancy. This attitude can manifest itself in the careful composing of the earlier example or in writing filled with cross-outs and
false starts:

> I have taken English course xxxx for six years in my home
> country, but it just xxxxx help me how to read English, no spe-
> cial course on writing. So I think the xxx xxxx xxx xxxxx prob-
> lem to me in English is writing—how to write a correct sen-
> tence.

Writers who develop the notion of good writing as correct writing have often also developed certain expectations about what the
relationship between writing student and teacher ought to be.
Here is one EFL student's description of an ideal composition
teacher:

> one who explains to the students, in detail, how to use the
> English *grammar* in written English and helps them to write
> in a *correct form* and then *checks theirs errors and teaches
> how to avoid them.*

This student's comment, with its emphasis on form, grammar
and error avoidance, reflects a view of writing as a science rather
than a craft; it focuses on information that can be conveyed didac-
tically. Notice that the student has placed the burden of skill
transmission on the teacher while taking a correspondingly passive role. The student not only views writing as something that
can be received relatively passively, but feels that the avoidance
of grammatical error is the primary criterion for good writing.

This student's view of composing is similar to that of the Saudi
Arabian student who told me that he hoped I could provide him
with "the master key for learning how to write English." Both
epitomize the unrealistic expectations of some EFL writers. Their
attitudes are almost certainly the result of instruction that encouraged them to think that writing—either in their mother tongue or
the target language—is primarily a matter of observing correct
grammar and mechanics rather than expressing an idea clearly and
coherently.

## Level Three Writers

After either passing over or through stage two, students at stage
three, like learners at stage one, use writing to express themselves.
The chief difference between levels one and three is one of maturity. At their best, level three students have the vocabulary and
syntactic skill to write with the power and authenticity of speech

while maintaining the conventions of writing. This is one such student's description of a former teacher:

> I can see his sharp eyes hidden in his wrinkled face and his big mustache moving rhythmically as he said, "I know you, Mr. Z. You can cheat very well and if we squeeze you we will get a barrell of wickedness, but if you just try to use your mind I bet you will answer it without cheating." I felt ashamed and never tried to cheat again.

This student, an Arab, uses strategies that would have been effective in either speech or writing: details, quotations, and analogy.

I do not mean to imply that a kind of miraculous transformation takes place when writers move from stage one or two to stage three. Rather, stage three itself is composed of a series of stages in which the student tests out the ways speech and writing differ. A major problem for stage three writers is adjusting linguistic register to meet audience needs and expectations, a problem they share with many native-speakers of English. For EFL writers, however, the problem is often more acute. Part of the reason is obvious: most EFL students have limited exposure to language varieties. Traditionally, language teaching has stressed *correct* rather than *appropriate* usage. EFL texts typically emphasize sentential grammar and only rarely include varieties of register or even authentic discourse. EFL teachers for whom English is a foreign language typically have had more exposure to literature than to practical conversation and writing. In Poland, for example, university English majors read Shakespeare and study transformational grammar, but have little opportunity to converse with native speakers of English. In Syria, English teachers have even less exposure to native speakers. I recently worked with a group of forty such teachers whose English was fluent and grammatical; yet most were unable to pick out the stylistic inconsistencies in the following sentences:

> Cease making that noise, you little rascal!
> What time do you plan to show up at the ceremony, Mr. President?
> Gentlemen, to arms! This is no time to be scared of the enemy!

If English teachers have problems spotting inappropriate usage, the problem will be even greater for their students. An EFL student suggests the patience needed to learn appropriateness:

> I just learned routine grammatical fragments of English in Korea, which doesn't help that much especially in expressive

> idiomatic writing and speaking. Having spent almost five
> years in U.S., I am now able to understand what American
> native people talk about except for the cases when they use a
> lot of slang terms. ...

This student was aware that his English was occasionally inappropriately formal. He was clearly at the stage of attempting to synthesize spoken and written forms, and well on his way to focusing on audience rather than on differences in the codes themselves. Because linguistic register is complex, we can expect students at this stage to sometimes miss the mark even though they are aware of the need to adapt tone to audience needs.

The following student's response to an assignment to write a letter requesting funds to start a small business is inappropriately stiff and bureaucratic:

> Dear Sir,
>     Re: Application for a business loan
>     Allow me to bring to your knowledge that the number children has been growing rapidly lately correspondingly the market for children's clothes has also increased. Because of this increase in the demand for children's clothes I have the intention of establishing a business in this area. However my capital at present is insufficient to establish the business. Because of this, my main purpose in writing to you is to obtain a small business loan.

The letter was written by a Chinese student who was described by his teacher as having weak oral language skills: he spoke with hesitation and refrained from taking part in class discussion. His writing, while better in grammar and mechanics than many of his classmates', tended to be inappropriately formal. For instance, "Allow me to bring to your knowledge" substitutes for "Let me tell you." Reliance on nouns instead of verbs, characteristic of officialese, is demonstrated in: "I have the intention of establishing" which should be revised for emphasis to "I intend to establish." Yet, the student's choice of register is not always inappropriate. His last sentence is preferable in this context to the more frank: "I don't have enough money to start the business."

While this student seems to have been influenced by written language, a second student responded to the same assignment in a way that helps illustrate the influence of speech or writing:

> In todays' style of living the clothing plays a very important role, in special our children, we always want them to look very nice & if we go shopping, sometimes we buy more clothes for our children than for ourselves. ... The purpose of this loan

> application is to purpose of build an small business for produc-
> ing and selling children clothing. . . . And ahead of all this will
> be myself.

The letter was written by a student from Latin America who was
living in a college fraternity and was described by his teacher as
glib and fluent in spoken English. The sample illustrates his attempt to connect with the reader (emulating certain features of
spoken dialogue) through the use of "our" and "we." Just as the
writer borrows part of his rhetorical strategy from oral language, so
he attempts to apply certain spoken conventions to his written
language. For example, the comma splice is probably a result of
oral interference, as are omitted endings (a common problem for
language learners who have difficulty hearing or making certain
sounds). Here, again, we observe the influence of spoken on written language. The student tries to affect a more formal tone and
interestingly uses the reflexive pronoun (myself) as a substitute for
the objective pronoun (me), a hyper-correction common in middle
class speech in the area where the student lives. The strategies of
this EFL student are no doubt familiar to teachers of native speakers: the student relies on oral language and the transfer of certain
aspects of oral language to the written mode.

## Implications for Teachers and Researchers

Models over-generalize and over-simplify complex problems, and
this one is no exception. I have tried to present a new perspective
on the relationship between oral and written language among
non-native speakers of English, an alternative to the simple notion
of oral interference. In itself the model offers no solutions to our
problems, but it is a necessary preliminary step to empirically-
based research. The model assumes: (1) the universality of a broad
writing problem—finding the fit between speaking and writing
and learning to make the appropriate adjustments in form and register to suit audience; (2) the developmental, fluid nature of the
oral and written relationship; (3) the importance of attitude and
instruction in determining the pace and direction of development.

What factors shape the nature and progress of the non-native
speaker's writing development? Although common sense tells us
that everything from orthographic to rhetorical differences between one's native tongue and the target language are a potential
source of difficulty, we have no precise knowledge of what these

difficulties will be. The contrastive analysis hypothesis, stressing mother-tongue interference, claimed that second language learning is primarily a process of acquiring those items which differ from the native language. This view has come under attack in recent years (Dulay & Burt, 1974) and is being replaced with the error analysis hypothesis. This approach recognizes that one's native language is only one of a variety of factors influencing second language learning. The learner also constructs hypotheses about the target language based on his limited knowledge of the target language as well as on his knowledge about the communicative function of language in general.

Language background may be less crucial in determining writing development than the learner's attitudes about the communicative function of speaking and writing. Teachers who are sensitive to these attitudes have a head start in diagnosing student errors and prescribing their treatment. Writes a speaker of Black English Vernacular:

> The reason essay make me mad because I can't think of anything to write on and my weakness is writting a Essay. The reason it so hard is because my spelling bad and I can't put my word togather my writting poor that the reason why I get mad. I get mad at myself. I get mad when I'am talking to somebody and do not listen to me.

An EFL student expresses similar feelings of frustration and fear of being misunderstood:

> in this class there are person who speak different languages but they try to talk and express their feeling in a common idion; the English. Many of their qualities are lost because with the new idiom they cannot show their knowledge. ... We have to hand in this paragraph to the teacher right now and then our ideas will be misunderstood for the teacher.

Students' attitudes about written language may have been shaped by their instructional background:

> My illiterate parents thought reading anything other than the Koran or textbooks was evil and so I was forced to hide my reading. When my parents discovered my books and magazines, they burned them. When I made mistakes in writing my teacher kept me after school to re-write the mistakes ten times. What kind of learning is this?

Awareness of student attitudes about written language is the first step in determining the stage of the learner's development. Is he/she struggling to express ideas (stage one), to achieve correct form above all else (stage two), or to synthesize oral and written codes to achieve language appropriate for a given situation (stage three)?

With students at the early stages of development, we must both avoid emphasizing correctness of form at the expense of meaningful, organized discourse and offer to provide students with practice encoding the language both in speech and writing. We must go beyond conventional exercises in grammar and transcription, which are typically the limits of writing in the beginning stages of traditional EFL instruction.

Students at stage two need more than exposure to the language and practice using it. Like other reluctant writers, these students need techniques which help them overcome their inhibitions about using the language for expression. Elbow's (1973) free writing technique combined with additional opportunities to express ideas in the target language under nonthreatening conditions can help the writer gain confidence. When grammatical problems occur, teachers need to keep in mind that these errors often arise out of an inability to *apply* rules rather than an absence of the rule itself. Students who can recite rules for using the present perfect and perform well in fill-in-the-blank style tests may still not be able to use the form correctly in their own writing. Exercises are not enough. Students need work in making the connection between form and function.

Students at stage three have at least vague notions about differences and similarities in speaking and writing. More than anything else, they need to see and hear various registers of English and to experiment with them. Exercises that involve writing and restating the same message for different audiences are useful. Journal-keeping allows students to practice expressive writing and can help them generate ideas which can be adapted for other purposes. Group composing and editing encourage the interaction of talking and writing. These techniques also provide an opportunity for problems with register to surface for group discussion.

At all levels form should be viewed as a means to function, not an end in itself, and writing should be related to work students do in other courses, for example, note-taking, summary writing, letter writing.

I offer these pedagogical suggestions with some hesitation for they are largely without empirical basis. Yet it is the lot of teachers to march on, with or without support from researchers. For the time being we must work with still largely undefined notions about the precise ways in which speaking and writing influence one another in the language development of the non-native speaker. Many important questions remain unanswered. How much transfer of learning can we expect from one language skill area to another? Will fluent speakers make good writers? Why do some students have particular difficulty with one mode or another? Are personality and cultural background the important variables our intuition suggests they are? Are the age and sex of the learner factors in mode preference or proficiency? Are the most effective methods for teaching written composition to non-native speakers comparable to those used by teachers of native speakers? Research in applied linguistics has been slow in seeking answers to such questions.

On the other hand, there are optimistic signs. We now realize a need for theory and research in the relationship between speaking and writing—long an area with recognized pedagogical implications. We are posing questions, designing new models and redesigning old ones. We are looking to other disciplines for insight at a time when research in composition itself is expanding at exponential rates. In recent years we have witnessed the value of such cross-disciplinary contacts. Just as an approach to analyzing the errors of foreign language learners has influenced the teaching of composition to native speakers of English, so research in first language development continues to provide important insights in EFL. Future solutions to our problems are likely to evolve from interdisciplinary work, perhaps conducted by research teams with experts from adjacent fields working on common problems.

More specifically, there are signs of parallels between first and second language learners beyond those previously acknowledged. Might age and culture be less important than certain universals of development? There are no simple answers. It is not enough to offer oral interference as an explanation for student writing problems. The time has come to try to understand what oral interference means and to arrive at developmental models of writing which illuminate its relationship to speech.

# 11 Written Language in a Visual World

J. G. Kyle
University of Bristol (England)

Most people in our culture learn to read and write—functionally, if not always as fluently as some teachers might like. If we, as educators, want to know something about how people succeed in becoming literate, studies which involve this large group of successful individuals may provide some insights into the processes of learning to read and write. However, if our interest lies instead with those who, despite schooling, fail to achieve literacy, then we need to study those exceptions to the normal pattern in order to gain insights into the processes which produce failures in reading and writing. Such a strategy seems logical, but it is neither simple nor free from problems. A vast literature on dyslexia highlights the problems of research on children with reading difficulties (see Valtin, 1979). Typically, researchers find children who do not read or write properly despite normal cognitive and manual skills (even better when one finds groups of superior intelligence) and set out the type of problems they have. This then gives us a model of reading, and the parts of the reading process which may be sources of failure can be identified. The problem, however, is that each child we study may be suffering from a different deficiency in the reading process.

Where, then, should we begin our study of reading difficulties? One apparently simple answer is to start with the "basic skills" which the child brings to his reading lesson. But what are these skills and how do they fit together to produce readiness for reading and writing? Kirk and Kirk (1971) list over 50 psycholinguistic skills and Guilford and Hoepfner's (1971) model of intellect has 120, each of which may be related to formal language in a whole series of ways. The "basic skills" answer is far from simple.

A better answer might be to find children deficient in specific skills and to track the effect of this deficiency throughout their development. If our particular interest is the relationship between oral language and formal systems of reading and writing—as it is in this book—it would seem that the perfect group to study would be children who do not produce or receive oral language: deaf children. Here are children whose intelligence is said to be normal (Ries & Vonieff, 1974), but who have no language (Furth, 1966) when they come to that first encounter with a teacher. If they have serious problems in reading and writing, then it seems clear that human oral and written systems are mutually dependent. If they can learn to read and write, then there is no necessary relationship between oral language and the written word.

Unfortunately, even this research strategy is too good to be true. Apart from problems of finding deaf children whose level of deafness can be easily and clearly specified (Dawson, 1979) or whose intelligence level is easily matched on standard tests to hearing children (Kyle, 1980a), deaf children are not really a "no language" control group (Blank, 1965). However, despite such problems, deaf children are a group with severe reading and writing difficulties, who do provide a unique opportunity for examining oral language in relation to reading and writing.

It may seem obvious to state that the hearing of speech, and more particularly the hearing of one's own speech, is critical in reading, but it is appropriate to point out that it is what is retained of the speech in memory which is critical to reading. This points to the difference between groups of people born deaf and those whose hearing loss arises at a later point in life. The former have to learn English by using what little hearing remains and trying to fit it to a limited internal knowledge of speech, while the latter have to fill in the gaps in what they lip-read or mis-hear from the vast store of English knowledge already accumulated. Adventitiously deaf people probably read more than they did when they were hearing. It may be that the language which exists beyond the eye and ear plays a significant role in their process of reading.

This point requires further examination, because it is at the heart of the similarities and differences between hearing children and congenitally deaf children. If we can establish the role of speech processing (not the language "out there" of communication, but rather the language "inside" us) in learning to read and write, we can begin to consider to what extent deaf children can cope with written language without access to external speech. By definition, written language is visual and deafness should therefore be no problem unless the way we think about words affects our understanding. If hearing people use speech, deaf people must use something else, and if the something else is successful then there is no reason for the absolute emphasis on speech in the education of both hearing and deaf children.

Our aim must be, therefore, to examine the role of speech in written language processing for hearing people, and then to determine (a) what happens when we take away this speech (written language without hearing), and (b) what happens when a different language form takes the place of speech (written language through sign language).

## The Role of Speech in Written Language

Smith (1978) argues the case for reading as a high level activity that involves the speech system and its link with short term memory. It is this approach to reading as a process rather than as a specific skill which will be examined here. Indeed there has often been a problem associated with the notion of "skills" in reading development. While one can distinguish a series of elements in the reading process and while certain children appear aware of these elements at certain stages of development, the subskills have often been given the status of a developmental stage when in reality they may be symptoms of reading instruction and a function of the reading process. If the process of reading is a specific example of information processing, then the capabilities are already there. What capabilities a child shows must have been drawn out by the task or materials the instructor has given the child. When children come to their first reading lesson they already have many fundamental capabilities in speech, in speech comprehension, and in cognition. Some even have the basics of reading. Thus, it is more fruitful to talk about reading development in terms of processes available and strategies used than in terms of subskills of reading or of reading readiness.

One of the emerging processes evident in young readers is the "silent speech" process, which may well be the link to the internal world of thinking. But exactly how such subvocal speech functions in relation to reading instruction is still the subject of debate. Robeck and Wilson (1974) maintain that poor comprehenders are children who continue to use the auditory symbol as a bridge between the written symbol and the semantic meaning of what they read silently. Fry (1972) suggests that subvocalization is a distraction—a crutch to help the very immature who have a better speaking than reading knowledge of the language. Nevertheless, Groff (1977), in his review of this field, very clearly indicates that the weight of evidence supports silent speech as a fundamental aspect of the reading process.

Moreover, a number of psychologists and developmental theorists have concluded that "inner" speech representation plays an important role in both information processing and language development. Much of the psychological work in this area has been on memory, and, in particular, short-term memory, where lists of items are presented and people have to recall the items immediately after presentation. For example, Conrad (1964) found that people's recall of letters was consistent with a process of speech storage. That is, in recall, whenever a mistake was made it was based on the acoustic or articulatory features of the original item. This was true even when materials were presented visually. Baddeley (1966) extended this research to words, and was able to separate speech representation, or coding in short-term memory, from the semantic representation that is used when items are stored in long-term memory. It seems that we use speech sounds as an immediate storage device but progress very quickly to using the meaning of the items. As we will see later, this basic principle of human information processing is relevant for understanding the process of reading.

Developmental research also supports the importance of inner speech. Developmental theorists at least agree on a very strong link between speech and thinking. It can be claimed that, in young children, speech carries thinking. For example, children's games are often characterized by role-playing where speaking aloud appears to be a complete expression of purpose and thought. At the age of five or so, a change begins to occur. Speech which was formerly vocalized becomes internalized and silent, and functions as a tool in thinking. Sokolov (1972) has linked internal speech and thinking in a series of studies using electromyographic (EMG) techniques (recording of impulses from the speech muscles). He showed that silent speech—where activation of the speech muscles occurred but no overt speech was produced—was apparent in a whole range of tasks. Strikingly, he found that silent speech accompanied even "nonverbal" tasks, such as the reasoning involved in Raven's matrices (Raven, 1960), where a missing pattern has to be chosen on the basis of logical rules. The electromyographic recordings increased as these nonverbal problems became more difficult. A similar pattern can be demonstrated in reading. Hardyck and Petrinovich (1970) showed that EMG activity increased in reading as text complexity increased. McGuigan (1970) did a similar study but asked people to say *when* they thought they were using subvocalization; he found very little relation between real and reported activity. So it seems that we are not necessarily adept at noticing our silent speech. McGuigan also demonstrated that this activity was related to verbal processes only, since in his comparison of copying words and drawing shapes the latter produced no measurable increase in EMG activity.

Subvocalization is not a new concept to most reading teachers, but there has been much confusion concerning its function and importance. People appear to gradually internalize speech for their thinking and reasoning, as the EMG studies show. Silent speech is also apparent in reading. But we need to know more about the functions of internal speech if we are ever going to be able to use it in written language instruction.

The question then is to what extent our ideas about the development of covert speech fit into our experimental findings of its use by adults in reading and remembering. At the very least we ought to be able to demonstrate a developmental pattern for the experimental findings.

Conrad (1972) did experiments with children where pictures were memorized. Some of the pictures had similar-sounding names like "hat," "bat," "rat" and some had dissimilar names like "girl," "spoon." Subjects were presented with items either from the similar sounding names, or dissimilar sounding names. Very young children showed no difference in remembering each set of pictures, but by the age of five or six years a difference began to emerge. At eight years of age there was a clear advantage for the dissimilar set (as there is for adults). This supports the notion that children use a phonological store and that it develops at the time when silent speech is reported.

Shankweiler et al. (1979) strengthen this finding in a study of eight-year-old children, where they compared good and poor readers. Good readers showed a marked speech coding effect (as defined by Conrad) while poor readers showed very little sensitivity to speech coding in memory. Interestingly, poor readers' lack of speech coding was not restricted to visual presentation as found in reading, but also was evident in auditory presentation. This suggests very clearly that the difficulty arises in speech processing generally and is not purely a function of reading ability.

Baddeley (1979) brings together many of these strands of the argument and tries to explain them within his model of Working Memory. Although this model is quite technical in detail, it is worth discussing its principles since it provides a framework for the analysis of deaf children's development. Based on a series of experiments on verbal reasoning, verbal memory, and comprehension, Baddeley proposed two parts to short-term memory:

*Central Executive:* a decision maker, choosing strategies for processing, and dealing with the meaning stored in long term memory.
*Articulatory Loop:* a system of rehearsing like a recording tape loop, which corresponds roughly to memory span.

In language processing, the Loop holds information in sequence, while the Executive assembles it into meaningful speech sounds. In support of this idea are findings that memory span is less for long words than short words (Baddeley, Thomson, & Buchanan, 1975) and that children with difficulties in blending and breaking up words have more errors on the final consonants than on the initial ones. What Baddeley claims is that the Articulatory Loop is required in early reading development when letter sounds have to be blended to make words and when words have to be processed in sequence to allow the Executive to "understand" the meaning of the whole sentence. Mature readers often do not require the Loop. For mature readers, the Executive samples from the written text, predicts what is coming next, and then matches to the next part of the sentence. Even when the Loop is suppressed by making the reader repeat a redundant word, like "the," over and over again during reading, it slows down the process but it does not affect the extraction of meaning for the mature reader. Only when a mismatch occurs or when the text becomes very complex, does the Articulatory Loop need to be brought into use. This may involve conscious inner speech to support the processing of the Executive.

We do not need to agree with all of Baddeley's model to see its usefulness as a conceptual tool. It very neatly brings together research concerning memory processes with the notion of inner speech. It also clearly separates the decision-making part from the speech part. The model clearly shows that we can use inner speech (the Articulatory Loop) to hold information long enough to extract meaning accurately, and that the Executive decides when we have to do this. If Conrad is right then this capability emerges when developmental theorists say speech becomes silent. The model opens up intriguing possibilities: people without speech should be able to use an Executive but not an Articulatory Loop. Does this mean that they should be able to read (as Baddeley's mature readers would), or do they get stuck at a developmental stage where silent speech is so important to reading? To test Baddeley's model—and the whole question of the role of speech in reading development—we need to turn to an exceptional group: deaf people.

### Written Language without Hearing: Reading Test Results

There is really no doubt about it: prelingually deaf children have very serious problems in learning to read English. Recent research in both the United Kingdom and in the United States confirms the difficulties which every teacher of the deaf experiences in helping deaf children learn to read. What is surprising is that the problem has received so little attention in the literature on deafness. Even recently, Moores (1978) spends only 3 of his 250 pages on "Educating the Deaf" specifically discussing reading problems. Nevertheless, we can illustrate the level of reading ability of deaf children.

Conrad (1979) has produced startling figures for the population of deaf school leavers in the United Kingdom. For the entire population aged fifteen to sixteen years who are placed in a school for the deaf or in a special unit attached to a normal school, the mean reading age is nine years when it should be nearly sixteen years. Di Francesca's (1972) report, based on Gallaudet's survey of reading ability for the same-aged children in the United States produces a reading age of nine years two months. (Some slight difference would be expected because of differences in test procedures and method of collecting data.) There is, therefore, remarkable concordance concerning the degree of the problem. Conrad (1980) emphasizes that

> when hearing loss reaches 85dB and beyond, we find a full 50% of school leavers are unable to begin a standard reading test at the seven-year-old level. ... We tested more than 450 children of school leaving age in schools for the deaf and partially-hearing units—almost the entire population. In all of these, we found five children who had a hearing loss greater than 85dB and who could read at the level of their chronological age. Just five—in all Britain. (p. 324)

At the same time it can be shown that prelingually deaf children speak and lip-read poorly (Conrad, 1979; Swisher, 1976) and therefore one can say that their spoken language experience and ability is very limited. It seems clear that those without speech processing (deaf children) are at a severe disadvantage in reading (and writing) when compared to those who can use speech properly. But it is unwise to treat this statement too superficially. People who have lost their hearing probably read more than at any other time in their lives, despite the disruption of their speech communication with others. Conversely, many people with normal speech and hearing have difficulties in reading. The emphasis has to be on the deeper processing—the representation involved in language use as it relates to reading and writing. We need to look very carefully at different aspects of processing—at when and where the difficulties of a deaf child arise—in order to understand the nature of the link between speech and written language.

Kyle (1980b) has begun to examine developmental aspects of reading in deaf children aged seven years and nine years. Despite my preoccupation with speech here, visual processes are important in the very early stages of reading, and it can be predicted that deaf children would not be disadvantaged at these early stages. This, in fact, tends to be the case. At seven years of age, partially hearing and profoundly deaf children (over 85dB better-ear average hearing loss) are not significantly different from hearing children in sight vocabulary. In letter discrimination, (matching letters in different type) and letter equivalence (identifying upper and lower case versions of the same letter), while being behind at seven years of age, these children begin to catch up by the age of eight and are not significantly different in these skills by the age of nine. However, at all levels there are differences between hearing and deaf children on comprehension measures. This finding is commonly confirmed by teachers' experiences: the deaf child progresses in vocabulary and other prereading skills but, when it comes to words in sequence in a sentence, cannot begin to process the meaning of the sentence.

Looking back to Baddeley's proposal of speech coding as critical in the Articulatory Loop, it seems likely that breakdown occurs here. Disturbed speech and lip-reading will affect the Articulatory Loop and result in difficulties in preserving longer chunks of written material. Processing of short units might not be affected if they can be associated directly to visual meaning; for example, the word "ball" might be identified directly, using only the Executive part of the process. Such a process would agree with Fowler's (1979) analysis of phonological coding in beginning reading. She claims there are two aspects to this coding, one which aids the comprehension of sentences and one which acts as a lexical access code, i.e. finds the place in memory where the word's meaning is stored. Deaf children may have found a substitute for the lexical access problem, but not for the preservation of longer pieces of information. But even these concepts are too simple, since they disallow *all* profoundly deaf children from learning to read. On the contrary, Conrad found five deaf children who could read at an advanced level. And even if the mean reading age of fifteen-year-old deaf children is nine years, there is still some comprehension occurring. It seems, therefore, that deaf children must use a system of representation other than speech coding, though how this works is not immediately apparent. An examination of the language structures involved in reading comprehension and particularly in writing provides a clearer window on these inner processes than does reading research.

## Written Language without Hearing: Examining Language Structures

The difficulty we experience in trying to understand deaf people's stories or free writing is probably similar to the difficulty they have in understanding our written English. That is, deaf people's writing does not look like "simple" English, or English written by a normal beginning writer; it is often completely different in character. Below are two examples, the first from a ten-year-old, profoundly deaf girl, and the second from a profoundly deaf woman in her thirties.

> One day boy ate fish. turtle sleep. turtle walk on water. turtle ate fish water. boys look eat fish. boy are sad. because he can not fish (from Quigley, 1979, p. 291).

> Fingerspellings are useful for borrow the English if there are no signs for the words sometimes it find useful for the names, addresses, etc. . . . But if the hearing people who learn the fingerspellings then will trapped in fingerspellings as they will use them instead of signings (taken from correspondence).

Different explanations have been offered for the nature of deaf people's English. A recent kind of explanation, one based on generative grammar, suggests that the deviant structures in deaf people's writings are rule based (Quigley, 1979). In general, however, most earlier studies focus on "deaf errors" and explain deaf people's sentence structure as an immature—or "retarded"—form of hearing people's syntax (Heider & Heider, 1940). Simmons (1962) measured the type-token ratio of writing samples generated from pictures and concluded that deaf children exhibited less diversity of vocabulary than normal children. Moores (1970) focused on deaf writers' restricted, stereotyped expression, as well as generally poor grammatical abilities. Cooper and Rosenstein (1966) comment on deaf writers' shorter, simpler sentences and the unusual distribution of parts of speech in these sentences. Myklebust (1964) identifies the common errors made by deaf writers as problems of omission, substitution, addition, and word order. He also highlights the undue use of "carrier phrases." In response to pictorial prompts a deaf girl of nine produced this story:

1. The boy play with doll house
2. He put on the table
3. The boy have many toys
4. He have tables
5. He have cars. (p. 339)

A hearing girl of nine produced the following:

> One day, I was in my room. In my room are lots of kinds of toys. First, I play with my little doll family and their little furnitures. Next, I . . . . (p. 339)

It is clear that these stories are quite different in approach and expression. Although this deaf girl has acquired some simple syntax, she is using it inappropriately. This same inappropriateness occurs with verb endings, articles, and pronouns. It is relatively easy to illustrate weaknesses in deaf people's syntax. Quigley, Martanelli, and Wilbur (1976) show that deaf children do not have well established rules for the use of auxiliary verbs, with the passive construction being most difficult. Quigley et al. (1974) show that questions are a problem too.

However in nearly all studies the emphasis has been on the deviant nature of deaf children's writing and reading, focusing on what Swisher (1976) calls a "quantitative level" (i.e., their sentences are shorter, with frequent errors). Only in summary do Quigley, Wilbur, Power, Martanelli, and Steinkamp begin to hint at underlying *processes* which supply the key to the differences between normal and deaf writers. When we focus on the processes, we see that deaf children show a considerable degree of language sophistication. Quigley et al. propose that deaf children view written English as a linear structure, rather than as a hierarchical one as the grammar demands. Moreover, deaf children acquire rule-generated structures not found in English. Both Taylor (1969) and Ivimey (1976) concur that deaf children use a different kind of internal representation of language. However, no one seems to get to the core of this representation problem—how our teaching strategies and deaf children's views of the world might combine to produce syntax problems.

Consider what the salient cues for deaf children are in their approach to written language. Their environment is visual, not auditory: the most striking features are visual-placement ones, and the most important sequences are visual-movement ones. This visual orientation is not a handicap in early reading instruction, where pictures and single words appear simultaneously and associations can be made. But the use of pictures with accompanying sentences can cause difficulties for the deaf child. A visual orientation becomes a problem for understanding sentences in which the visual order of words does not correspond to the visual placement of objects in the accompanying picture. Suppose that the deaf child is trying to read the sentence "The boy is throwing the ball." Assume further that there is a single picture showing this action. In the picture, the ball does not have to be on the right (as the word "ball" is in the sentence); it could be above or to the left of the boy. Furthermore, in the picture the concepts "the boy" and "throwing" are integrated, not separate. The picture conveys the meaning by trying to show the boy in the act of throwing. So the deaf child has to learn not only how to separate parts of the picture (boy and ball), but also how to divide concepts within a single illustration (boy and throwing).

A simple solution might be to make the sentence concrete by giving the gestures—"(the) boy"—"throw." Either take the part of the boy or point to a picture of the boy, and then do a throwing action. But then there is another problem: the "throw" gesture must incorporate some of the characteristics of the ball in order to make sense visually, so there is another separation problem. And finally, to gesture "(the) ball" as the last part of the sentence doesn't make any sense at all, since you have just thrown it away!

Profoundly deaf children have serious problems in understanding and using English word order because we do not understand their notion of visual order. To sign the sentence using American Sign Language (ASL) or British Sign Language (BSL) would produce, most commonly, "ball (boy-throw)," that is, boy and throw signed closely together or even simultaneously with different hands. In learning written English, deaf children must learn rules for syntactic transformation which very often disturb these salient, visual rules. It is a tribute to teachers that deaf children do learn some transformations, and it is not surprising that one of the major findings in Quigley, Wilbur, et al. (1976) is that there is a strong tendency for deaf children to over-use simple sentence patterns, such as "subject-verb-object."

The matter of representation is, therefore, a recurrent one: hearing people's speech plays an important role in reading development, while in deaf people's poorer reading and written expression another linguistic system seems to be at work. The question of how visual representation might be used to better advantage to encourage easier written language production and reception will be explored later. It seems appropriate to consider first how deaf people, on their own, have learned to use sign language as a formal language system—a system which may form the representation needed to comprehend the English language.

## Written Language through Sign Language

Conrad (1980a) makes it quite clear that for a significant proportion of all deaf people—certainly for a vast majority of the profoundly deaf—the language of sign is an efficient linguistic form. Although profoundly deaf people's speech is almost unintelligible according to teacher's ratings and objective measurements, they do exhibit language potential and learn to use language in the medium of sign language. Goldin-Meadow (1979) presents evidence that the natural gestural/sign forms developed by deaf children without deaf parents ("home-signing") exhibit very important characteristics of early language processes. The first example of the deaf girl's writing above is consistent with a visual representation of the story with continual change of referent; thus, "boys look eat fish" is likely to be boys–look (turtle) eat–fish. The turtle is understood because the direction the boys are looking designates the previously established position of the turtle. It would certainly form an acceptable representation in basic sign language. The key question is whether sign language can perform the same function as the speech code in the hearing child.

It has been very difficult to identify the nature of the code used by deaf people in memory tasks. Some work has been done on comparing the performance of deaf and hearing individuals on the same kind of memory tasks. Although in early research deaf people's memory performance was "disadvantaged," it seems likely that task characteristics were biased because of response incompatability (Green, 1980) or because of no proper hearing control groups (Conrad, 1979). When these problems are solved, the performance of deaf people is similar to that of hearing people. However, what is of most concern is *how* deaf people perform such tasks. Kyle (1981) discusses some of the problems in the research which tries to find a sign code in memory tasks. The growing assumption that deaf people use sign language codes in short term memory has largely been based on the work of Bellugi, Klima, and Siple (1974) and extended in Klima and Bellugi (1979). The difficulty is that very small numbers of deaf people took part in these studies and the evidence on the critical confusions in memory based on sign language is based on a relatively small number of errors. Nevertheless, findings support the theory that sequential processing may be done in sign language as it is in speech. Kyle (1981) agrees, showing a relative superiority for deaf people's recall in sign when they have to repeat the sign as it appears. For hearing people, repeating the word in speech helps recall because it acts as an external Articulatory Loop.

In sentence recognition, Dawson (1981) reports a massive improvement in memory when the syntax of presented sentences corresponds to the form of British Sign Language (BSL) used by the children. She compared standard English sentences like "we arrived late in London" with BSL forms such as "we arrive to London late." Significantly better recall was found for BSL forms than for standard forms. This finding agrees with the conclusions of Odom and Blanton (1970) that deaf people understood sentences better when they were written in a format following American Sign Language (ASL) rather than in standard English. Brewer, Caccacmise, and Siple (1979) show that in the process of sentence recognition deaf people do make the same inferences from propositions. Their study used manually coded English (or signs in English word order), but it implies that when deaf people do these tasks involving recall or recognition they are processing sign information in a way similar to hearing people's coding through speech.

This type of research emphasizes the strength of deaf people's representation in sign and highlights the similarities with speech when sign is forced into a sequential mode. Sign language functions as a language representation in memory. Sign should therefore be available as the linguistic device for reading and writing *development*. However, one possible problem with teaching English through sign is that sign language does not share the grammar of English, nor does it share the same parts of speech or tense markers. Is it necessary to supply these in order for deaf children to learn to use English for writing and reading?

The issue is a very complex one and one fraught with statements of belief rather than properly researched views. At least in theory it is possible to teach one language through another. If one wishes to teach written French to English-speaking children, current practice is to expose them to structured texts in French with corresponding English translations. It would be very unusual to have a mediating language of "Franglais" in order to bridge the gap between the two languages; rather, one would accept the differences between their syntax and their idioms. However, sign languages, because of their use of hands, body posture, facial expression, and eye gaze, leave open the possibility of the simultaneous presentation of signs and speech. Thus, a combination of the two languages—sign language and spoken English—could occur. This usually means that signs are made to follow English word order (although it could mean English made to follow sign order, as in deaf people's writing). This combined system may offer a better approach to deaf people's problems with English syntax.

A number of signing systems are actually using such combinations: Signed English, Seeing Essential English, Signing Exact English, and Paget-Gorman Sign System [compared by Bornstein (1979) and Wilbur (1979)]. Such systems form the basis of the greater part of Total Communication programs for deaf children in English speaking communities in the United States and in the United Kingdom. When ASL or BSL have been used it usually quickly becomes a pidgin form where redundant parts of speech are dropped (Bornstein, 1979) and this is often the mainstay of conversation between deaf adults and hearing adults. In all cases educators have claimed that such systems improve communication in the classroom, are easy to learn by parents and teachers, and encourage English language growth. However, as Conrad (1981) points out, there has been no presentation of evidence that such systems have improved children's reading or writing.

The evidence suggests that deaf people use sign codes in ways similar to speech codes, but there is also neurological evidence that tends to support the idea that these are the only codes which can be used (Kyle, 1978; Ruben & Rapin, 1980). It therefore seems likely that, in order to teach reading, we have to begin to use visual cues and to use sign language with sequences corresponding to the syntax stages set out by Quigley et al. (1976). This means that teachers of deaf children should understand sign language principles (whether they use them directly or not) and that they should consider visual elements very carefully in presenting materials. Materials should stress visual sequences. Sentences such as "The boy is throwing the ball" should be supported by three pictures, rather than a single one: (1) a picture of "the boy," (2) a picture of the "the boy throwing," and (3) a picture of "the boy throwing the ball." Done systematically and early, such training will provide strategies which will enable a deaf child to deal with his visual world in a form which can transfer to written sentences.

However, there is still one difficulty which, although it is not easily solved, must at least be recognized if we are to make clear the requirements of the deaf child. Sign languages have a particular characteristic which we can call "simultaneity." It is the capability of building "pictures" or phrases by presenting different signs simultaneously, so that the "sentence" consists not of a sequence, but rather a unified meaning created by building one sign simultaneously on another. This closely parallels the construction of a visual illustration where all the elements are present at the same time. Klima and Bellugi (1979) discuss it in ASL, Kyle and Woll (in press) and Brennan (1975) consider it in BSL, Sorensen and Hansen (1976) examine Danish deaf children's use of it, while Goldin-Meadow (1979) shows it exists in children even where no formal sign language exposure is evident. If this were the basis of the representation of language, then sequential processing in short-term memory tasks may be a case of forcing the natural code to work differently. Fortunately, simultaneity is not used all the time in sign languages; it may be more a characteristic of informal than formal conversations.

## Implications

Finally, then, we have developed a picture of deaf children with a different internal world struggling to understand a sequential language to which they have limited access. Unlike children learning to read a second language, who are also experiencing the second language aurally, deaf children must use their own code or their own strategies to try to do the things that hearing children do with a speech code. The task for deaf children is not impossible, but it will help greatly if educators have a clear idea of the nature and magnitude of the problems such children face.

Deaf children's difficulties with reading and writing help us appreciate the importance of speech for the development of written language in normal children. Whether or not one accepts the developmental picture of speech—speech coding—reading as set out in the early stages of this essay, it seems that the sequential speech experience of hearing children fits very neatly into the reading books we provide. In the early stages, a hearing child can use picture-word associations for vocabulary learning, and a deaf child can do this as well; but as soon as the hearing child finds a picture with a sentence underneath, he or she can switch strategies to a more useful one. That is, the task becomes one of decoding text into speech and, by doing this, the child strengthens the link to overt conversational speech and thereby to a whole range of speech experience. The fact that a deaf child does not or cannot adequately do this illustrates its importance for hearing children.

According to Valtin (1979), hearing children with reading problems at some stage very often have had a speech disturbance (or a minor hearing loss). This may not produce a deaf child's world but it may upset the salience of speech decoding as a way to the internal world of representation. The speech coding process as set out by Baddeley (1979) and Conrad (1979) is directly involved in getting meaning from external events, and the model of the process provides insights into the features which might be prone to disorder.

The tactic of teaching children with reading problems through other codes is theoretically viable. That is, words or letters can be taught to a child by emphasizing their visual parts, and the feel and rhythm of them as they are written. Such tactics must support the speech decoding process, and one hopes that they allow the normal speech coding process to take over very quickly, and thus facilitate progress in reading and in writing.

The problems of deafness are complex. Deaf people are not just people who cannot hear but, when the deafness occurs before spoken language develops, they may be people using a very different language code. The fact that even a very, very small number read very well indicates that speech and speech coding are not the only ways of learning to read, and that other language forms may be possible. We have only begun to consider these. The fact that so many hearing children learn to read and write too quickly for us to be able to work out how illustrates how closely speech and spoken language experience may be implicated in developing reading. To understand the process of reading and writing is to understand something of the internal world of the child, and this must be our task.

# 12 Integrating Oral and Written Business Communication

Don Payne
Iowa State University

In the course of this article I argue that speech can provide useful metaphors for the teaching of business writing. Although many of my remarks will apply to writing courses in general, I want to show specifically how business communications courses can integrate oral and written discourse—with emphasis on the word *integrate.*

## Problems with Business Communications Courses

First, a fundamental question. Why should there be any uneasiness about uniting speech and writing, whether we're teaching a full business communications course or just a brief unit on letters, memos, or reports? One answer is that such a proposal must face a tradition of neglect. A recent article by Wyllie (1980) points out that in the seventies less than 15 percent of the articles that the American Business Communication Association published in its *Bulletin* dealt with oral communications. In the past, textbooks in business communication have given minimal coverage to oral skills, and most courses have followed the lead of the texts. Thus writing dominates these courses, even though evidence already exists to challenge such a priority. Repeatedly, studies have shown that those in business spend most of their time communicating orally and that they place primary value on speaking skills.

### Neglect of Oral Communications

A decade ago a survey of thirty-five California-based *Fortune 500* corporations found that 94 percent of the business executives questioned made extensive use of oral communication skills. Ben-

184

nett (1971), in summarizing the study, made the first of several pleas for redesigning business communication courses:

> These findings indicate that the oral communication skills should not be neglected and that courses should be offered to business administration students in oral as well as written communication. Studies of schools of business curricula have shown that most business communications courses have emphasized written and in many cases excluded oral communications. (p. 8)

Bennett's argument was strengthened when Huegli and Tschirgi (1974) found that oral communication skills were even more important at entry-level positions, where, we might suppose, the impact of our courses is likely to be highest since those hired at this level will have most recently had our high school and college business courses.

In 1979 a study by Stine and Skarzenski of more than eighty Iowa-based businesses asked business executives, "What percentage of your workers' time on this job is spent in written communication?" As a whole, these executives estimated that almost half (48 percent) of their workers' time involved oral communication compared to only 28 percent for written communication. An even more recently published study by Swensen (1980) showed that forty-five chief executive officers of large industrial corporations rated face-to-face communication within a firm as the most important form of communication. The reasons are practical ones. Montoux and Porte (1980), for instance, have shown that even "phatic communication has a positive influence on turnover, absenteeism, production, and efficiency to the extent that attitudes affect the performance variables" (pp. 10-11). If such benefits can result from communication aimed primarily at sociability rather than factual information, then oral skills may deserve even more emphasis than business and industry have realized.

This dominance of speaking over writing should not surprise us. An informal check on communication in our own lives would reveal roughly the same proportion, even for those of us whose professions center on the production and teaching of writing. But the sheer amount of time those in business spend in oral communication does not prove that such skills need a proportional attention in formal education or that the place for such teaching is in the business communications course. Students themselves would be the first to argue that their speaking skills, perhaps by virtue of greater practice, are superior to their writing skills. When I ask my students on the first day of class to write a paragraph on their attitudes toward writing, responses like the following are typical:

> Sometimes it is easier to just "talk" than to "write." That way if there is any misunderstanding between you and the receiver of the message, it can be cleared up right away. Also you can, or at least I can, express myself a little better.

> Although I know that writing is important, I don't care to write. I have always been weak in paper and letter writing ever since high school. No matter what kind of paper I write, or how much time I put into it, I still receive a poor grade. This is probably the main reason for not liking to write. Also, with the telephone so nice and handy, I would just as soon pay the extra and talk, for business and otherwise.

> I sometimes feel writing to be a waste of time and much prefer face-to-face communication. However, since that isn't always possible, the knowledge of writing effectively must be undertaken. My own personal problem is the fact that it doesn't always come easy for me.

In these comments the students not only praise the spoken word, they prefer it, and echo it in their writing.

### Writing Modeled on Speech

Some have turned this preference for the oral style into a compositional maxim. Gunning (1968), famous for his readability counseling begun in the 1940s, entitles one of the chapters of his writing text "Writing Like You Talk." He opens that chapter with a quotation from the October 1962 *Bulletin of the Bureau of Naval Weapons,* a publication sent to individual naval stations. Here is part of that material:

> Our biggest problem in communications is that you're there and we're here! *We'd have no problem if we could all get together and talk whenever we wanted to.* But we can't do that so we have to resort to writing to "talk" to each other.
> *At best, writing is a poor substitute for talking.* But *the closer our writing comes to conversation, the better our exchange of ideas will be.* (p. 119, emphasis mine)

I have italicized portions of this statement because they suggest three distinct assumptions that deserve our attention, some of the same assumptions we have already seen in the students' comments:

1. We are better speakers than writers. (Problems would vanish "if we could all get together and talk.")

2. Speech is inherently superior to writing. (Writing is "a poor substitute.")
3. Good writing approximates conversation.

We should of course grant that the purpose behind this communication from the Bureau of Naval Weapons may have encouraged the writer to overstate the case. But we would not have to look far to find advice similar to the Bureau's or to Gunning's. We could find it in Pascal's preference for "a natural style," in Flesch's notion of "plain talk," in Lesikar's advocacy of the "conversational style," or in Trimble's advice to develop prose with "a natural, conversational rhythm."

Much of this advice is defensive, an attempt to help beginning writers avoid the straightjacketed prose of a misguidedly formal style. And, to be sure, rather than directly equate speech and writing, most of these writers hedge with the usual caveats and qualifiers, though their approach runs the risk that many students may never perceive the distinction between writing that is conversation and writing that merely achieves the effect of good conversation, what Somerset Maugham called "the conversation of a well-bred man."

## Piecemeal Design of Communications Courses

I suggest, then, that the first problem in proposing to integrate speech and writing in business communications is a neglect of oral communication *per se,* and the second is a pedagogy that attempts to transform writing into speech. The third problem I wish to raise grows out of the way many of us have chosen to redesign our courses. With pressures to combine the teaching of oral and written communications, our response has been too piecemeal. Of the twenty business communications texts sitting on my office shelf, for instance, sixteen have at least one chapter on oral communication in addition to whatever material may be included on job interviews or communication theory.[1] It is clear that Lesikar (1980), in the preface to the fourth edition of his *Business Communication: Theory and Application,* expresses the thinking of many business textbook writers, "Because we in the field are embracing oral communications more and more, I expanded the coverage of this area" (p. v).

But I would argue that the "embrace" of oral communication is in fact closer to a handshake. Texts have taken the expeditious route of adding separate chapters on the subject. As a result, the two forms of discourse merely coexist; they have not been integrated. Predictably, course designs for teaching oral communication have adopted this same additive approach by simply creating discrete units of new material. The assignments—interview simulations, committee work, oral reports, sales presentations—may be connected by content to written assignments but the distinction between speaking and writing is largely implied, not explicitly taught.[2] It is the same segregation of subject matter one might expect from a course created by administrative fiat from separate speech and writing courses taught by faculty in different departments.

Surely then we would like some way to afford oral communication the prominence in our classrooms that it already has in the businesses and industries where our students are to be employed. And we would like to distinguish speech and writing as separate modalities without denying their common linguistic parentage. At this point we're probably conditioned to ask, "What do the researchers say?" But, in this case, if we must depend upon the aid of "scientific" truth or the comfort of statistics, we face paralysis. Empirical research has proved confusing, contradictory. Historically, however, rhetoricians have not hesitated to rely upon their linguistic sense to define an oral style. Thomas (1956) gives us this list of traits collected from rhetoricians spanning more than two hundred years:

> accurate expression, suggestive words, specific words, vivid speech, colorful words, direct quotations, loaded words, questions, comparisons and contrasts, homely words, illustrations, informal English, simple words, short words, concise statements, figures of speech, short sentences, figurative language, direct address, personalizations, informal syntax, simple syntax, summary, suspense and climax, euphony, transitions, repetition. (pp. 47-48)

Since Aristotle first wrote with confidence that "the style of written prose is not the same as that of controversial speaking" (Cooper, 1953, p. 211), the identity of oral style and the specific traits offered as proof of it have been pervasive *a priori* assumptions in our study of language. But the intuitive consensus about oral style has not yet been corroborated by researchers. And such proof does not seem readily forthcoming. The primary categories, speech and writing, are simply too large for investigation; those subcategories small enough for practical research are simply too limited for any extrapolated conclusions. So each study remains distinct, tentative, focused on a single writer or a group, on novices or professionals, on taped informal conversations or published formal speeches. Some conclusions contradict; some even question the basic hypothesis by finding that general linguistic differences among speaker-writers are more pronounced than any oral-written differences (these studies summarized in Einhorn, 1978).

## A Problem-Solving Approach to Speaking-Writing Integration

Nevertheless, whether we look for "truth" in empiricism, phenomenology, or intuition, there are still directions we can take in the classroom. First of all, I would suggest that we use students' oral confidence to teach prewriting. One of the solutions I've found comes out of the case approach, which has long been a mainstay for business communication courses and more recently has been recommended as a general method for teaching composition (Field & Weiss, 1978; Tedlock & Jarvie, 1981).

The writing in my own classes is centered on problems in real business situations. Much of the term is spent training students to recognize the primary nature of the problem, to anticipate their readers' responses, and to choose appropriate writing strategies. Here is a typical writing assignment (I'll be referring to it throughout the following discussion)—a problem which my wife encountered a few years ago when she worked as a bookstore manager and which I frequently use in my classes:

> The stores of a Midwest bookstore chain have been averaging three bad checks a week, and the general manager decides to require all managers to hold refresher meetings on check handling procedures in the hopes of reducing the problem. The student, assuming the general manager's role, must write a memo that informs the managers of his or her decision.[2]

### Discussion

The analysis of this problem would begin in the mode with which students are most confident—the oral mode—the informal atmosphere of class discussion, where statements are more tentative, communal, exploratory. The students, whether they realize it or not, are participating in a prewriting stage and developing a heuristic for future analyses.

Characteristically, the authoritarian students will propose threatening the managers with loss of job if all bad checks aren't eliminated in sixty days while the more humanitarian ones will labor over ways of offsetting the burdensome request for meetings, usually with tantalizing offers of Christmas bonuses or increased profit-sharing. In between are those who recognize the more routine, informative nature of the memo. All in all, this oral analysis will raise more questions than it answers. Thus the questions lead naturally to an intermediate stage, one designed to ease the transition from the associative thought process of class discussion or personal brainstorming to the carefully defined logic of the final communication. For my classes, that transition is the written problem analysis.

## Written Problem Analysis

Such an analysis basically asks students to do three things—to define their primary task, to propose strategies, and to justify their choices. But how do I maintain the hybrid nature of this assignment? By specific suggestions like these:

1. Think of the analysis as a way of sharing with me the thinking you do about the assignment after you leave class.
2. Think of the analysis as the transcript of your half of a conference, as a dialogue between the two of us. Ask me those specific questions you have trouble answering.
3. Imagine your eventual writing assignment as a telephone conversation between you and your reader and record how it might proceed.
4. Present choices you're considering but are uncertain about—anything from different plans of overall organization to alternative wordings for a particular idea.

This analysis serves as a link between speaking and writing in a number of useful ways. It bridges the oral student-teacher relationship (typified by the individual conference) and the written relationship (typified by the graded letter, memo, or report). It reinforces the the state-clarify-defend cycle of dialogue, a cycle that must become in a more rigorous way (without audience prompts) a key writer's habit. It requires, too, an increasing accountability for one's ideas, a state in between group anonymity and sole authorship. It recognizes the value of open-ended exploration of both form and content while giving such brainstorming the linear control and permanence of a written form. Finally, by eliminating I-have-only-one-shot-at-the-topic paralysis and by encouraging no-penalty experimentation ("Would it be too gimmicky to begin my memo with . . . ?"), the problem analysis also reduces the writer's block associated with beginning the "real" assignment.

What effect does this approach have on the writing? For one thing, it just gives students more writing practice. Though I make no length requirement, the analyses are often much longer than the formal assignments. And, I've found, the more thorough the analyses, the better the corresponding assignments. Because the questions in the analyses are student-initiated and goal-directed, the students' commitment to finding answers often leads beyond my direct comments to individual conferences or to more focused class discussions, thus continuing the interplay between oral and written thought. Moreover, the security of an audience with whom they have more direct access reduces the communicator-audience distance. I am especially pleased that the problem analysis makes me as instructor only a temporary audience, an intermediary between the student and a remote, unfamiliar reader instead of the false final audience for the assignment.

## Writing for a Reader

For teaching speaking and writing as distinct modalities, this question of audience is especially important. In the problem analysis students become attuned to their readers. While telling me bluntly what they want their imaginary reader to know, they recognize that the same tone will be unacceptable when they confront the reader directly in the eventual letter or memo. Students can readily provide examples from oral communication of the tones they want to achieve in writing. Then they face the realization that writing cannot be mere transcription. The entire area that Trager (1958, 1961) has denoted as "paralanguage," those extralinguistic speech noises that we refer to as "tone of voice," are difficult or impossible to approximate in writing, as those who've suffered from the oratorical approach to punctuation (place a comma wherever you pause) can attest. Even in speech, of course, we can unknowingly distress our audience—offend it, bore it, patronize it. But writing by its very nature excludes key elements of the larger interactive situation within which it tries to communicate. Hasan (1973) explains these lost elements this way:

> In spoken communication more information regarding the relevant immediate situation is available extralinguistically to the participants of the discourse. . . . In written communication, on the other hand, extralinguistically provided information is of a

> very limited kind and depends much upon the shared contexts
> between the participants. In order to be decoded appropri-
> ately, the relevant components of the meaning of the message
> must be encapsulated explicitly in language, since whatever is
> not encapsulated may not be available to the decoder. (p. 280)

To decide what meaning should be "encapsulated," the student
writer must gauge the information gap or, more simply, compare
what the reader knows to what the writer knows. One way is to
focus students' attention on the exact source of the reader's
knowledge. "What does the reader know?" is a preliminary but
inadequate question. To use my earlier example, the students
might merely ask: "Do the bookstore managers know check-
handling procedures?" A misleading answer may cause them to
omit this information entirely from their memos. But there are
other critical questions related to the *source* of information, questions that integrate oral and written skills. Students should be asking *where* the reader got his information, whether from the current
text, from previous spoken or written texts, or from extralinguistic
features.

One question then might be an intratextual one: "Does the
reader find out the information from my letter or memo?" This
line of thinking should lead to improvements in diction, in transitions, in completeness. In the bookstore example, a student might
ask these specific questions: "Is my meaning of procedural review
clear?" "Will the managers know I expect a meeting with all the
employees and not just a posting of procedures?" "Did I include
necessary details about the where, when, and how of the meetings?"

A second question might be a pretextual one: "Does my reader
know this information from previous communication?" If the answer is yes and the communication was written, then a brief summary and reference (date, page, invoice number or some other appropriate identification) may be enough. If the earlier communication was oral—a conference, a luncheon meeting, a telephone
conversation—then the accuracy and extent of that communication
may have been affected by situational interference and may need
to be repeated more thoroughly in the present communication. In
some cases, especially in international business correspondence,
these questions of situation can even become questions of culture
and necessitate explanations that would be needless for writer-
readers in a common cultural context.

Perhaps the most useful of these questions about the source of
information is the extralinguistic one: "Does the reader's knowl-

edge come from the words at all?" Though we use terms like "tone of voice" and "audience" in referring to writing, it's all too easy to equate writing with the words on the page. In practice, the visible presence of words asserts itself; the invisible extralinguistic meaning hides behind and between these words. But by using students' experience in oral communication we can teach them, like bird hunters, to flush out these situational meanings.

## Mastery of Extralinguistic or Situational Meaning

One way is to teach the basics of semantic and communication theory, to have students, for example, read a simple narrative like this one suggested by Haney (1979):

> A businessman had just turned off the lights in the store when a man appeared and demanded money. The owner opened a cash register. The contents of the cash register were scooped up, and the man sped away. A member of the police force was notified promptly. (p. 249)

Based on these few words my students confidently answer a series of true-false statements, claiming to "know" a number of "facts"—that there was a robbery, for instance, or that the cash register contained money, or that the owner and the businessman are the same person, or that the police officer is a man, or that the man (which one?) entered the store, left in a car, or fled the police. Forced to defend their "knowledge" solely by the words in the text, students soon recognize how much meaning results from inference. They have classified an event into a situational category (a robbery) that shares certain definable traits (business, night, money, cash register, rapid departure, police) and then have built inferential knowledge on this assumption. Some feel tricked. "If it isn't a robbery, then the writer is misleading us. He should tell us why the man demanded money." Exactly! The linguistic and extralinguistic meanings complement each other. Much of a writer's task is shifting meaning from the invisible to the visible, from the assumed to the stated, and vice versa.

If your point as a writer (there was a robbery) coincides with the common contextual inference from the facts (a man who demands money at night from a business is probably committing robbery), extralinguistic meaning is sufficient. At first, of course, students will ignore assumptions. One wrote this sentence in a memo to the bookstore managers: "Checks are a convenient means of exchange." Making this business truism linguistically explicit implies doubt that such knowledge exists in the managers' assump-

tions about their work. This contextual fact creates the written
equivalent of tone of voice—in this case a tone of preachiness,
condescension, even insult.

A second productive way to flush out situational meanings is to
treat writing as dialogue. By viewing individual sentences from
their rough drafts as the utterances of one of the speakers in a
conversation, students readily see that the sentence "checks are a
convenient means of exchange" is not a performative or provocative statement. It leads to no response except "so what?" Statements that generate only nods of agreement from the listener are
little more than monologues. With no uncertainty, no reason for
involvement, the reader of this written monologue slows, yawns,
stops.

But when students rethink their writing as dialogues, they learn
to detect a divergence in logic, a missing detail, a faulty transition,
a vague word. These converted dialogues, whether treated as a
private exercise or an inclass dramatization, can sharpen still further the distinctions between speech and writing. Consider this
sentence, for instance:

> I have decided that you managers conduct 'refresher meet-
> ings."

Dramatized, this sentence works only if speaker and audience assume some formal arrangement, one that identifies the roles so
strongly underscored in "you managers." Face to face with
another student, the speaker quickly feels uncomfortable with the
words, recognizing key linguistic and extralinguistic features—the
coldness of the plural when only one reader is involved at a time,
the excess of the title "managers" when that should be assumed
knowledge, the needless reference to the speaker when there is
only one authority in either the oral or written situation. Students
point out that this sentence "feels right" only if spoken in a tone of
controlled anger. They note other problems, too. "How do you
translate quotation marks into speech?" "Why are they there?"
The writer in focusing on the words alone has used his punctuation carelessly, ignoring the extralinguistic ambiguity. When de-
livering the words orally, however, he halts at the marks, like an
actor without the proper stage directions.

## Oral-Written Interaction

By making students more conscious of what they do when they
speak we can hope to transfer that consciousness to writing, with-

out in the process implying that the modes are interchangeable. Zoellner (1969) has proposed one intriguing method for bringing speaking and writing closer together. He suggests that we teach writing by turning our classrooms into art studios with large blackboards or pads of newsprint mounted on freestanding frames. By doing so, he argues, the distance between the thought and the record can be shortened and de-formalized. He suggests that students would benefit from a talk-write dialogue of "successive approximates" (p. 297), revisions of the students' intended meanings through a process of leaping rapidly from thinking aloud to writing down these oral thoughts to responding orally again to the just-written words. As a heuristic the talk-write approach can combine the best of spontaneity and permanence, of security and doubt.

Business communication gives us models for this oral-written interaction in its dictation and word processing techniques. Like the sketch pad or portable blackboard, the cassette recorder, dictating machine, and computer terminal give the student instantaneous feedback. With computers, especially, the rapid interchange of aural-visual symbols can narrow the gap between the spoken and written word. Computerized word processing systems can give students a valuable freedom to think and to control the form of their thoughts. With the split screen, student writers can easily choose from different draft versions or rearrange material, but they always know that the obliteration of an ill-formed phrase can be accomplished with the quiet finality of a single keystroke. Not since the typewriter have we had such a dramatic change in the tools for composing. And surely one of the intriguing questions about this new tool is its potential for rapid talk-write interaction in the classroom and its ultimate effect on our notions of speaking and writing as distinct activities.

Both simple and complex technologies, of course, bring us, like Zoellner, to the question we so often ask students about their writing, "What in the world were you trying to tell me here?" Surely most of us have observed responses like the one he describes:

> The student . . . launches into the cortical utterance or visceral blurt, in the course of which *he says the thing he was unable to write,* producing in the vocal modality a word-pattern which is protoscribal and to a greater or lesser degree rhetorically viable. (p. 296)

We have frightened students with writing's permanence and aloneness. We need to restore its tentativeness and communality. Among the types of composition being taught in our classes today, business writing has some special advantages for accomplishing this goal. By using "real world" situations it can offset the distance and artificiality of much classroom writing. By using a problem-solving approach, it can draw upon a technique natural to business yet broadly applicable in human communication. By using the dialogue as a metaphor and a practical method for composing, it can help students differentiate speaking and writing in a way critical for their careers. In using the technological bridges between oral thought and its eventual transcription, it can lessen some of the harmful barriers between the two modes. It would, after all, be a shame to departmentalize speech and writing when, taught together, they offer us so much.

## Notes

1. Eight of the texts include an entire section (2-5 chapters) on speaking and listening skills:

> Barr, D. W. *Communication for business, professional and technical students* (2nd ed.). Belmont, Calif.: Wadsworth, 1980.
>
> Himstreet, W. C., & Baty, W. M. *Business communications: Principles and methods* (5th ed.). Belmont, Calif.: Wadsworth, 1977.
>
> Lee, L. W., Benoit, S. S., Moore, W. C., & Powers, C. S. *Business communication*. Chicago: Rand McNally, 1980.
>
> Leonard, D. J. *Shurter's communication in business* (4th ed.). New York: McGraw-Hill, 1979.
>
> Level, D. A., & Galle, W. P. *Business communications: Theory and practice*. Dallas: Business Publications, 1980.
>
> Makay, J. J., & Fetzer, R. C. *Business communication skills: A career focus*. New York: D. Van Nostrand, 1980.
>
> Murphy, H. A., & Peck, C. E. *Effective business communications* (3rd ed.). New York: McGraw-Hill, 1980.
>
> Treece, M. *Communication for business and the professions*. Boston: Allyn and Bacon, 1978.

Of these only Barr attempts to integrate speaking, writing, and listening. Eight texts contain a single chapter on oral communications:

> Bowman, J. P., & Branchaw, B. *Successful communication in business*. New York: Harper & Row, 1978.
>
> Brown, H. M., & Reid, K. K. *Business writing and communication: Strategies and applications*. New York: D. Van Nostrand, 1979.
>
> Burtness, P. S., & Clark, A. T. *Effective English for business communication* (7th ed.). Cincinnati: South-western, 1980.
>
> Janis, H. J. *Writing and communication in business* (3rd ed.). New York: Macmillan, 1978.

Lesikar, R. J. *Business communication: Theory and application* (4th ed.). Homewood, Ill.: Richard D. Irwin, 1980.

Sigband, N. B. *Communication for management and business* (2nd ed.). Dallas: Scott, Foresman, 1976.

Wilkinson, C. W., Clarke, P. B., & Wilkinson, D. C. M. *Communicating through letters and reports* (7th ed.). Homewood, Ill.: Richard D. Irwin, 1980.

Wolf, M. P., Keyser, D. F., & Aurner, R. R. *Effective communication in business* (7th ed.). Cincinnati: South-western, 1979.

And the following contain little or no material on oral communication:

Andrews, C. A. *Technical and business writing.* Atlanta: Houghton Mifflin, 1975.

Hatch, R. *Communicating in business.* Chicago: Science Research Associates, 1977.

Shepherd, R. *This business of writing. . . .* Chicago: Science Research Associates, 1980.

Weeks, F. W., & Jameson, D. A. *Principles of business communication* (2nd ed.). Champaign, Ill.: Stipes, 1979.

2. A full version of this assignment has been included in F. W. Weeks and K. O. Locker, *Business writing cases and problems* (Champaign, Ill.: Stipes, 1980), pp. 60-61. For an analysis of the assignment see J. Fleming, "My favorite assignment: Practice in editing for clarity and conciseness," *ABCA Bulletin,* 1977, *41,* 38.

# 13 Speaking, Writing, and Teaching for Meaning

James L. Collins
State University of New York at Buffalo

In this final chapter I will explore some of the implications of the preceding chapters for teaching. Although many of the chapters offer pedagogical suggestions, my purpose is to show what these suggestions have in common and how they add up to sound practical advice for teachers. I will use examples of student writing and of teacher-student writing conferences to clarify and illustrate the suggestions I discuss. My focus will be on the teaching of writing to unskilled writers, particularly at high school and college levels.

My major argument can be simply stated: This book's meaning for teaching is that we need to place a greater priority on *teaching for meaning*. Foremost among the reasons for that necessity are two important relationships between speaking and writing.

## Semantic and Developmental Relationships

The first relationship is a semantic one and is seen in key differences between spoken and written language. In spoken dialogue meaning is the creation of more than one person; as speaker and listener roles shift, participants may alternately contribute to the construction of meaning. Meaning is established through cooperation and collaboration. And just as speakers share the construction of meaning, they can also share features of the linguistic environment that supports and contributes to meaning: gestures, facial expressions, pitch, intonation, and contexts of situation and culture. With writing, though, these shared aspects of meaning diminish or disappear. Writing is produced without an interlocutor and, unless the audience is intimately known, without shared referential contexts. As a result, writing must represent meaning more fully than does speaking. What is meaningful when conversing, including what is tacitly shared, must be adequately stated when writing. Speaking and writing, in short, represent meaning in different ways.

The second relationship is a developmental connection between speaking and writing. There is an identifiable stage in the development of writing abilities where writing becomes increasingly differentiated from speaking. During this stage writers learn to make meaning more fully elaborated—more explicit and autonomous—in writing than in speaking. As writers learn to represent meaning sufficiently within written texts, their writing moves away from context-dependence toward context-independence.

Taken together, the semantic and developmental relationships between speaking and writing suggest that meaning ought to be the basis of teaching language and writing, especially to unskilled writers. The relationships indicate that meaning is what connects speaking and writing and the development of language skill. Lack of meaning is the basis of a definition of weak student writing and of an understanding of development, both of which are implicit in the relationships I have outlined.

Weak writing can be defined as writing produced through the mediation of spoken language. Inexperienced or unskilled or basic writers write as if readers will cooperate and collaborate to produce meaning as participants in spoken dialogue often do. For speakers, the assumption that language is supplemented by unspoken contexts which support and complete the structuring of meaning works quite well. And because it works for speakers, the same assumption influences the semantics of unskilled writing. What is adequately elaborated meaning in speaking becomes abbreviated meaning in writing, meaning that points toward, but does not explicitly represent, contextual referents. This tenth grader's sentence can be taken as an example: "One night me and my two friends went to the store." By itself, the sentence does not tell us which night, which friends, or which store. The referents for those words are not supplied by the writer. Those items refer to information outside of the text, to information that remains part of the situation surrounding the event alluded to in the sentence. It is the implication that further information should have been specified that ties a text to a situational context and makes it context-dependent. The sentence, furthermore, is tied to a cultural context. Given a certain socio-cultural context, such as a neighborhood or peer group, the expression "me and my two friends" might take on a fuller meaning in that the identities of writer and friends would be clear from the context. The expression, thus, depends on familiarity with a particular socio-cultural context for its full semantic value, just as the sentence depends on familiarity with a particular situational context.

The understanding of the development of writing abilities which this book emphasizes can also be discussed in terms of meaning and familiarity. Development is not construed as a series of abrupt changes, as a sequence of stages in which what comes later shows a clean break with what is prior. Rather, development is described as a process of actively incorporating or integrating old skills within new ones. Existing skills become transformed as new skills are acquired. Thus, the primacy of spoken or written language is not the issue; the real issue is the primacy of the familiar. The writer of the sentence, "One night me and my two friends went to the store," in this interpretation is writing in familiar language to a familiar audience. She is writing as she is accustomed to speaking. It is tempting to change "me and my two friends" to "my two friends and I," hoping that by doing so, the writer will learn something about the correct forms of standard written English. By itself, though, that strategy is inappropriate for several reasons. The strategy asks for an abrupt change from familiar spoken language to conventional written language, not a gradual transition. The change, furthermore, ignores the semantic level of language; "my two friends and I" communicates no more information than does "me and my two friends." The change, finally, is not actively controlled by the writer; it is a change that she is asked to accept passively. A better strategy is to ask first the writer what she means, to ask her to identify the two persons (and the time and place in the rest of the sentence) that she has in mind. This latter strategy places a priority on meaning. It is consistent with semantic and developmental relationships between speaking and writing.

## Addressing the Problems of Unskilled Writers

Placing a priority on meaning amounts to making the construction of meaning a major and initial concern in the composition classroom. Meaning usurps the place traditionally given to error elimination. Finding and correcting errors becomes a minor and final concern, something that happens at the editing stage of the writing process, not before. Because speaking and writing are so dissimilar in the demands each makes on language and logic, unskilled writers must produce writing through the mediation of spoken language, and two sets of problems result. The most obvious set of problems, the surface one, shows up as violations of the norms of standard written English. Unskilled writers resort to the sound and syntax of everyday speech to produce writing, and that leads to orthographic and syntactic errors. We should, of course, teach writers to eliminate these errors. Deviations from standard English stand out in writing like static on a poorly functioning television set; the reader, like the viewer, is distracted, and the message is blurred. Still, teaching error elimination is not synonymous with teaching writing. The second set of problems that result from the tendency to resort to familiar spoken language while writing concerns what I have called abbreviated meaning. Such problems are deeper than surface errors. Unskilled writers rely not only on the sound and syntax of everyday speech, but on its sense as well. The result is meaning that is context-bound and cryptic, and therefore we are faced with writing that fails to communicate to an audience, whether such writing is error-free or not.

## The Priority of Meaning over Error-Avoidance

That point can be illustrated with an example of college basic writing. In a recent class of open admissions, first year university students, I had many writers who had apparently learned their lessons in error avoidance well. Their writing was typically brief, less than one handwritten page, and virtually error-free. The writing, though, was vacuous and impersonal, polite and innocuous. Here is an example:

> I would like to describe a very pleasant place. This place has miles and miles of green grass. It has tall green trees, the leaves are very huge. The flowers are bright and beautiful. Their animals are wild and playful. This place has beautiful pastures, also filled with tall green grass with big brown barns surrounding it. This place has a tall green house with glass windows, it also contains a narrow road that leads to a little pond with huge rocks. This pleasant place is the country.

The paragraph shows a lack of sufficiency of content, probably attributable in part to the apparent tendency by the writer to use only "safe" words and sentences, those that she is confident will not produce error. The writer wants to avoid error and its risks, and thus the trees are only tall and green, the flowers bright and beautiful, the animals wild and playful, the barns big and brown, the house tall and green. Certainly more could be said about each of those items. The suggestion of ownership, in "their animals," and the suggestion of habitation, in "house" and "barns," could also be further developed; these suggested meanings possibly contradict the conclusion that the "pleasant place is the country."

Clearly, the writer of that paragraph has not learned to represent meaning sufficiently within written texts. She is not writing with the reader's expectation for full and explicit meaning in mind. Rather, she appears to believe that readers want error-free writing at all costs, even at the cost of meaning. This is the real basis of my argument that meaning should take precedence over error elimination. Both are important, but making meaning ought to come before making meaning conform to standard English. Reversing that order places error avoidance in the way of structuring meaning in written language.

As teachers of writing, our approach to error should not get in the way of our approach to meaning. By worrying about mistakes in writing before we have helped students with the more important problem of adequately representing meaning in writing, we may be teaching students to do the same. Students might develop a warped sense of audience, a sense that readers expect error-free writing more than writing which has been made meaningful, and a distorted sense of writing, a sense that teacher-inspired language and meaning can be substituted for the writer's own. Such teaching, in short, is not consistent with semantic and developmental relationships between speaking and writing. It does not teach students to transform spoken language gradually into writing by making meaning more explicit. Instead, we can say that context-dependent meaning is changed rather abruptly into teacher-dependent meaning.

## A Teacher-Dominated Conference

To illustrate that idea, I will present a transcript which contains an excerpt from a taped conference between a teacher and a tenth-grade writer. The writing conference was recorded during regular class time, and like the writing discussed in the transcript, the tape was produced under normal classroom conditions. I will use brackets in the transcript to coordinate the tape with the student's writing and with the teacher's written changes of that writing. The subject of the transcript is this first draft of a paragraph written by the student as part of an essay entitled "Selecting a Drum Set":

You should try to get something in "your class". Time after time people make that mistake. They will either get a set that is too small and unexpandable. By this I mean that it is hard to add on to your set, or they will get one that is so big that they don't know what to do with them.

That paragraph changes as the teacher and student discuss it during the conference. The teacher opens with a statement of written language convention:

Teacher: When you use an "either," you have to come up with an "or," and if you don't come up with an "or," your sentence is incomplete.

Student: Or. [Apparently pointing to that word in the text.]

T: But it's way down here, and this is a capital [*By*]. This threw me off. Did you mean another sentence here?

S: No; I think I meant a comma, see, see cause I . . .

T: But this is really a separate sentence.

S: Right, but when I said "unexpandable," I wanted to uh, tell'm what I meant by "unexpandable," you know. 'Cause I didn't want to just leave it like that, 'cause then they'll be thinking: What does he mean by "unexpandable"?

T: Ok, you're right. So let's see if there's a better way that we can do it, because you've actually injected a separate sentence in here, and you should make it a clause.

S: So, so why don't I just, um, take out "unexpandable" and put in the meaning instead, saying, "it's too small, and it's too hard to add on to . . .".

T: Right. All you . . .

S: And so forth.

T: Right. All you need to do is cross out this. [Crosses out *By this I mean that it is.*] "They will either get a set that is too small and unexpandable" comma "hard to add on to." And that explains that. [Apparently pointing to revision of student's sentence.]

S: Well I . . .

T: This is a . . . set off by commas, "unexpandable, hard to add on to." It's an explanation of unexpandable, "or." [Brief pause.] Now, you can't do this. Them is a plural. You've started by talking about "a set." Set is singular, so you have to come up with a singular pronoun, because it refers back to "set." Unless you want to change "set" to a plural: "They will either get sets that are too small and unexpandable, or . . .".

S: I think I'd rather keep that "a set." What word for "them"?

T: "It." "They will get one that is so big that they don't know what to do with *it.*"

The student's paragraph changes during that conference. The changes, adding an appositional phrase in place of a prepositional phrase and making a plural pronoun singular, are directed by the teacher. In the case of the plural, the teacher lets the student decide. In the case of the apposition, the student would if permitted change his paragraph differently (see his comment about halfway through the transcript, where he, ironically, mentioned "put in the meaning"). The second draft of the paragraph incorporates the teacher's changes:

> You should try to get something in "your class." Time after time people make that mistake. They will either get a set that is too small and unexpandable, hard to add on to, or they will get one that is so big that they don't know what to do with it.

If the first and second drafts of the paragraph are compared, it is clear that the second draft communicates more clearly and violates fewer writing conventions. The writer, though, has not made those improvements. The teacher has.

The interaction between student and teacher in that conference is marked by imbalance. The teacher does most of the talking. The teacher determines that the focus of the talk will be a few of the rules governing standard written English. The student is limited to brief comments which he is several times not allowed to complete. The student would, it seems, prefer that the focus of talk be the same as the focus of his writing. Another of the student's comments, again ironically, indicates that he is concerned about the impact of his writing on his audience: "They'll be thinking: What does he mean . . .". It is the teacher, however, who makes the writing conform to a surface level of audience expectations.

It can be argued that the temptation to change and correct student writing is a natural one for teachers, especially when working with students for whom literacy presents real difficulties. The concern for process rather than written product and the growing popularity of immediate oral feedback about writing from peers and teachers reflect the desire to provide as much useful assistance to writers as we can. Still, there is a difference, subtle but crucial, between helping writers and dominating their writing processes. Deciding what to mean and how to write it are, finally, the tasks of the writer. We need to give our students opportunities to practice completing these tasks, and that means that we ought to temporarily resist the temptation to make surface corrections. Granted, there are times when writers get stuck and need someone else's skills to help solve particular problems.

We can draw an analogy with the woodworking student who asks his or her teacher how to glue and clamp two pieces of wood. The student is stuck; the task exceeds the student's skill; so it is fitting and even necessary for the teacher to take over the gluing and clamping, to show the student how pieces of wood can be joined together. Joining sentences is very similar to joining pieces of wood, and so far the analogy holds up. The differences between woodworking and writing, of course, are where the analogy breaks down. In writing, the parts of discourse must be made, words and sentences must be constructed, and not just shaped and joined together as when rough-sawn boards are turned into the parts of a finished piece of furniture. Words and sentences, paragraphs and whole pieces of discourse, are representations of meaning, and meaning must be made, not just packaged for delivery to readers. In the above transcript, the teacher's attempt to join the student's sentences using a standard conjunction shows that the teacher has taken over and changed the meaning the writer is trying to construct.

## Encouraging the Discovery and Elaboration of Meaning

Avoiding an initial emphasis on eliminating errors is not enough by itself to help writers learn to state meaning explicitly in writing. The preceding chapters suggest that we do other things as well. We can teach students to be aware of differences between speaking and writing. We can integrate talk and writing in the composition classroom. We can make discussion a part of prewriting and revising, and we can use oral presentations to teach audience awareness by having students face, and practice satisfying, an audience. What these strategies have in common is a method I will call discovering and elaborating the meaning which is latent in language. We can help students clarify and elaborate what they say, and what they write, by asking for more information, information that connects with and expands what has already been said or written. When student writing only suggests or "points toward" meaning that we, as concerned and helpful readers, consider necessary to understand the text adequately, we should ask writers to complete the representation of meaning.

The method of teaching writing by getting writers to discover and elaborate meaning which is latent in their writing assumes particular attitudes toward writers by their teachers. Writers are thought to be capable of learning to explicitly state meaning. Unskilled writers are simply not accustomed to doing that; they are more familiar with the relatively implicit manner of representing meaning typical of spoken dialogue. Unskilled writers can be taught to realize meaning, to push written language far enough to discover and communicate the full import of their thought and words. Unskilled writers, as I have said, are unfamiliar with the demands writing makes on language and logic. But that skill develops as we make them familiar with those demands.

I favor intuition as the means by which writers learn to discover and develop meaning which is latent in their writing. Spoken language is largely learned intuitively as children go about the business of making sense of their environments. Written language, too, can be learned intuitively as writers and readers go about the business of making sense of print. In a "normal" course of development, familiarity with the semantics of written language is gained unconsciously as a product of reading, writing, and increasingly formal speaking practice. For unskilled or basic writers, development has been minimized through severely limited practice. We need to maximize practice so that the intuitive channel to development will be activated. I see nothing wrong with direct teaching of differences between speaking and writing; I am only presenting the caution that telling students that writing requires explicit and autonomous meaning does not take the place of having them produce such meaning in writing. Like a good coach, we have to get the players out of the locker room and onto the practice field.

## Sufficiency of Content and Patterns of Logic

Placing a priority on teaching for meaning in the composition classroom involves having students revise toward explicit writing. When the meaning of a student's writing is abbreviated, the student should be asked to recognize and develop what is meant by the writing. Two aspects of meaning are particularly important to that method: sufficiency of content and discernible patterns of logic. I will illustrate each of these aspects in turn.

Writing produced through the mediation of spoken language often shows a lack of sufficiency of content. The following essay, in which an eleventh-grade writer describes a favorite place, can be taken as an example:

> Half way down the river there is a place ware there is a water fall. The water flows over and around some flat rocks and falls down. At the bottom of waterfall to the corner of the other side is a hollow log wich looks like its ben thair for years. Its falling apart.

> There are big flat rocks and other rocks all down the side of the river and some in the water sticking out. There are trout in the river.
>
> On the other side of the river there are blue Berry bushes. There are trees and other bushes too.
>
> On this side of the river is a big flat rock wich is around ten feet long and maby six feet wide. Thare is a big oak tree next to the rock and other oak trees along the side of the river. On one of those trees in the woods is a sine that ses no deer hunting. Thair are akorns and lievs all over the ground.

Clearly, that example shows a reliance on the sounds of spoken English. The three different spellings of *there,* the spelling of *sign* and of *maybe,* for example, suggest that the writer is spelling phonologically, either by the way words sound, or by analogy with similar sounding words. Her spelling is idiosyncratic, not rule-governed, especially in the case of *there.*

To assume, however, that the level of abstraction consisting of transforming the sounds of spoken language into written signs accounts for all, or even most, of the problems in this example of student writing is to make a serious error. The writer is not only abstracting from the sounds and syntax of speech, but from sight and experience as those are represented in speech as well. In the description of the waterfall the writer appears to assume that the reader will locate the river and find the place "half way down" without having a map or cognitive representation of territory. Similarly, the writer apparently assumes that her identification of the river's sides will make sense to the reader who does not share her vantage point. Words point to referents, as if the writer is describing a photograph that the reader cannot see. The frequency of *there,* used nine times in the essay, suggests that the writer is using that word to indicate or point out attributes of the place she is describing. The text depends on the context—the waterfall as it has been seen by the writer—for meaning. The writer apparently assumes that the reader has also viewed the scene. Meaning is insufficiently represented in the text; the reader, quite literally, had to be there to understand the content of the essay.

The writer needs, therefore, to hear from the reader. We can call the writer's attention to the words that make her text context-bound (halfway down, side, there) and ask her to explain the referents for those words. Or we can ask the writer to draw a picture of the waterfall and then represent the picture in the writing to help the reader locate features of the place she has in mind. Or we can ask the writer to change her point of view from her own to the reader's: "If you visited the place I am describing ..." might make a good beginning, one which encourages the writer to keep in mind an audience which has not seen the place. In each of these strategies is the message that, for an unfamiliar audience, the content of the essay is insufficient to serve the purpose of description. In each, furthermore, is the message that latent meaning can be developed in the direction of explicit meaning.

The second aspect of meaning, the necessity of discernible patterns of logic, can be illustrated by this example in which a tenth-grade writer describes his sister:

> She is a girl she stands about 5'4". She has black hair. It is naturally curly its cut short because its easier to take care of. She has brown eyes. She doesn't wear any make up. She's averagely pretty also has pierced ears She is 18 years old. She wears jeans and pullover tops to school. smokes cigarettes. wears furry socks and earth shoes shes very picky about things everyone else does she is very sensitive but trys to hide it by acting tough But she can't hide it. The only thing she has for breakfast is a glass of milk. When she is done with her gum she just rolls it up in a ball and puts it on the coffee table. Most of the time she gets late she is in twelfth grade and is too lazy to get a job and she admits it. her report card is no big deal at all. Her hobbies she collects giraffes and assorted stuffed animals.

In this example, as in the last one, words seem to point to a real context, to what has been observed by the writer. The writer is describing visible, observed attributes and habits of his sister. The attributes and habits do not adequately portray the sister, though, because they are not presented coherently in the writing. A pattern of connectedness is missing. The reader, for example, cannot tell if the writer wanted the various references to his sister's not exerting herself—suggested in hair length as "easier to take care of," in casual dress, in the disposal of gum, in eating habits, in getting up late, getting a job or getting grades—to be related or not. Those attributes are related only by collection or juxtaposition. The writer is concentrating on a subject, a person, and listing predicates. As a result, attributes that could be connected to the subject are in fact only juxtaposed, not related, in the writing. Perhaps the most significant evidence of juxtaposition is that the writer randomly mixes behavioral and physical description.

This time the content of the writing is sufficient. The writing is quite specific. What is missing is a pattern of logic or coherence; specific percepts are not connected to a controlling concept. We can ask the writer what "topic sentence" he would use to summarize what he has written. Or we can ask the writer to supply connections that are missing: How can your sister be "lazy" and "very picky about things" at the same time? Or we can ask that the writer separate the physical and behavioral descriptions by organizing them into separate paragraphs, then revising for an introduction, transition and conclusion for those paragraphs. What these strategies share is the message that the writer's logic must be apparent to the reader. In each, furthermore, is the message that latent patterns of logic can be made explicit.

## A Student-Supportive Conference

Implicit in my discussion of two important aspects of meaning, the substantive and the logical, is a recommended pedagogical stance for teachers of unskilled writers. I will clarify that stance by using another transcript of an actual student-teacher conference to illustrate its significance. This time the writer is a high school senior, and the writing discussed during the taped conference is this first draft:

| | |
|---|---:|
| My parents are usually nice with me. To me they tell | 1 |
| me what to do too much. | 2 |
| Their not my parents their my aunt and uncle. | 3 |
| They have taken care of me since I was eight years old. | 4 |
| Now I'm 18 and they still tell what to do. | 5 |
| Anyway I know one thing and is they love me alot. | 6 |
| Sometimes they hurt my feelings and so ma different ways. | 7 |
| That I just feel like going back to my own mother. | 8 |
| But I have to stay over her because the only way I | 9 |
| could make a future for myself is staying over here. If I | 10 |
| were to go to P. Rico I couldn't get a job because I don't | 11 |
| know any Spanish. | 12 |
| Anyway if though they are not my mother and father | 13 |
| I like a lot because they have taught me whats right and | 14 |
| wrong. | 15 |

The student writer initiated the following conference by asking the teacher what was wrong with her essay:

Teacher: You want to know what's wrong with it?

Student: Right. I know it's between this paragraph [the first] and this [third paragraph]. Right? From the beginning.

T: What do you mean?

S: Ok. You see: "My parents are usually nice," then you go to here, uh, "They have been taking care of," right? So I should have added that on to.

T: You should have what?

S: I should have added, like, "They have been taking care of me," I should have put it right on top. Together with the first paragraph.

T: How would it read?

S: Uh, "My parents are usually," let me see, "nice to me. My parents," I should just switch, "they're my aunt and uncle, they have been taking care of me since I was eight years old, and now I am eighteen." That would sound better, right?

T: Yep.

S: Then, uh, and I would add a little bit more about how they hurt my feelings.

T: Where would, where does that come now?

S: Right there. [line 7].

T: Where you say, "Sometimes they hurt my feelings . . .".

S: "In so many different ways."

T: "In so many different ways." This is "many?"

S: Right. This was written fast.

The student changes what she has written during that conversation. She moves part of what was written in the third paragraph to the first, probably because *taken care of me,* line 4, helps to explain *nice,* line 1. Also, she changes *and,* line 7, to *in; ma,* line 7, to *many; with,* line 1, to *to;* and *have taken,* line 4, to *have been taking.* (This may be typical of what happens when we place an instructional priority on meaning. In research conducted for one of my graduate courses, a teacher recently discovered that his students, fifth and sixth graders, made 25 percent fewer errors in their second drafts, as compared to their first drafts, when they were asked to revise for further meaning without any mention of error. I suspect that requiring elaborated meaning causes students to read their writing closely, and close reading leads to the elimination of some errors. And when writers find some of their mistakes, our job at the error-correcting stage of the writing process becomes easier.)

The teacher in the transcript does not call the writer's attention to surface errors. Instead, the student is given a chance to talk about her sense that something is wrong, to talk about what is on her mind, not the teacher's. As the writer talks, we can almost see meaning being constructed, as when she notices that calling her surrogate parents both "parents" and "aunt and uncle" (lines 1 and 3) is a source of confusion. As the writer talks, she also notices the need for further elaboration. She mentions that "hurt my feelings" (line 7) can be expanded, and that phrase is discussed later in the transcript:

Teacher: What would be an example of the way they hurt your feelings?

> Student: Uh-h-h. The times when they call me stupid. That's
> sometimes. They tell me I don't know how to do things.
> That's, that's one thing that really hurts you a lot. Being called
> stupid.
> T: Why do they call you stupid?
> S: Um. Something happened last time, I remember, and they
> just call me that. That was 'cuz what happened to my niece.
> And it wasn't my fault.
> T: And they called you stupid . . .
> S: Right.
> T: . . . because of what happened to your niece?
> S: Right.
> T: But you don't want to write that as an example?
> S: No. Some, uh, they hurt my feelings, sometimes like when
> this weekend came, it's what happened to their daughter.
> They're trying to take it out on me.
> T: Your aunt and uncle had a daughter of their own?
> S: Right.
> T: And what happened to her?
> S: Well, she got pregnant, and she left home and lived with
> her boyfriend.
> T: And that shows up in the way they treat you?
> S: Right. 'Cuz they really loved her a lot, and they wanted,
> like. I could put. That's true, I could. They really loved her a
> lot, and they, um, wanted to give her everything. But, they
> couldn't.

When the writer says, "I could put," in her final comment, she
is referring to her writing. The teacher has questioned the writer
and suggested an example to illustrate "hurt feelings." The writer
discovers that example as she talks with the teacher. The pedagogical stance her is one of helpful and concerned reader. The reader,
furthermore, is a general one, representative of an audience that
needs more information, and a genuinely interested one, representative of an audience that cares about meaning. In contrast to
the transcript I provided earlier, this teacher is less the critic or
judge and more the editor of student writing. The teacher prods
and probes, not as an examiner, but as a person who quite simply
encourages the writer to say more, to pack more meaning into the
text of writing.

### Dealing with Errors

Now for errors. Just as talk can be a profitable route to the
achievement of explicit meaning, talk can be a means to the elimi-

nation of error. At the editing for correctness stage of the writing process, we can confer with students to make them responsible for proofreading their own work. We can do that by calling the writer's attention to patterns of error and by discussing each pattern with the writer. I have learned to avoid working from the first line of writing to the last in a single editorial conference, pointing out all the errors along the way. It is better, I have found, to discuss one problem at a time, beginning with the most frequently committed error. Two problems, for example, stand out in the following tenth grader's paragraph (which uses a blank space in place of a person's name originally contained in the writing):

> One day I was walking home from school when _____ come and push me around so I push her around. So she smack me in my face. So I smack her back. So she swear. So I scrached her in her face. So I gave her a bloody nose. And I rip her shirt. So _____ broke my glasses. their was grass where we were fighting. We were puling on each other hairs. this happened at the mercy hospital park. _____ got mad at me. So then my boyfriend came in and broke it up. he grab _____. And she told him to leave her alone. So I went away with my boy friend.

Because the writer of that paragraph is writing as she would speak, many variations from standard written English show up. Foremost among those problems, in terms of frequency, are the over-reliance on the conjunction *so*, used nine times, and the deletion of *ed* to indicate the past tense of regular verbs, committed six times. *So* is a semantic problem here, and the writer needs to talk about when she means sequence, cause, and consequence by that word and not only about how to substitute other conjunctions and combine sentences. The *ed* problem, on the other hand, is a syntactic error, and the writer needs to edit that problem out of the writing. The teacher can help by first calling the writer's attention to places wnere she has used the *ed* form correctly ("scrached" and "happened," for example) and then asking the writer to find other words where *ed* is needed. The writer, I suspect, does not need a lesson in verbs or in the past tense. She needs to find her errors and correct them, one pattern of error at a time.

A note of caution. I am advocating teaching for meaning before teaching for error elimination because traditionally teachers of writing often reverse that order and because the pedagogical implications of the preceding chapters add up to a renewed concern for the priority of meaning. I am not arguing, however, that meaning and error are never related. In fact, the writer's attempt to realize meaning often overlaps with surface features of the writer's language. In the elimination of error, we should not forget our concern for meaning. In the tenth grader's sentence, "Acorn be falling from the trees," for example, the writer might mean that acorns seem to be always falling from the trees; changing the uninflected *be* to *are* would not capture that meaning precisely. It is better, again, to ask the writer what is meant at the error-correcting stage than to simply change the writer's words.

## Conclusion

Asking what is meant is probably the most fundamental and important question we can present to our students. The question, as I have shown, permits the integration of spoken and written language in the classroom. The question differentiates between informal dialogue and sustained monologue, between casual conversation with intimate friends and purposeful speech for an academic audience, between spoken and written language. The question teaches students to become aware of these differences, and it encourages them to practice and master language skills inherent in the differences.

Asking what is meant, furthermore, is a question that not only teachers can ask. We can train students to ask each other for adequately full and explicit meaning. And we should. The individual student-teacher conference, which I have used to illustrate language interaction in the teaching of basic writing, is not always possible. Given the large class sizes in most secondary English classrooms, given the pressure of getting writers to "catch up" in a semester of college work, given the abundance of writing that persistent practice produces in both high school and college, we all recognize the necessity of having students share the burden of reading and responding to writing. That necessity is not undesirable: in training students to ask for explicit meaning during peer conferences, we are asking students to place a priority on meaning, we are teaching audience expectations, and we are teaching students to be aware of meaning when they write. In class discussions that precede and follow the act of writing, or the reading of literature, a focus on what is meant is again a good idea, especially if discussions allow students to construct meaning for themselves and to share meaning with others. (Rather than identifying a "correct" meaning for students in response to literature, it has often been said, we can teach students to responsibly interpret for themselves.)

Finally, asking what is meant gets us out from under the criticism that we dominate classroom language. Studies of language interaction in classrooms show that teachers say too much, that students are often treated as passive recipients of knowledge. Such studies suggest that we are working too hard. It is the student's task to make the subject meaningful. Instead of asking students to receive prescribed meaning conveyed by teacher and textbook language, we should train students, as frequently as possible, to use language to construct meaning for themselves and others. Language learning is an active process, one in which skill is acquired through practice. A good deal of the task of the language teacher consists of getting students to use language to produce meaning, since meaning is what connects speaking and writing and the development of language skill.

# References

Abrahams, R. D. *Positively black*. Englewood Cliffs, N.J.: Prentice-Hall, 1970.

Anderson, P. The relationship between observed and elicited written and oral language of adult learners of English as a second language. Unpublished doctoral dissertation, Indiana University, 1980.

Arapoff, N. *Writing through understanding*. New York: Holt, Rinehart & Winston, 1970.

Armstrong, R. G. A West African inquest. *American Anthropologist*, 1954, *56*, 1051-1075.

Baddeley, A. D. B. Short term memory for word sequences as a function of acoustic, semantic and formal similarity. *Quarterly Journal of Experimental Psychology*, 1966, *18*, 362-365.

Baddeley, A. D. B. Working memory and reading. In P. A. Kolers, M. Wrolstad, & H. Bouma (Eds.), *The processing of visible language*. New York: Plenum, 1979.

Baddeley, A. D. B., Thomson, N., & Buchanan, M. Word length and the structure of short term memory. *Journal of Verbal Learning and Verbal Behavior*, 1975, *14*, 575-589.

Baker, S. *The practical stylist* (4th ed.). New York: Thomas Y. Crowell, 1977.

Barthes, R. *S/Z* (R. Miller, Trans.). New York: Hill and Wang, 1974. (Originally published, 1970.)

Bartholomae, D. The study of error. *College Composition and Communication*, 1980, *31*, 253-269.

Bates, E. *Language and context: The acquisition of pragmatics*. New York: Academic Press, 1976.

Bauman, R. Speaking in the light: The role of the Quaker minister. In R. Bauman & J. Sherzer (Eds.), *Explorations in the ethnography of speaking*. London: Cambridge University Press, 1974.

Becker, A. L. A tagmemic approach to paragraph analysis. *College Composition and Communication*, 1965, *16*, 237-242.

Bellugi, U., Klima, E. S., & Siple, P. Remembering in signs. *Cognition*, 1974, *3*, 92-125.

Bennett, J. C. The communications needs of business executives. *The Journal of Business Communication*, 1971, *8*, 5-11.

Bereiter, C., Hidi, S., & Dimitroff, G. Qualitative changes in verbal reasoning during middle and late childhood. *Child Development*, 1979, *50*, 142-151.

Bereiter, C., & Scardamalia, M. From conversation to composition: The role of instruction in a developmental process. To appear in R. Glaser (Ed.), *Advances in instructional psychology* (Vol. 2). Hillsdale, N.J.: Lawrence Erlbaum, in press.

Bergson, H. L. *Matter and memory.* New York: Macmillan, 1911.

Bernstein, B. Social class and linguistic development: A theory of social learning. In A. H. Halsey, J. Flood, & C. A. Anderson (Eds.), *Education, economy & society.* New York: Free Press, 1961.

Bernstein, B. *Class, codes and control* (Vol. 1). London: Routledge and Kegan Paul, 1971.

Bever, T. G. Cerebral asymmetries in humans are due to two incompatible processes: Holistic and analytic. *Annals of the New York Academy of Science,* 1975, *263,* 251-262.

Black, H. *The American schoolbook.* New York: William Morrow, 1967.

Blank, M. Use of the deaf language in language studies: A reply to Furth. *Psychological Bulletin,* 1965, *63,* 442-444.

Blankenship, J. A linguistic analysis of oral and written style. *Quarterly Journal of Speech,* 1962, *48,* 419-422.

Bloch, M. Astrology and writing in Madagascar. In J. Goody (Ed.), *Literacy in traditional societies.* Cambridge: Cambridge University Press, 1968.

Bloch, M. (Ed.). *Political language and oratory in traditional society.* London: Academic Press, 1975.

Bloomfield, L. Review of *The Philosophy of Grammar* by Otto Jespersen. *Journal of English and Germanic Philology,* 1927, *26,* 444-446.

Bloomfield, L. *Language.* New York: Holt, Rinehart & Winston, 1933.

Bogen, J. E. The other side of the brain, II: An appositional mind. *Bulletin of Los Angeles Neurological Societies,* 1969, *34,* 135-162.

Bogen, J. E. Some educational implications of hemispheric specialization. In M. C. Whittrock (Ed.), *The human brain.* Englewood Cliffs, N.J.: Prentice-Hall, 1977.

Bolinger, D. *Aspects of language* (2nd ed.). New York: Harcourt Brace Jovanovich, 1975.

Bornstein, H. Systems of sign. In L. J. Bradford & W. G. Hardy (Eds.), *Hearing and hearing impairment.* New York: Grune and Stratton, 1979.

Bower, G. H. Analysis of a mneumonic device. *American Scientist,* 1970, *58,* 496-510.

Brennan, M. Can deaf children acquire language? *American Annals of the Deaf,* 1975, *120,* 463-479.

Brewer, L., Caccamise, F., & Siple, P. Semantic integration in the adult deaf. *Directions,* 1979, *1,* 15-25.

Britton, J. Talking and writing. In E. Evertts (Ed.), *Explorations in children's writing.* Champaign, Ill.: NCTE, 1970.

Britton, J., Burgess, T., Martin, N., McLeod, A., & Rosen, H. *The development of writing abilities (11-18).* London: Macmillan Education, 1975.

Brown, R. *A first language: The early stages*. Cambridge: Harvard University Press, 1973.

Brown, T. A. Foreword to J. Piaget, *Adaptation and intelligence: Organic selection and phenocopy*. Chicago: University of Chicago Press, 1980.

Bruner, J. S. *Toward a theory of instruction*. Cambridge, Mass.: Harvard University Press, 1966.

Bruner, J., Olver, R., Greenfield, P., Hornsby, J., Kenney, H., Maccoby, M., Modiano, N., Mosher, F., Olson, D., Potter, M., Reisch, L., & Sonstroem, A. *Studies in cognitive growth*. New York: John Wiley, 1966.

Bullock Report. *A language for life*. London: Her Majesty's Stationery Office, 1975.

Burling, R. An anthropologist among the English teachers. *College Composition and Communication*, 1974, 25, 234-242.

Burns, P. C., & Broman, B. L. *The language arts in childhood education* (4th ed.). Chicago: Rand McNally, 1979.

Burrows, A. T., Monson, D. L., & Stauffer, R. G. *New horizons in the language arts*. New York: Harper & Row, 1972.

Burton, D. L., Donelson, K. L., Fillion, B., & Haley, B. *Teaching English today*. Boston: Houghton Mifflin, 1975.

Buytendijk, F. J. J. The meaning of pain. *Philosophy Today*, 1959, 3-4, 180-185.

Cambourne, B. L. The processing of text-book prose. *Proceedings of 4th Australian Reading Conference*. Sydney: Ashton-Scholastic, 1977. (a)

Cambourne, B. L. *The comprehensibility of textbooks in first year college courses*. Riverina College, Wagga Wagga, Australia, 1977. (b)

Cambourne, B. L. *Some psycholinguistic dimensions of the silent reading process in proficient, average and low ability readers*. ERDC research report, Riverina College, Wagga Wagga, Australia, 1980.

Carter, J., & Muir, P. (Eds.). *Printing and the mind of man: The impact of print on the evolution of western civilization during five centuries*. Cambridge: Cambridge University Press, 1967.

Cayer, R. L., & Sacks, R. K. Oral and written discourse of basic writers: Similarities and differences. *Research in the Teaching of English*, 1979, 13, 121-128.

Chomsky, N. *Syntactic structures*. The Hague: Mouton, 1957.

Chomsky, N. Review of B. F. Skinner's *Verbal Behavior*. In J. Fodor & J. Katz (Eds.), *The structure of language: Essays in the philosophy of language*. Englewood Cliffs, N.J.: Prentice-Hall, 1964.

Cicourel, A. *Cognitive sociology*. New York: Free Press, 1974.

Cipolla, C. M. *Literacy and development in the west*. Baltimore: Penguin, 1969.

Clark, R. A., & Delia, J. G. The development of functional persuasive skills in childhood and early adolescence. *Child Development*, 1976, 47, 1008-1014.

Clay, M. M. *Reading: The patterning of complex behavior*. Auckland, New Zealand: Heinneman, 1972.

Cole, M., Gay, J., Glick, L., & Sharp, D. M. *The cultural context of learning and thinking.* New York: Basic Books, 1971.

Conrad, R. Acoustic confusion in STM. *British Journal of Psychology,* 1964, *55,* 75-84.

Conrad, R. The developmental role of vocalizing in short term memory. *Journal of Verbal Learning and Verbal Behavior,* 1972, *11,* 521-533.

Conrad, R. *The deaf school child: Language and cognitive function.* London: Harper & Row, 1979.

Conrad, R. Let the children choose. *International Journal of Pediatric Otorhinolaryngology,* 1980, *1,* 317-329.

Conrad, R. Sign language in education: Some consequent problems. In B. Woll, J. G. Kyle, & M. Deuchar (Eds.), *Perspectives on BSL and deafness.* London: Croom Helm, 1981.

Cooper, C. R., & Odell, L. Considerations of sound in the composing process of published writers. *Research in the Teaching of English,* 1976, *10,* 103-115.

Cooper, L. (Ed.). *The rhetoric of Aristotle.* New York: Appleton-Century-Crofts, 1953.

Cooper, R. L., & Rosenstein, J. Language acquisition of deaf children. *Volta Review,* 1966, *68,* 58-67.

Cooper, T. C. Measuring written syntactic patterns of second language learners of German. *Journal of Educational Research,* 1976, *69,* 176-183.

Corbett, E. P. J. *Classical rhetoric for the modern student.* New York: Oxford University Press, 1965.

Cornett, O. R., Knight, D. L., Reynolds, H. N., & Williams, C. M. A theoretical model of reading in hearing impaired children. *Directions,* 1979, *1,* 43-68.

Cramer, R. L. *Writing, reading, and language growth: An introduction to language arts.* Columbus, Ohio: Charles E. Merrill, 1978.

Critchley, M. *The parietal lobes.* London: Arnold, 1953.

Crowhurst, M. On the misinterpretation of syntactic complexity data. *English Education,* 1979, *11,* 91-97.

Crowhurst, M., & Piché, G. L. Audience and mode of discourse effects on syntactic complexity in writing at two grade levels. *Research in the Teaching of English,* 1979, *13,* 101-109.

Dasen, P. R. Cross-cultural Piagetian research: A summary. *Journal of Cross-cultural Psychology,* 1972, *3,* 23-39.

Dawson, E. H. Are the deaf really a homogenous population. *Teacher of the Deaf,* 1979, *3,* 188-193.

Dawson, E. H. Psycholinguistic processes in prelingually deaf adolescents. In B. Woll, J. G. Kyle, & M. Dencher (Eds.), *Perspectives on BSL and Deafness.* London: Croom Helm, 1981.

Deese, J. Behavior and fact. *American Psychologist,* 1969, *24,* 512-522.

Delia, J. G., & Clark, R. A. Cognitive complexity, social perception and the development of listener-adapted communication in six-, eight-, ten-, and twelve-year-old boys. *Communication Monographs,* 1977, *44,* 326-345.

Delia, J. G., & O'Keefe, B. J. Constructivism: The development of communication in children. In E. Wartella (Ed.), *Children communicating*. Beverly Hills, Calif.: Sage, 1979.

Delia, J. G., O'Keefe, B. J., & O'Keefe, D. J. *A perspective on communication theory*. Reading, Mass.: Addison-Wesley, in press. (a)

Delia, J. G., O'Keefe, B. J., & O'Keefe, D. J. The constructivist approach to communication. In F. E. X. Dance (Ed.), *Comparative human communication theory*. New York: Harper & Row, in press. (b)

De Saussure, F. *Course in general linguistics* (C. Bally & A. Sechehaye, Eds.; W. Baskin, Trans.). New York: McGraw-Hill, 1959. (Originally published, 1916.)

DeVries, T. D. Writing writing and talking writing. *Elementary English*, 1970, *47*, 1067-1071.

Dewey, J. *Experience and education*. New York: MacMillan, 1938.

DiFrancesca, S. *Academic achievement test results of a national testing program for hearing impaired students—U.S.—Spring 1971*. (Series D No. 9) Washington, D.C.: Gallaudet College, Office of Demographic Studies, 1972.

Dilena, M. *Reading comprehension as information processing*. Unpublished qualifying paper, Harvard University, 1975.

Dilena, M. Computer models of language understanding and implications for teaching reading comprehension. Paper delivered at the 2nd Australian Reading Conference, Sydney, 1976.

Dimond, S. J. *The double brain*. Baltimore: Williams and Wilkins, 1972.

Dimond, S. J., & Beaumont, J. G. A right hemisphere basis for calculation in the human brain. *Acta Psychologia*, 1972, *36*, 443-449.

Dulay, H., & Burt, M. Errors and strategies in child second language acquisition. *TESOL Quarterly*, 1974, *8*, 129-136.

Duncan, S. Toward a grammar for dyadic conversation. *Semiotica*, 1973, *9*, 29-46.

Durkheim, E. *The elementary forms of religious life*. New York: Macmillan, 1954.

Durnford, M., & Kimura, D. Right hemisphere specialization for depth-perception reflected in visual field differences. *Nature*, 1971, *231*, 394-395.

Einhorn, L. Oral and written style: An examination of differences. *Southern Speech Communication Journal*, 1978, *43*, 302-311.

Einstein, A. Letter to Jacques Hademard. In B. Ghislen (Ed.), *The creative process: A symposium*. New York: The American Library, 1952.

Eisenstein, E. J. Some conjectures about the impact of printing on western society and thought: A preliminary report. *Journal of Modern History*, 1968, *40*, 1-56.

Elbow, P. *Writing without teachers*. New York: Oxford University Press, 1973.

Emig, J. *The composing processes of twelfth graders*. Urbana, Ill.: NCTE, 1971.

Emig, J. Writing as a mode of learning. *College Composition and Communication*, 1977, *28*, 122-128.

Erwin-Tripp, S. Is second language learning like the first? *TESOL Quarterly*, 1974, *8*, 111-129.

Ewoldt, C. *Psycholinguistic research in the reading of deaf children.* Unpublished doctoral dissertation, Wayne State University, 1977.

Farrell, T. Literacy, the basics, and all that jazz. *College English*, 1977, *38*, 443-459.

Ferris, D. R. Teaching children to write. In P. Lamb (Ed.), *Guilding children's language learning.* Dubuque, Iowa: Wm. C. Brown, 1967.

Field, J. P., & Weiss, R. H. *Cases for composition.* Boston: Little, Brown, 1978.

Filbey, R. A., & Gazzaniga, M. S. Splitting the brain with reaction time. *Psychometric Science*, 1969, *17*, 335-336.

Finnegan, R. *Oral literature in Africa.* Oxford: Clarendon Press, 1970.

Finnegan, R. Literacy and literature. Unpublished manuscript, 1979.

Firth, J. R. The technique of semantics. In *Papers in linguistics, 1934-1951.* London: Oxford University Press, 1957. (Originally published, 1935.)

Fisher, C. J., & Terry, C. A. *Children's language and the language arts.* New York: McGraw-Hill, 1977.

Flavell, J. H., Botkin, P. T., Fry, C. L., Wright, J. W., & Jarvis, P. E. *The development of role-taking and communication skills in children.* New York: John Wiley, 1968.

Flesch, R. *The art of plain talk.* New York: Macmillan, 1951.

Fodor, J. *The language of thought.* New York: Thomas Y. Crowell, 1975.

Fodor, J., & Bever, T. The psychological reality of linguistic segments. *Journal of Verbal Learning and Verbal Behavior*, 1965, *4*, 414-421.

Fowler, C. Phonological coding in beginning reading. *Status Report on Speech Research, Haskin Labs*, 1979, 139-145.

Frake, C. "Struck by Speech": The Yakan concept of litigation. In J. Gumperz & D. Hymes (Eds.), *Directions in sociolinguistics.* New York: Holt, 1972.

Freire, P. *Pedagogy of the oppressed* (M. B. Ramos, Trans.). New York: Seabury Press, 1970.

Fry, E. *Reading instruction for classroom and clinic.* New York: McGraw-Hill, 1972.

Furth, H. *Thinking without language.* London: Collier Macmillan, 1966.

Gadamer, H. G. *Truth and method.* New York: The Seabury Press, 1975.

Gardner, H. *The shattered mind: The person after brain damage.* New York: Alfred A. Knopf, 1975.

Gardner, H. The loss of language. *Human Nature*, 1978, *1*, 84.

Garrett, N., Bever, T., & Fodor, J. The active use of grammar in speech perception. *Perception and Psychophysics*, 1966, *1*, 30-32.

Gay, J., & Cole, M. *The new mathematics and an old culture.* New York: Holt, Rinehart & Winston, 1967.

Gazzaniga, M. S. *The bisected brain.* New York: Appleton-Century-Crofts, 1970.

Gazzaniga, M. S., & Hilljard, S. A. Language and speech capacity of the right hemisphere. *Neuropsychologia,* 1971, *9,* 273-280.

Gazzaniga, M. S., & Sperry, R. W. Language after section of the cerebral commissures. *Brain,* 1967, *90,* 131-148.

Gibson, J. W., Gruner, C. R., Kibler, R. J., & Kelly, F. J. A quantitative examination of differences and similarities in written and spoken messages. *Speech Monographs,* 1966, *33,* 444-450.

Giorgi, A. *Psychology as a human science.* New York: Harper & Row, 1970.

Giorgi, A. Phenomenology and psychology. In W. J. Arnold (Ed.), *Nebraska symposium on motivation, 1975.* Lincoln: University of Nebraska Press, 1976.

Glassner, B. Preliminary report: Hemispheric relationships in composing. *Journal of Education,* 1980, *162,* 72-95.

Gleason, H. A., Jr. *Linguistics and English grammar.* New York: Holt, Rinehart & Winston, 1965.

Goldin-Meadow, S. Structure in a manual communication system developed without a conventional model: Language without a helping hand. *Studies in Neurolinguistics,* 1979, *4,* 125-209.

Goldstein, L. Some relationships between quantified hemispheric EEG and behavioral states in man. In J. Gruzelier & P. Flor-Henry (Eds.), *Hemisphere asymmetries of function in psychopathology.* Elsevier: North-Holland Biomedical Press, 1979.

Goodman, K. S., & Burke, C. *Theoretically based studies of miscues in oral reading performance.* (Report No. 9-0375). U.S. Dept. of Health, Education and Welfare, 1973.

Goody, E. N. Towards a theory of questions. In E. N. Goody (Ed.), *Questions and politeness: Strategies in social interaction.* Cambridge: Cambridge University Press, 1978.

Goody, J. *Literacy in traditional societies.* Cambridge: Cambridge University Press, 1968. (Originally published, 1963.)

Goody, J. *The domestication of the savage mind.* Cambridge: Cambridge University Press, 1977.

Goody, J., & Watt, I. The consequences of literacy. In J. Goody (Ed.), *Literacy in traditional societies.* Cambridge: Cambridge University Press, 1968. (Originally published, 1963.)

Gough, K. Literacy in Kerala. In J. Goody (Ed.), *Literacy in traditional societies.* Cambridge: Cambridge University Press, 1968. (Originally published, 1963.)

Graves, D. Research update: Andrea learns to make writing hard. *Language Arts,* 1979, *56,* 569-576. (a)

Graves, D. Research update: Research doesn't have to be boring. *Language Arts,* 1979, *56,* 76-80. (b)

Graves, D. Research update: What children show us about revision. *Language Arts,* 1979, *56,* 312-319. (c)

Green, B. L. Performance of deaf children on memory tasks. *New York University Educational Quarterly,* 1980, *11,* 20-28.

Greenfield, P. Oral and written language: The consequences for cognitive development in Africa, the United States and England. *Language and Speech*, 1972, *15*, 169-178.

Groff, P. Subvocalization and silent reading. *Reading World*, 1977, *16*, 231-237.

Groff, P. The effects of talking on writing. *English in Education*, 1979, *13*, 33-37.

Guilford, J. P., & Hoepfner, R. *The analysis of intelligence*. New York: McGraw-Hill, 1971.

Gumperz, J. C., & Gumperz, J. J. From oral to written culture: The transition to literacy. In M. F. Whitehead (Ed.), *Variation in writing*. New York: Lawrence Erlbaum, 1979.

Gunning, R. *The technique of clear writing* (Rev. ed.). New York: McGraw-Hill, 1968.

Hakuta, K., & Cancino, H. Trends in second-language acquisition research. *Harvard Educational Review*, 1977, *47*, 294-316.

Halliday, M. A. K. Notes on transitivity and theme in English, Part 2. *Journal of Linguistics*, 1967, *3*, 177-274.

Halliday, M. A. K. *Explorations in the functions of language*. London: Edward Arnold, 1973.

Halliday, M. A. K., & Hasan, R. *Cohesion in English*. London: Longman, 1976.

Haney, W. V. *Communication and interpersonal relations: Text and cases* (4th ed.). Homewood, Ill.: Richard D. Irwin, 1979.

Hardyck, C. D., & Petrinovich, L. R. Subvocal speech and comprehension level as a function of the difficulty of reading material. *Journal of Verbal Learning and Verbal Behavior*, 1970, *9*, 647-652.

Harpin, W. *The second "R": Writing development in the junior school*. London: George Allen & Unwin, 1976.

Harrell, L. E., Jr. A comparison of the development of oral and written language in school-age children. *Monographs of the Society for Research in Child Development*, 1957, *22*, (3, Serial No. 66).

Harris, M. M. Oral and written syntax attainment of second graders. *Research in the Teaching of English*, 1977, *11*, 117-132.

Hartwell, P. Dialect interference in writing: A critical view. *Research in the Teaching of English*, 1980, *14*, 101-118.

Hasan, R. Code, register, and social dialect. In B. Bernstein (Ed.), *Class, codes and control* (Vol. 2). London: Routledge and Kegan Paul, 1973.

Hasan, R. Text in the systemic-functional model. In W. U. Dressler (Ed.), *Current trends in textlinguistics*. New York: Walter de Gruyter, 1978.

Havelock, E. *Prologue to Greek literacy*. Toronto: OISE Press, 1976.

Heidegger, M. *Being and time*. London: SCM Press, 1962. (Originally published, 1927.)

Heider, F., & Heider, G. A comparison of sentence structure of deaf and hearing children. *Psychology Monographs*, 1940, *52*, 52-103.

Hewing, P. H. A practical plan for teaching oral communication in the business communication course. *The ABCA Bulletin*, 1977, *40*, 9-11.

Higgins, E. T. Written communication as functional literacy: A developmental comparison of oral and written communication. In R. Beach & P. D. Pearson (Eds.), *Perspectives on literacy.* Minneapolis: College of Education, University of Minnesota, 1978.

Hirsch, E. D., Jr. *The philosophy of composition.* Chicago: University of Chicago Press, 1977.

Hodes, P. *A psycholinguistic study of reading miscues of Yiddish-English bilingual children.* Unpublished doctoral dissertation, Wayne State University, 1976.

Horton, R., & Finnegan, R. (Eds.). *Modes of thought.* London: Faber & Faber, 1973.

Houts, P. L. (Ed.). *The myth of measurability.* New York: Hart Publishing Co., 1977.

Householder, F. *Linguistic speculations.* Cambridge: Cambridge University Press, 1971.

Howard, D. R. *The idea of the Canterbury Tales.* Berkeley: University of California Press, 1976.

Huegli, J. M., & Tschirgi, H. D. Communication skills at the entry job level. *The Journal of Business Communication,* 1974, *12,* 24-29.

Hunt, K. W. Syntactic maturity in school children and adults. *Monographs of the Society for Research in Child Development,* 1970, *35,* (Serial No. 134).

Hymes, D. H. Models of the interaction of language and social life. In J. J. Gumperz & D. Hymes (Eds.), *Directions in sociolinguistics: The ethnography of communication.* New York: Holt, Rinehart & Winston, 1972. (a)

Hymes, D. H. On communicative competence. In J. B. Pride & J. Holmes (Eds.), *Sociolinguistics.* Middlesex, England: Penquin Books, 1972. (b)

Innis, H. *The bias of communication.* Toronto: University of Toronto Press, 1951.

*International Herald Tribune,* May, 1979.

Irvine, A. L. *Reading narrative and technical prose: A psycholinguistic study of year 6 children.* Unpublished dissertation, University of New England, Australia, 1979.

Ivimey, G. The written syntax of an English deaf child: An exploration in method. *British Journal of Disorders of Communication,* 1976, *11,* 103-120.

Jackson, J. H. *Selected writings of John Hughlings Jackson.* New York: Basic Books, 1958.

Jahn, J. *Muntu* (M. Green, Trans.). New York: Grove Press, 1961.

Johnson, T. D. Language experience: We can't all write what we can say. *The Reading Teacher,* 1977, *31,* 297-299.

Joos, M. *The five clocks.* New York: Harcourt, Brace and World, 1961.

Kantor, K. J. Developmental aspects of sense of audience in written discourse. *Studies in Language Education,* Report No. 33. Athens, Ga.: Department of Language Education, University of Georgia, 1978.

Kantor, K. J., & Perron, J. D. Thinking and writing: Creativity in the modes of discourse. *Language Arts,* 1977, *54,* 742-749.

Katz, J. J., & Fodor, J. A. The structure of a semantic theory. In J. A. Fodor & J. J. Katz (Eds.), *The structure of language*. Englewood Cliffs, N.J.: Prentice-Hall, 1964.

Kelly, G. *A theory of personality: The psychology of personal constructs*. New York: W. W. Norton, 1963.

Kimura, D. Cerebral dominance and the perception of verbal stimuli. *Canadian Journal of Psychology*, 1961, *15*, 355-358.

Kimura, D. Left-right differences in perception of melodies. *Quarterly Journal of Psychology*, 1964, *16*, 355-358.

Kimura, D. Dual functional asymmetry of the brain in visual perception. *Neuropsychologia*, 1966, *4*, 275-285.

Kimura, D. Spatial localization in the left and right visual fields. *Canadian Journal of Psychology*, 1969, *23*, 445-448.

Kinneavy, J. L. *A theory of discourse*. Englewood Cliffs, N.J.: Prentice-Hall, 1971.

Kirby, D. R., & Kantor, K. J. Toward a theory of developmental rhetoric. Paper presented at the Canadian Council of Teachers of English Conference on Learning to Write, Ottawa, Ontario, May, 1979.

Kirk, S. A., & Kirk, W. D. *Psycholinguistic learning disabilities*. Urbana, Ill.: University of Illinois Press, 1971.

Klima, E. S., & Bellugi, U. *The signs of language*. Cambridge, Mass.: Harvard University Press, 1979.

Knight, D. L. A general model of English language development in hearing-impaired children. *Directions*, 1979, *1*, 9-28.

Koch, S. Language communities, search cells, and the psychological studies. In W. J. Arnold (Ed.), *Nebraska symposium on motivation, 1975*. Lincoln: University of Nebraska Press, 1976.

Kolers, P., & Katzman, M. T. Naming sequentially presented letters and words. *Language and Speech*, 1966, *9*, 54-95.

Kozol, J. *The night is dark and I am far from home*. Boston: Houghton Mifflin, 1975.

Kroll, B. Combining ideas in written and spoken English: A look at subordination and coordination. In E. O. Keenan & T. L. Bennett (Eds.), *Discourse across time and space*. Southern California Occasional Papers in Linguistics, 1977, *5*, 69-108.

Kroll, B. M. Cognitive egocentrism and the problem of audience awareness in written discourse. *Research in the Teaching of English*, 1978, *12*, 269-281.

Kroll, B. M., & Lempers, J. D. Effect of mode of communication on the informational adequacy of children's explanations. *Journal of Genetic Psychology*, 1981, *138*, 27-35.

Kyle, J. G. The study of auditory deprivation from birth. *British Journal of Audiology*, 1978, *12*, 37-39.

Kyle, J. G. Measuring the intelligence of deaf children. *Bulletin of British Psychology and Sociology*, 1980, *33*, 30-32. (a)

Kyle, J. G. The reading development of deaf children. *Journal of Research on Reading*, 1980, *3*, 86-97. (b)

Kyle, J. G. Representation and memory in deaf people: The search for the code. In B. Woll, J. G. Kyle, & M. Deuchar (Eds.), *Perspectives on BSL and Deafness.* London: Croom Helm, 1981.

Kyle, J. G., & Woll, B. The sign language of deaf people: The other English language. *Special Education Forward Trends,* in press.

Labov, W. *Language in the inner city.* Philadelphia: University of Pennsylvania Press, 1972.

Labov, W., & Fanshell, D. *Therapeutic discourse.* New York: Academic Press, 1977.

Ladefoged, P., & Broadbent, D. Perception of sequence in auditory events. *Quarterly Journal of Experimental Psychology,* 1960, *12,* 162-170.

Larson, R. L. "Rhetorical writing" in elementary school. In R. L. Larson (Ed.), *Children and writing in the elementary school: Theories and techniques.* New York: Oxford University Press, 1975. (Reprinted from *Elementary English,* 1971, *48,* 926-931.)

Lashley, K. S. The problem of serial order in behavior. In L. A. Jeffress (Ed.), *Cerebral mechanisms in behavior.* New York: John Wiley, 1951.

Lassan, A., Ingvar, D. H., & Skinhoj, E. Brain functions and blood flow. *Scientific American,* 1978, *239,* 62-71.

Lenneberg, E. H. *Biological foundations of language.* New York: John Wiley, 1967.

Lesikar, R. V. *Business communication: Theory and application* (4th ed.). Homewood, Ill.: Richard D. Irwin, 1980.

Levin, S. R. Langue and parole in American linguistics. *Foundations of Language,* 1965, *1,* 83-94.

Levine, M. Scientific method and the adversary model: Some preliminary thoughts. *American Psychologist,* 1974, *29,* 661-677.

Levy, J. Psychobiological implications of bilateral asymmetry. *Hemispheric functions in the human brain.* New York: Halsted Press, 1974.

Levy, J., Trevarthen, C., & Sperry, R. W. Perception of bilateral chimeric figures following hemispheric deconnexion. *Brain,* 1972, *95,* 74-75.

Lieberman, P. Some effects of semantic and grammatical context in the production and perception of speech. *Language and Speech,* 1963, *6,* 172.

Linde, C. *Information structures in discourse* (NWAVE *III*). Washington, D.C.: Georgetown University, 1974.

Loban, W. *Language development: Kindergarten through grade twelve.* Urbana, Ill.: NCTE, 1976.

Lopate, P. Helping young children start to write. In C. R. Cooper & L. Odell (Eds.), *Research on composing: Points of departure.* Urbana, Ill.: NCTE, 1978.

Lord, A. B. *The singer of tales.* Cambridge: Harvard University Press, 1960.

Lundsteen, S. W. *Children learn to communicate: Language arts through creative problem solving.* Englewood Cliffs, N.J.: Prentice-Hall, 1976.

Luria, A. R. *The working brain: An introduction to neuropsychology* (B. Haigh, Trans.). New York: Basic Books, 1973.

Luria, A. R. Language and brain: Towards the basic problems of neurolinguistics. *Brain and Language*, 1974, *1*, 1-14.

Luria, A. R., & Simernitskaya, E. G. Interhemispheric relations and the functions of the minor hemisphere. *Neuropsychologia*, 1977, *15*, 175-178.

Luria, A. R., Simernitskaya, E. G., & Tubylevich, B. The structure of psychological processes in relation to cerebral organization. *Neuropsychologia*, 1970, 8, 13-18.

Luria, A. R., & Yudovich, F. I. *Speech and the development of mental processes in the child* (J. Simon, Trans.). Baltimore: Penguin, 1971.

Lyons, J. *Introduction to theoretical linguistics*. Cambridge: Cambridge University Press, 1968.

Lyons, J. *Semantics* (Vol. 2). Cambridge: Cambridge University Press, 1977.

Mackay, D., Thompson, B., & Schaub, P. *Breakthrough to literacy: The theory and practice of teaching initial reading and writing* (2nd ed.). London: Longman, 1978.

Macrorie, K. *Uptaught*. New York: Hayden Press, 1970.

Macrorie, K. *Writing to be read*. Rochelle Park, N.J.: Hayden Book, 1976.

Maheu, R. World congress of ministers of education on the eradication of illiteracy. Speeches and messages, UNESCO, Teheran, 1966. Quoted in R. Horton & R. Finnegan (Eds.), *Modes of thought*. London: Faber & Faber, 1973.

Malinowski, B. The problem of meaning in primitive languages. Supplement to C. K. Ogden & I. A. Richards, *The meaning of meaning*. London: Kegan Paul, Trench, Trubner & Co., 1923.

Malinowski, B. *Coral gardens and their magic* (Vol. 2). London: George Allen & Unwin, 1935.

Mallett, M., & Newsome, B. *Talking, writing and learning 8-13*. London: Evan/Methuen Educational, 1977.

Maratsos, M. Non-egocentric communication abilities in preschool children. *Child Development*, 1973, *44*, 679-700.

Marcus, M. *Diagnostic teaching of the language arts*. New York: John Wiley, 1977.

Martin, N., D'Arcy, P., Newton, B., & Parker, R. *Writing and learning across the curriculum, 11-16*. London: Ward Lock Educational, 1976.

Maugham, W. S. *The summing up*. New York: Literary Guild, 1938.

McGuigan, F. J. Covert oral behavior during silent performance of language tests. *Psychological Bulletin*, 1970, *74*, 309-326.

McLeod, A. This is what came out. *English in Education*, 1969, *3*, 86-120.

McLuhan, M. *The Gutenberg galaxy*. Toronto: University of Toronto Press, 1962.

Mead, G. H. *Mind, self, and society*. Chicago: University of Chicago Press, 1934.

Medway, P. *From talking to writing.* London: Writing Across the Curriculum Project, 1973.

Meggitt, M. Uses of literacy in New Guinea and Melanesia. In J. Goody (Ed.), *Literacy in traditional societies.* Cambridge: Cambridge University Press, 1968. (Originally published, 1963.)

Merleau-Ponty, M. *Phenomenology of perception.* New York: Humanities Press, 1962.

Meyers, R. E. Functions of corpus callosum in interocular transfer. *Brain,* 1956, *79,* 358-363.

Miller, G. The magical number seven plus or minus two: Some limits on our capacity for processing information. *Psychological Review,* 1956, *73,* 81-97.

Miller, G., Heise, A., & Lichten, W. The intelligibility of speech as a function of the context and the test materials. *Quarterly Journal of Experimental Psychology,* 1951, *40,* 329-335.

Milner, B., Branch, C., & Rasmussen, T. Observations on cerebral dominance. In R. Oldfield & J. Marshall (Eds.), *Language.* Middlesex, England: Penguin, 1964.

Mishler, E. Meaning in context: Is there any other kind? *Harvard Educational Review,* 1979, *49,* 1-19.

Moffett, J. *Teaching the universe of discourse.* Boston: Houghton Mifflin, 1968.

Monroe, J. H. Measuring and enhancing syntactic fluency in French. *The French Review,* 1975, *48,* 1023-1031.

Moores, D. F. An investigation of the psycholinguistic functioning of deaf adolescents. *Exceptional Children,* 1970, *36,* 645-652.

Moores, D. F. *Educating the deaf: Psychology, principles and practices.* Boston: Houghton Mifflin, 1978.

Moutoux, D., & Porte, M. Small talk in industry. *The Journal of Business Communication,* 1980, *17,* 3-11.

Mukarovsky, J. Dialogue and monologue. In J. Burbank & P. Steiner (Eds. and trans.), *The word and verbal art.* New Haven: Yale University Press, 1977. (Originally published in 1940.)

Murray, D. Internal revision: A process of discovery. In C. R. Cooper & L. Odell (Eds.), *Research on composing: Points of departure.* Urbana, Ill.: NCTE, 1978.

Myklebust, H. R. *The psychology of deafness.* New York: Grune and Stratton, 1974.

Neisser, U. *Cognitive psychology.* New York: Appleton-Century-Crofts, 1967.

Ochs, E. Planned and unplanned discourse. In T. Givon (Ed.), *Syntax and semantics* (Vol. 12). New York: Academic Press, 1979.

Odom, P. B., & Blanton, R. L. Implicit and explicit grammatical factors and reading achievement in the deaf. *Journal of Reading Behavior,* 1970, *2,* 47-55.

O'Donnell, R. C. Syntactic differences between speech and writing. *American Speech,* 1974, *49,* 102-110.

O'Donnell, R. C., Griffin, W. J., & Norris, R. C. *Syntax of kindergarten and elementary school children: A transformational analysis.* Urbana, Ill.: NCTE, 1967.

Olson, D. R. Oral and written language and the cognitive processes of children. *Journal of Communication,* 1977, *27,* 10-26. (a)

Olson, D. R. From utterance to text: The bias of language in speech and writing. *Harvard Educational Review,* 1977, *47,* 257-281. (b)

Olson, D. R. The languages of instruction: The literate bias of schooling. In R. C. Anderson, R. J. Siro, & W. E. Montague (Eds.), *Schooling and the acquisition of knowledge.* Hillsdale, N.J.: Lawrence Erlbaum, 1977. (c)

Olson, D. R., & Hildyard, A. Assent and compliance in children's comprehension. In P. Dixon (Ed.), *Children's oral communication skills.* New York: Academic Press, 1981.

Olson, D. R., & Hildyard, A. Writing and literal meaning. In M. Martlew (Ed.), *The psychology of writing.* New York: John Wiley, in press.

Olson, D. R., & Nickerson, N. G. Language development through the school years: Learning to confine interpretation to the information in the text. In K. E. Nelson (Ed.), *Children's language,* (Vol. 1). New York: Gardner Press, 1978.

Ong, W. *Interfaces of the word.* Ithaca: Cornell University Press, 1977.

Ong, W. *Rhetoric, romance, and technology.* Ithaca: Cornell University Press, 1971.

Ong, W. The writer's audience is always a fiction. *PMLA,* 1975, *90,* 9-21.

Ornstein, R., Herron, J., & Johnstone, J. Differential right hemisphere involvement in two reading tasks. Unpublished paper, Langely Porter Institute, San Francisco, Calif., 1979.

Paivio, A. *Imagery and verbal processes.* New York: Holt, Rinehart & Winston, 1971.

Parry, M. The making of Homeric verse. In A. Parry (Ed.), *The collected papers of Milman Parry.* Oxford: Clarendon Press, 1971.

Pascal, B. *Pensees* (J. Warrington, Trans.). New York: Dutton, 1967.

Perron, J. The impact of mode on written syntactic complexity. *Studies in Language Education.* Reports No. 24, 25, 27, 30. Athens, Ga.: Department of Language Education, University of Georgia, 1976-77.

Petty, W. T. The writing of young children. In C. R. Cooper & L. Odell (Eds.), *Research on composing: Points of departure.* Urbana, Ill.: NCTE, 1978.

Petty, W. T., Petty, D. C., & Becking, M. F. *Experiences in language: Tools and techniques for language arts methods* (2nd ed.). Boston: Allyn and Bacon, 1976.

Philips, S. U. Literacy as a mode of communication on the Warm Spring Indian Reservation. In E., & E. Lenneberg (Eds.), *Foundations of language development* (Vol. 2). San Francisco: Academic Press, 1975.

Phillips, B. Starting points. *Radical Teacher,* 1978, *8,* 1-5.

Piaget, J. *Biology and knowledge: An essay on the relations between or-*

*ganic regulations and cognitive processes.* Chicago: University of Chicago Press, 1971.

Pianko, S. A description of the composing processes of college freshman writers. *Research in the Teaching of English,* 1979, *13,* 5-22.

Poincaré, H. Mathematical creativity. In B. Ghislen (Ed.), *The creative process.* New York: The New American Library, 1952.

Polanyi, M. *Personal knowledge: Towards a post-critical philosophy.* Chicago: University of Chicago Press, 1958.

Pollack, I., & Pickett, J. The intelligibility of excerpts from conversations. *Language and Speech,* 1964, *6,* 165-171.

Popper, K., & Eccles, J. C. *The self and its brain: An argument for interactionism.* New York: Springer International, 1977.

Porter, G. R. *The progress of the nation.* London: J. Murray, 1851.

Postovsky, V. Effects of delay in oral practice at the beginning of second language learning. Unpublished doctoral dissertation, University of California at Berkeley, 1970.

Quigley, S. P. Environment and communication in the language development of deaf children. In L. J. Bradford & W. G. Hardy (Eds.), *Hearing and hearing impairment.* New York: Grune and Stratton, 1979.

Quigley, S. P., Martanelli, D. S., & Wilbur, R. B. Some aspects of the verb systems in the language of deaf students. *Journal of Speech and Hearing Research,* 1976, *19,* 536-550.

Quigley, S. P., Smith, N. L., & Wilbur, R. B. Comprehension of relativized sentences by deaf students. *Journal of Speech and Hearing Research,* 1974, *17,* 325-341.

Quigley, S. P., Wilbur, R. B., Power, D. J., Martanelli, D. S., & Steinkamp, M. W. *Syntactic structures in the language of children.* Urbana, Ill., 1976.

Raven, J. C. *Guide to the standard progressive matrices.* London: H. K. Lewis, 1960.

Rensburger, B. Language ability found in the right side of the brain. *New York Times,* 1975, *14.*

Ricoeur, P. *Interpretation theory: Discourse and the surplus of meaning.* Fort Worth: Texas Christian University Press, 1976.

Riegel, K. The dialectics of human development. *American Psychologist,* 1976, *31,* 689-700.

Ries, P. W., & Vonieff, P. Demographic profile of hearing impaired students. *PRWAD Deafness Annual,* 1974, *4,* 17-42.

Rivers, W. M., & Temperly, M. S. *A practical guide to the teaching of English as a second or foreign language.* New York: Oxford University Press, 1978.

Robeck, M. C., & Wilson, J. A. R. *Psychology of reading: Foundations of instruction.* New York: John Wiley, 1974.

Robins, R. H. *A short history of linguistics.* Bloomington: Indiana University Press, 1967.

Rosen, C., & Rosen, H. *The language of primary school children.* Harmondsworth, England: Penguin Education, 1973.

Rousch, P. D., & Cambourne, B. L. *A psycholinguistic model of the reading process as it relates to proficient, average and low ability readers.* ERDC research report. Riverina College, Wagga Wagga, Australia, 1979.

Rousseau, J. *Discourse upon the origin and foundation of the inequality between mankind.* London: R & J Dodsley, 1761.

Ruben, R. J., & Rapin, I. Theoretical issues in the development of audition. In L. T. Taft & M. Lewis (Eds.), *Symposium in developmental disabilities in the preschool child.* New York: Spectrum, 1980.

Rubin, D. *Teaching elementary language arts.* New York: Holt, Rinehart & Winston, 1975.

Rubin, D. L. Adapting syntax to varying audiences as a function of social cognition: A developmental comparison. Paper presented at the Annual Meeting, American Educational Research Association, Boston, April, 1980.

Rubin, D. L., & Piché, G. L. Development in syntactic and strategic aspects of audience adaptation skills in written persuasive communication. *Research in the Teaching of English,* 1979, *13,* 293-316.

Sacks, H. Lecture notes, 1967.

Sacks, H. An analysis of the course of a joke's telling in conversation. In R. Bauman, and J. Sherzer (Eds.), *Explorations in the ethnography of speaking.* London: Cambridge University Press, 1974.

Sacks, H. On the analyzability of stories by children. In J. J. Gumperz & D. Hymes (Eds.), *Directions in sociolinguistics.* New York: Holt, Rinehart & Winston, 1972.

Salus, P. (Ed.). *On language: Plato to von Humboldt.* New York: Holt, Rinehart & Winston, 1969.

Samuels, S. J. The age-old controversy between holistic and subskill approaches to beginning reading instruction revisited. In C. M. McCullough (Ed.), *Inchworm, inchworm: Persistent problems in reading education.* Newark, Del.: IRA, 1980.

Sartre, J. P. *Being and nothingness.* New York: Washington Square Press, 1956.

Schegloff, E. A. On some questions and ambiguities in conversation. In W. U. Dressler (Ed.), *Current trends in text-linguistics.* New York: Walter de Gruyter, 1978.

Schegloff, E. A., & Sacks, H. Opening up closings. *Semiotica,* 1973, *8,* 289-327.

Schofield, R. S. The measurement of literacy in pre-industrial England. In J. Goody (Ed.), *Literacy in traditional societies.* Cambridge: Cambridge University Press, 1968. (Originally published, 1963.)

Schultz, J. Story workshop: Writing from start to finish. In C. R. Cooper & L. Odell (Eds.), *Research on composing: Points of departure.* Urbana, Ill.: NCTE, 1978.

Scinto, L. F. Textual competence: A preliminary analysis of orally generated texts. *Linguistics,* 1977, *194,* 5-34.

Scott, C. T. The linguistic basis for the development of reading skill. *Modern Language Journal,* 1966, *50,* 535-544.

Scribner, S., & Cole, M. Literacy without schooling: Testing for intellectual effects. *Harvard Educational Review,* 1978, *48,* 448-461.

Searle, J. R. *Speech acts.* London: Cambridge University Press, 1969.

Selman, R. L., & Byrne, D. F. A structural developmental analysis of levels of role-taking in middle childhood. *Child Development,* 1974, *45,* 803-806.

Shankweiler, D., Liberman, I. Y., Mark, L. S., Fowler, C. A., & Fisher, F. W. The speech code and learning to read. *Status Report on Speech Research, Haskin Labs,* 1979, 83-104.

Shaughnessy, M. P. *Errors and expectations: A guide for the teacher of basic writing.* New York: Oxford University Press, 1977.

Shuy, R. Health care for women: Current social and behavioral issues. The medical interview. *Problems in Communication,* 1976, *3,* 265-280.

Simernitskaya, E. G. On two forms of writing defects following local brain lesions. In S. J. Dimond & J. G. Beaumont (Eds.), *Hemispheric functions in the human brain.* New York: Halsted Press, 1974.

Simmons, A. A. A comparison of the type-token ratio of spoken and written language of deaf children. *Volta Review,* 1962, *64,* 417-421.

Sims, R. *A psycholinguistic description of miscues generated by selected young readers during the oral reading of text material in black dialect and standard English.* Doctoral dissertation, Wayne State University, 1972. (University Microfilms No. 76-08365, 1976.)

Sinclair, J. M., & Coulthard, R. M. *Towards an analysis of discourse: The English used by teachers and pupils.* London: Oxford University Press, 1975.

Skinner, B. F. *Verbal behavior.* Englewood Cliffs, N.J.: Prentice-Hall, 1957.

Smith, E. B., Goodman, K. S., & Meredith, R. *Language and thinking in school* (2nd ed.). New York: Holt, Rinehart & Winston, 1976.

Smith, F. *Comprehension and learning.* New York: Holt, Rinehart & Winston, 1975.

Smith, F. Making sense of reading and of reading instruction. *Harvard Educational Review,* 1977, *47,* 386-395.

Smith, F. *Reading.* Cambridge: Cambridge University Press, 1978.

Smith, F. Address to teacher educators. Riverina College of Advanced Education, Wagga Wagga, Australia, 1980.

Sokolov, A. N. *Inner speech and thought.* New York: Plenum Press, 1972.

Sorensen, R. K., & Hansen, B. *The sign language of deaf children.* Copenhagen: Doves Center for Total Kommunikation, 1976.

Spender, S. The making of a poem. In B. Ghislen (Ed.), *The creative process.* New York: The New American Library, 1952.

Sperry, R. W. Cerebral organization and behavior. *Science,* 1961, *133,* 1749-1757.

Sperry, R. W., & Gazzaniga, M. S. Language following surgical disconnection of the hemispheres. In F. L. Darley (Ed.), *Brain mechanisms underlying speech and language.* New York: Grune and Stratton, 1967.

Spiegelberg, H. *The phenomenological movement: A historical introduction.* The Hague: Martinum Nijhof, 1972.

Spiegelberg, H. *Doing phenomenology*. The Hague: Martinum Nijhoff, 1975.

Stine, D., & Skarzenski, D. Priorities for the business communications classroom: A survey of business and academe. *The Journal of Business Communications*, 1979, *16*, 15-30.

Swensen, D. H. Relative importance of business communication skills for the next ten years. *The Journal of Business Communication*, 1980, *17*, 41-49.

Swisher, L. The language performance of the oral deaf. In H. Whitaker & H. Whitaker (Eds.), *Studies in neurolinguistics, Vol. 2*. New York: Academic Press, 1976.

Taylor, J. *Reading and writing in the first school*. London: George Allen & Unwin, 1973.

Taylor, L. *A language analysis of the writing of deaf children*. Unpublished doctoral dissertation, State University of Florida, 1969.

Tedlock, D., & Jarvie, P. A. *Casebook rhetoric: A problem-solving approach to composition*. New York: Holt, Rinehart & Winston, 1981.

Thomas, G. L. Effect of oral style on intelligibility of speech. *Speech Monographs*, 1956, *23*, 46-54.

Tough, J. *Focus on meaning: Talking to some purpose with young children*. London: George Allen & Unwin, 1973.

Tough, J. *The development of meaning*. New York: John Wiley, 1977. (a)

Tough, J. *Talking and learning: A guide to fostering communication skills in nursery and infant schools*. London: Ward Lock Educational, 1977. (b)

Trager, G. L. Paralanguage: A first approximation. *Studies in Linguistics*, 1958, *13*, 1-12.

Trager, G. L. The typology of paralanguage. *Anthropological Linguistics*, 1961, *3*, 17-21.

Trimble, J. R. *Writing with style: Conversations on the art of writing*. Englewood Cliffs, N.J.: Prentice-Hall, 1975.

Vachek, J. *Written language: General problems and problems of English*. The Hague: Mouton, 1973.

Valtin, R. Dyslexia. *Reading Research Quarterly*, 1979, *14*, 201-221.

Van Dijk, T. A. Semantic macro-structures and knowledge frames in discourse comprehension. In M. A. Just & P. A. Carpenter (Eds.), *Cognitive processes in comprehension*. New York: John Wiley, 1977. (a)

Van Dijk, T. A. *Text and context: Explorations in the semantics and pragmatics of discourse*. London: Longman, 1977. (b)

Van Mannen, M. An experiment in educational theorizing. The Utrecht School. *Interchange*, 1978-79, *10*, 48-66.

Vann, R. Oral and written syntactic relationships in second language learning. In C. Yoria, K. Perkins & J. Schachter (Eds.), *On TESOL'79: The learner in focus*. Washington, D.C.: TESOL, 1979.

Vansina, J. *Oral tradition: A study in historical methodology* (H. M. Wright, Trans.). Chicago: Aldine Publishing Co., 1965. (Originally published, 1961.)

Vygotsky, L. S. *Thought and language*. (E. Hanfmann & G. Vakar, Eds.

and trans.), Cambridge, Mass.: M.I.T. Press, 1962. (Originally published, 1934.)

Wallas, G. *The art of thought.* New York: Jonathan Cape, 1926.

Walpole, J. Why must the passive be damned? *College Composition and Communication,* 1979, *30,* 251-254.

Wanner, E. Do we understand sentences from the outside-in or the inside-out? *Daedalus,* 1973, *102,* 163-184.

Weaver, C. *Grammar for teachers.* Urbana, Ill.: NCTE, 1979.

Wells, C. G. Language use and educational success: An empirical response to Joan Tough's "The development of meaning." *Research in Education,* 1977, *18,* 9-34.

Wells, C. G. *Learning through interaction: The study of language development.* Cambridge: Cambridge University Press, 1981.

Werner, H. The concept of development from a comparative and organismic point of view. In D. B. Harris (Ed.), *The concept of development.* Minneapolis: University of Minnesota Press, 1957.

Western, R. *Children's interpretation of form-function ambiguity.* Unpublished doctoral dissertation, University of Minnesota, 1974.

Whale, R. B., & Robinson, S. Modes of students' writings: A descriptive study. *Research in the Teaching of English,* 1978, *12,* 349-355.

Whittrock, M. C., et al. *The human brain.* Englewood Cliffs, N.J.: Prentice-Hall, 1977.

Wilbur, R. B. *American sign language and sign systems.* Baltimore: University Park Press, 1979.

Wilkinson, A. *The foundations of language: Talking and reading in young children.* London: Oxford University Press, 1971.

Wilkinson, A., & Swan, P. The development of style in children's writing. *Educational Review,* 1980, *32,* 173-184.

Wilks, I. The transmission of Islamic learning in the western Sudan. In J. Goody (Ed.), *Literacy in traditional societies.* Cambridge: Cambridge University Press, 1968. (Originally published, 1963.)

Williams, J. Defining complexity. *College English,* 1979, *40,* 595-609.

Williams, P. J. *The oral and silent reading of avid and non-avid readers.* Unpublished master's thesis, University of New England, Australia, 1980.

Wixon, V., & Stone, P. Getting it out, getting it down: Adapting Zoellner's talk-write. *English Journal,* 1977, *66,* 70-73.

Wolf, T. Reading reconsidered. *Harvard Educational Review,* 1977, *47,* 411-429.

Wyllie, J. Oral communications: Survey and suggestions. *The ABCA Bulletin,* 1980, *43,* 14-17.

Zaidel, E. *Linguistic competence and related functions in the right hemisphere of man following cerebral commissurotomy and hemispherectomy.* Unpublished doctoral dissertation, California Institute of Technology, 1973.

Zaidel, E. Auditory vocabulary of the right hemisphere following brain bisection or hemidecortication. *Cortex,* 1966, *12,* 199-211.

Zoellner, R. Talk-write: A behavioral pedagogy for composition. *College English,* 1969, *30,* 267-320.

# Contributors

**Loren Barritt** is Professor of Education at The University of Michigan where he teaches about the development of language and thinking. His list of publications is short but diverse. It includes articles about the language of normal and retarded children, phonetic symbolism, and black dialect. His most recent publication was a study of the children's game, hide and seek. In 1978/79 he wrote, with colleagues in the Netherlands, a handbook for the conduct of *Meaningful Educational Research*. He is now revising the text.

**Brian Cambourne** is Director of the Reading-Language Centre at Riverina College in Wagga Wagga, Australia. Prior to his university post, he taught for fifteen years in primary and secondary schools in New South Wales. Since completing his doctoral work on children's language, he has been involved in teacher education and has been active in research into oral and silent reading processes in Australian children. In 1975-76 he was awarded a Fulbright Scholarship to take up a post-doctoral fellowship at Harvard, where he worked with Professors J. Chall, C. Cazden, and C. Chomsky. In 1980-81, he was awarded an Australian Government Research Fellowship to work at the Center for the Study of Reading (Illinois) and the Center for the Study of Literacy and Language (Arizona). He is currently funded for research into the processing of textbook prose and the relationship between retellings and miscues.

**James L. Collins** is Assistant Professor of English Education at the State University of New York at Buffalo. He formerly taught English in a large urban high school for ten years and chaired the English Department for five. His publications include articles on writing and the teaching of writing and on language and schooling. Currently his research focuses on developmental and instructional relationships between spoken and written language.

**Anne Ruggles Gere** is Associate Professor of English at the University of Washington, where she directs the Puget Sound Writing Program and teaches courses in writing, rhetorical theory, and literature. Author of *Language, Attitudes and Change* (with Eugene Smith) and numerous articles in NCTE journals, she is currently working on a book-length study of rhetoric.

**Benjamin M. Glassner,** Instructor of Rhetoric and Composition at Michigan Technological University, is currently completing work on an examination of hemispheric relationships in composing, a dissertation study codirected by Janet A. Emig, Rutgers University, and Leonide Goldstein, Rutgers Medical School. The project is funded by the NCTE Research Foundation.

**Kenneth J. Kantor** is Associate Professor in the Department of Language Education at the University of Georgia. His primary areas of research interest are developmental processes in composition, contexts for writing, and English curriculum theory and history. Articles by Kantor have appeared in *Research in the Teaching of English, Language Arts, English Journal,* and *English Education.* He is presently serving as a member of the NCTE Research Committee, associate editor of *Research in the Teaching of English,* and coordinator of the Research in Composition Network.

**Barry M. Kroll** is Associate Professor of English at Iowa State University, where he teaches courses in writing, composition theory, and English education. He has also taught middle-school English, and has spent two years in Europe—one as a lecturer in English at Mainz, West Germany, and one as a research fellow at the Centre for the Study of Language and Communication, University of Bristol, England. His publications include articles in a number of NCTE journals, as well as in several educational and psychological journals. He is currently working on studies of children's writing development, with a focus on the development of audience-adapted writing abilities.

**J. G. Kyle** is Research Fellow in the School of Education Research Unit, University of Bristol, England. He is a teacher of psychology and reading, and is tutor in special education. He is currently director of funded research projects on British Sign Language Learning, Deaf People and the Community, and Reading Development in Deaf Children. He has published journal articles on the psychology and education of deaf children, and is coeditor of *Perspectives on British Sign Language and Deafness* (London: Croom Helm, 1981). He has two books on deafness in preparation.

**Barbara J. O'Keefe** is Assistant Professor in the Department of Speech Communication at the University of Illinois at Urbana-Champaign. She held faculty appointments at Wayne State University and Pennsylvania State University. Her published research has focused on the relationship of social cognition to communication and the development of communication skills in children. Her current research is focused on structures and processes involved in informal, face-to-face, social interaction in children and adults.

**David R. Olson** is Professor of Applied Psychology at the Ontario Institute for Studies in Education. He received his Ph.D. in educational psychology from the University of Alberta, Edmonton. He was a Fellow at the Center for Cognitive Studies, Harvard University in the 1960s and he was recently a Fellow at the Netherlands Institute for Advanced Study, Wassenaar, The Netherlands. Professor Olson is author of *Cognitive Development: The Child's Acquisition of Diagonality* and editor of *Media and Symbols: The Forms of Expression, Communication and Education* and of *The Social Contexts of Language and Thought: Essays in Honor of Jerome S. Bruner.* He is currently completing a volume on the development of spatial cognition.

**William D. Payne** is Assistant Professor of English at Iowa State University where he teaches courses in general composition as well as business and technical writing. His current interests are composition bibliography, the computerized composing process, and scientific rhetoric.

**Donald L. Rubin** is Assistant Professor in the Departments of Speech Communication and Language Education at the University of Georgia. His interest has focused particularly on the development of social perspective taking and audience adaptation skills in children's speech and writing. He has had articles published in *Research in the Teaching of English, Child Development,* and *Communication Monographs.*

**John C. Schafer** is Assistant Professor of English and Director of Freshman English at Tulane University. He has published several articles on text analysis and rhetorical theory and is the coauthor of a writing textbook, *Strategies for Academic Writing: A Guide for College Students* (University of Michigan Press, forthcoming).

**Roberta J. Vann** is Assistant Professor of English at Iowa State University, where she directs the Intensive English and Orientation Program for foreign students. A former Fulbright lecturer in Poland, she has done EFL teacher-training in Eastern Europe, Syria, and the United States and has published a number of articles on foreign language learning.